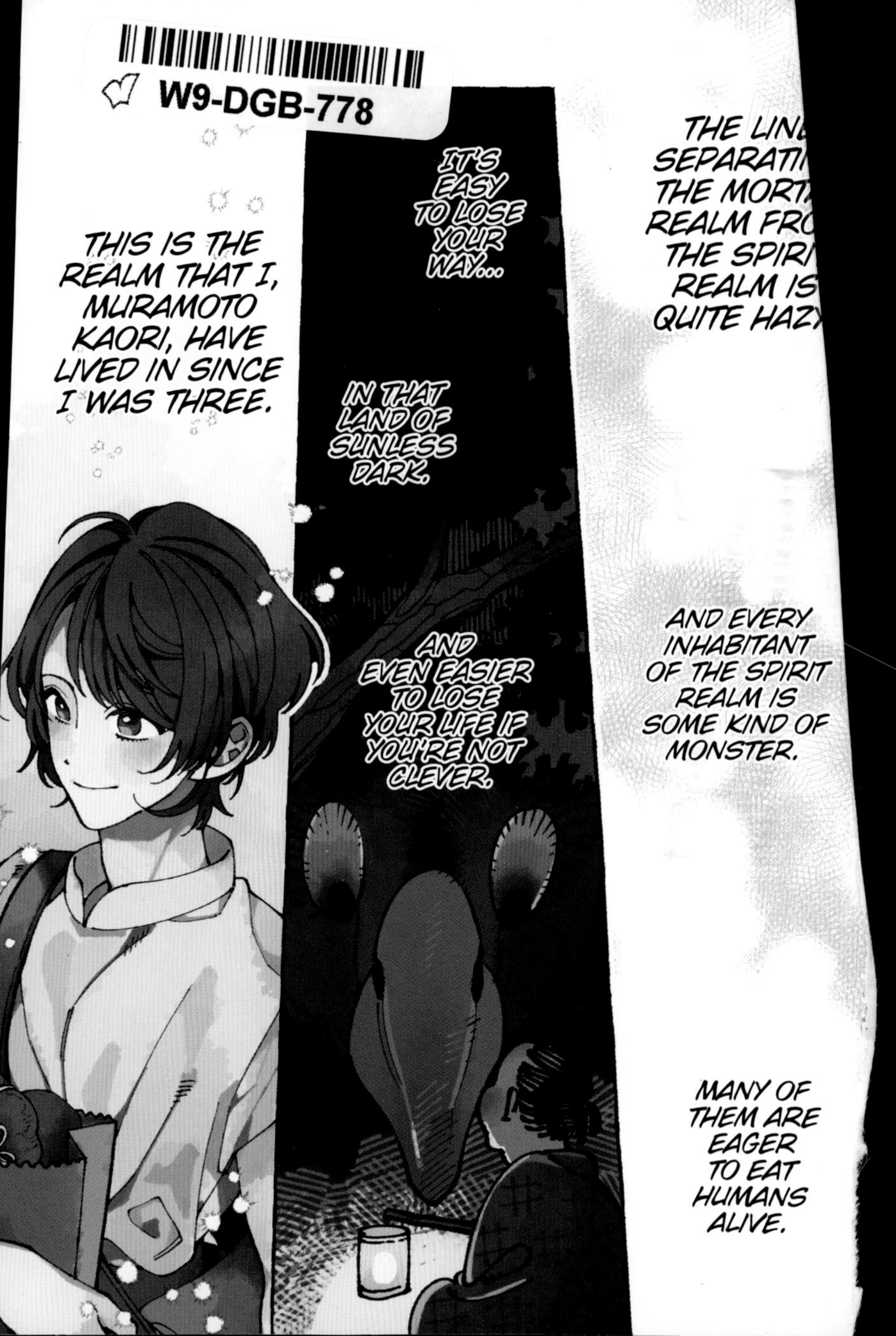
THE LIN SEPARATI THE MORT REALM FR THE SPIRI REALM IS QUITE HAZ
AND EVERY INHABITANT OF THE SPIRIT REALM IS SOME KIND OF MONSTER.
MANY OF THEM ARE EAGER TO EAT HUMANS ALIVE.
IT'S EASY TO LOSE YOUR WAY...
IN THAT LAND OF SUNLESS DARK.
AND EVEN EASIER TO LOSE YOUR LIFE IF YOU'RE NOT CLEVER.
THIS IS THE REALM THAT I, MURAMOTO KAORI, HAVE LIVED IN SINCE I WAS THREE.

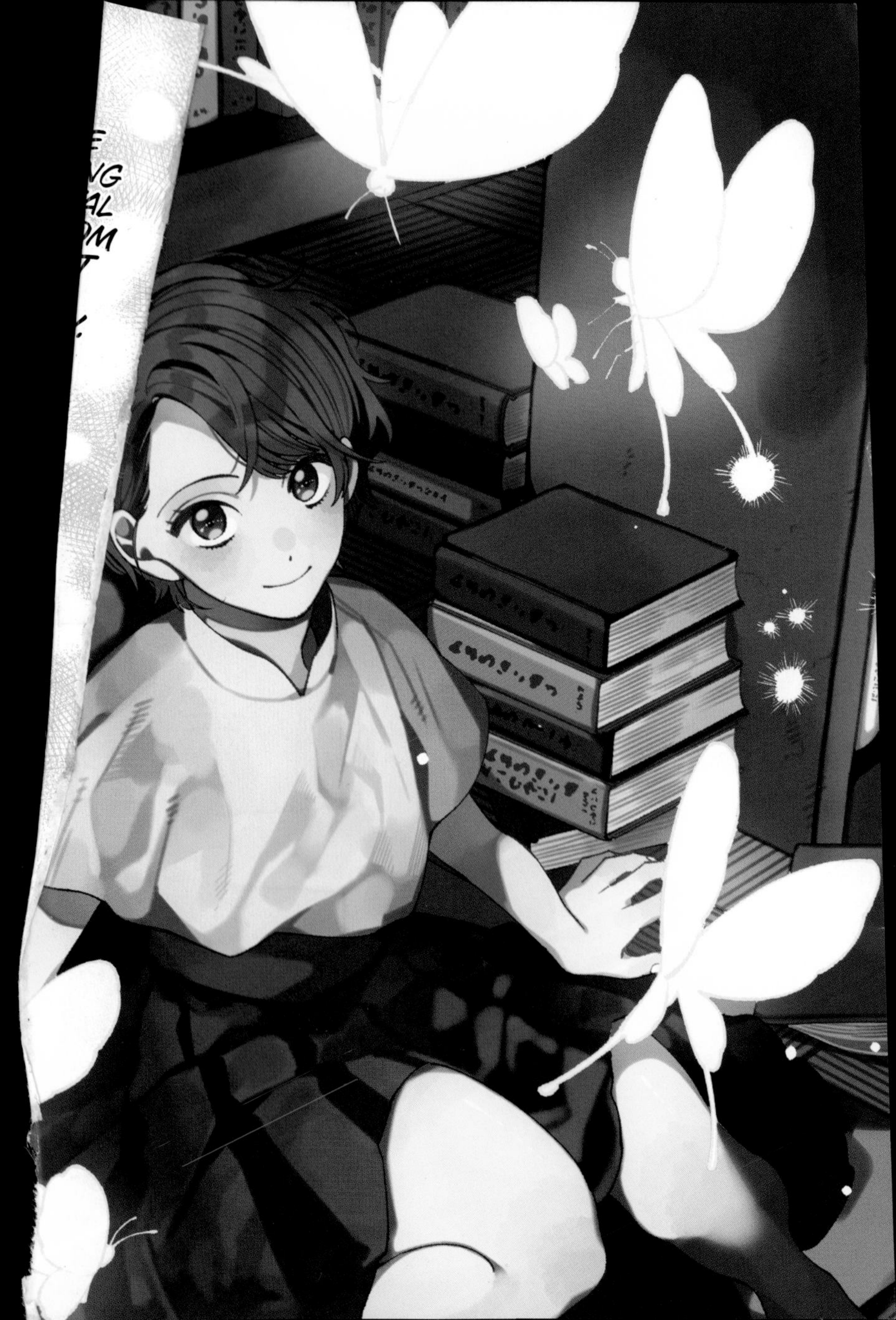

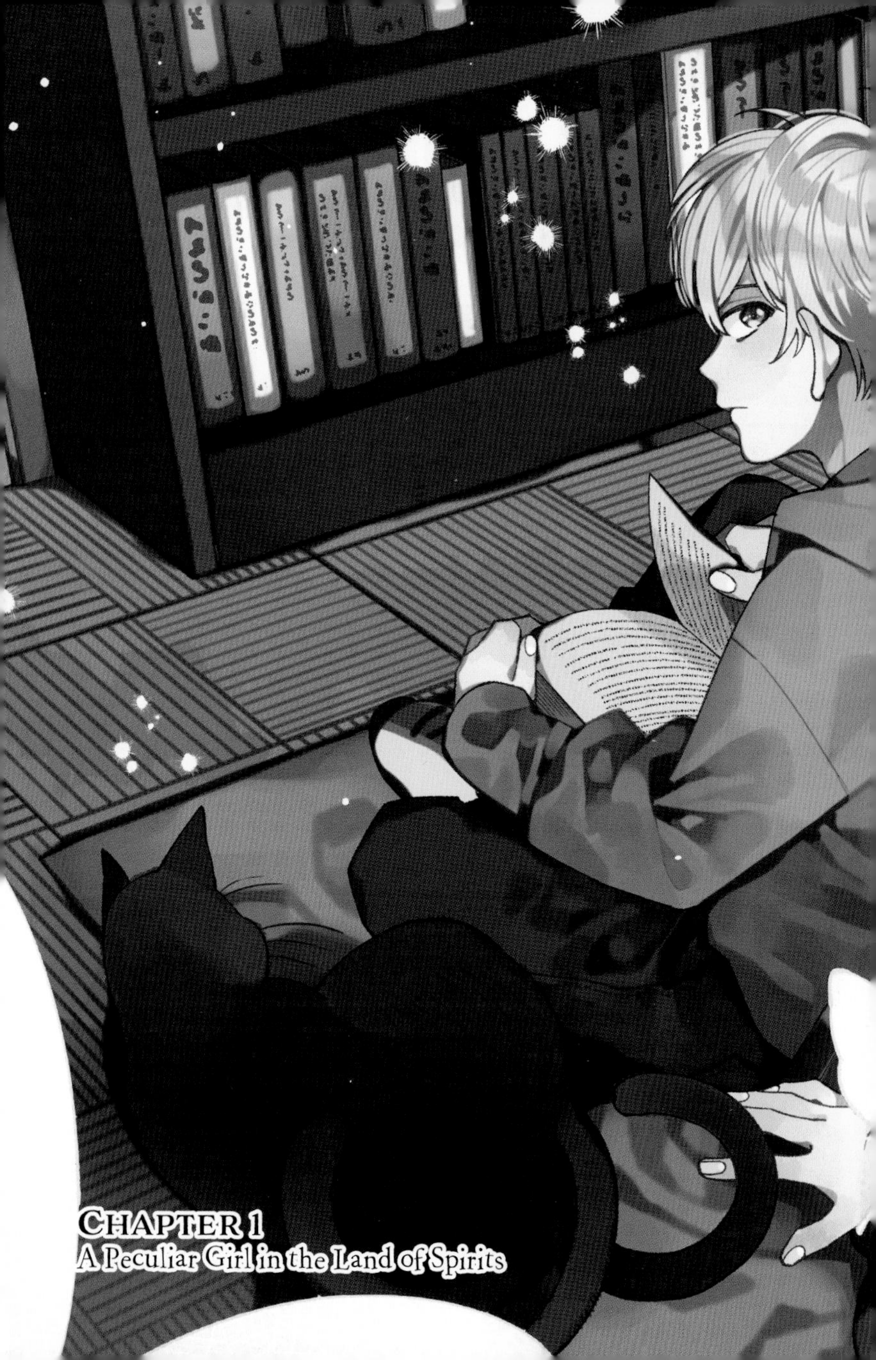
CHAPTER 1
A Peculiar Girl in the Land of Spirits

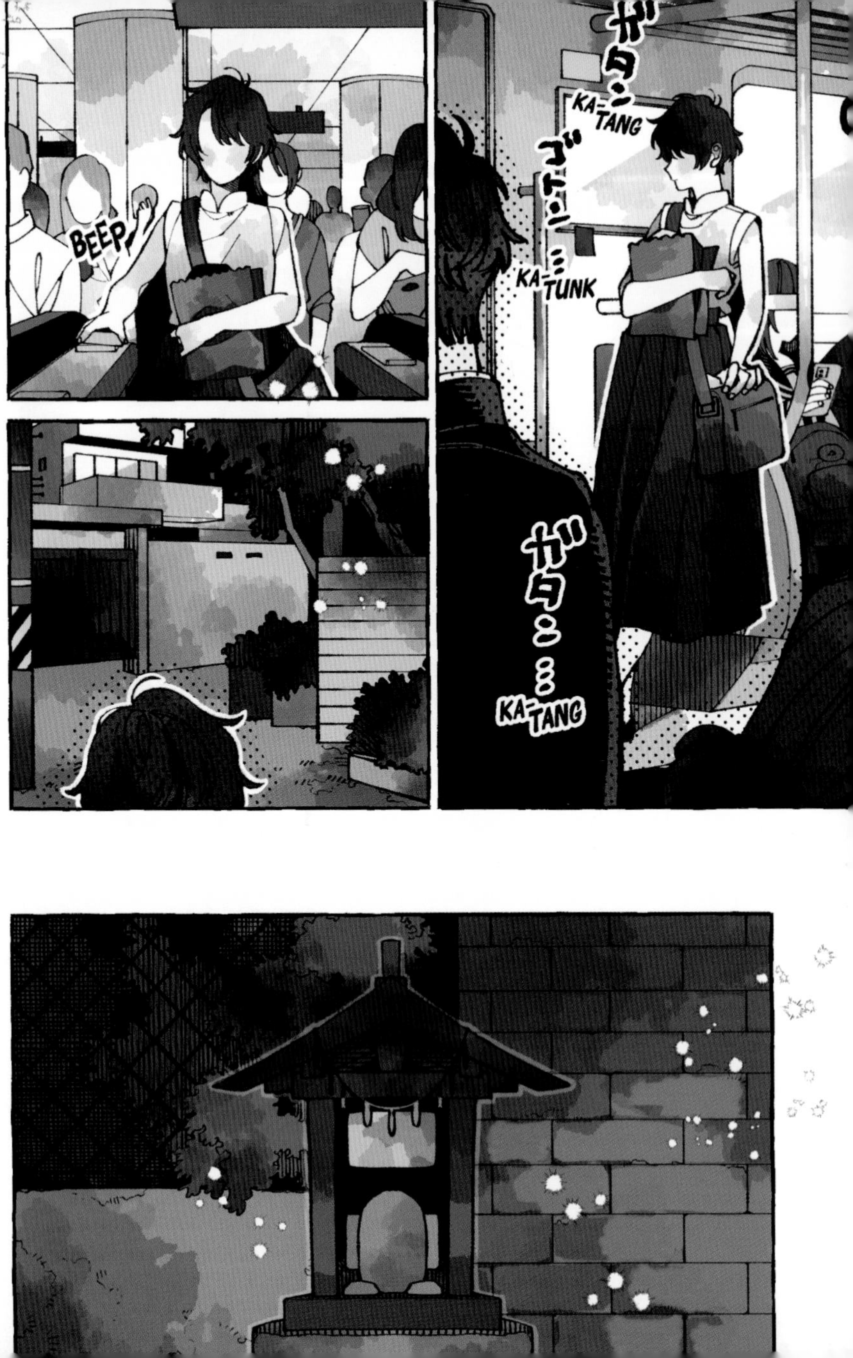
ガタン
KA-TANG
ゴトン…
KA-TUNK
ガタン……
KA-TANG
BEEP

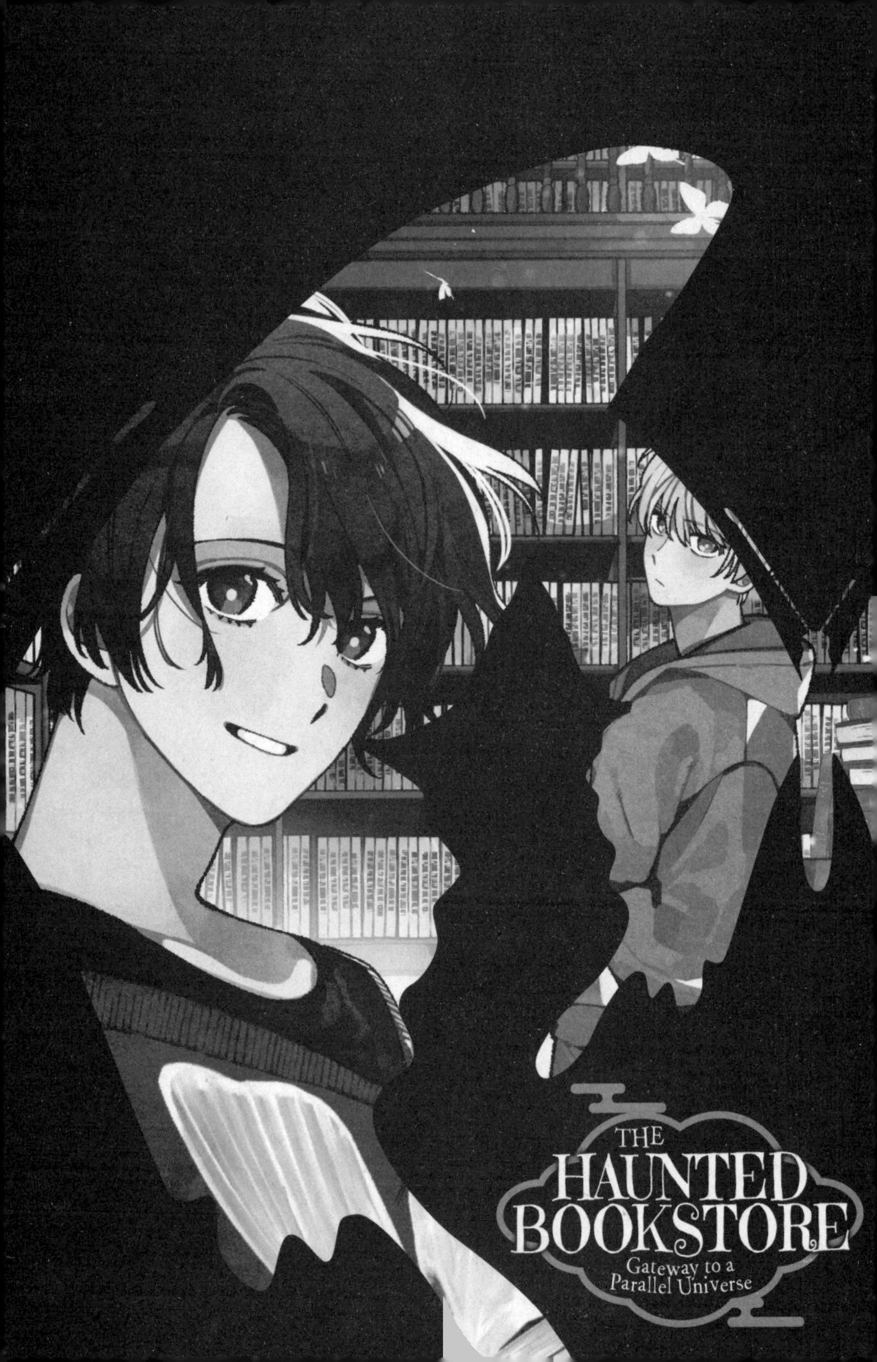
THE
HAUNTED
BOOKSTORE
Gateway to a
Parallel Universe

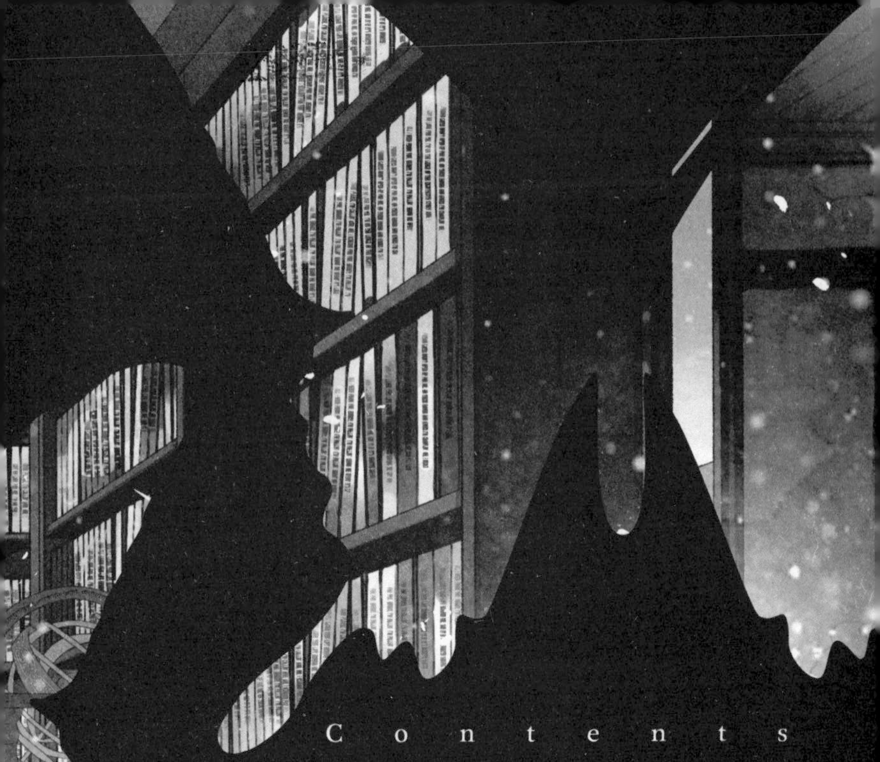

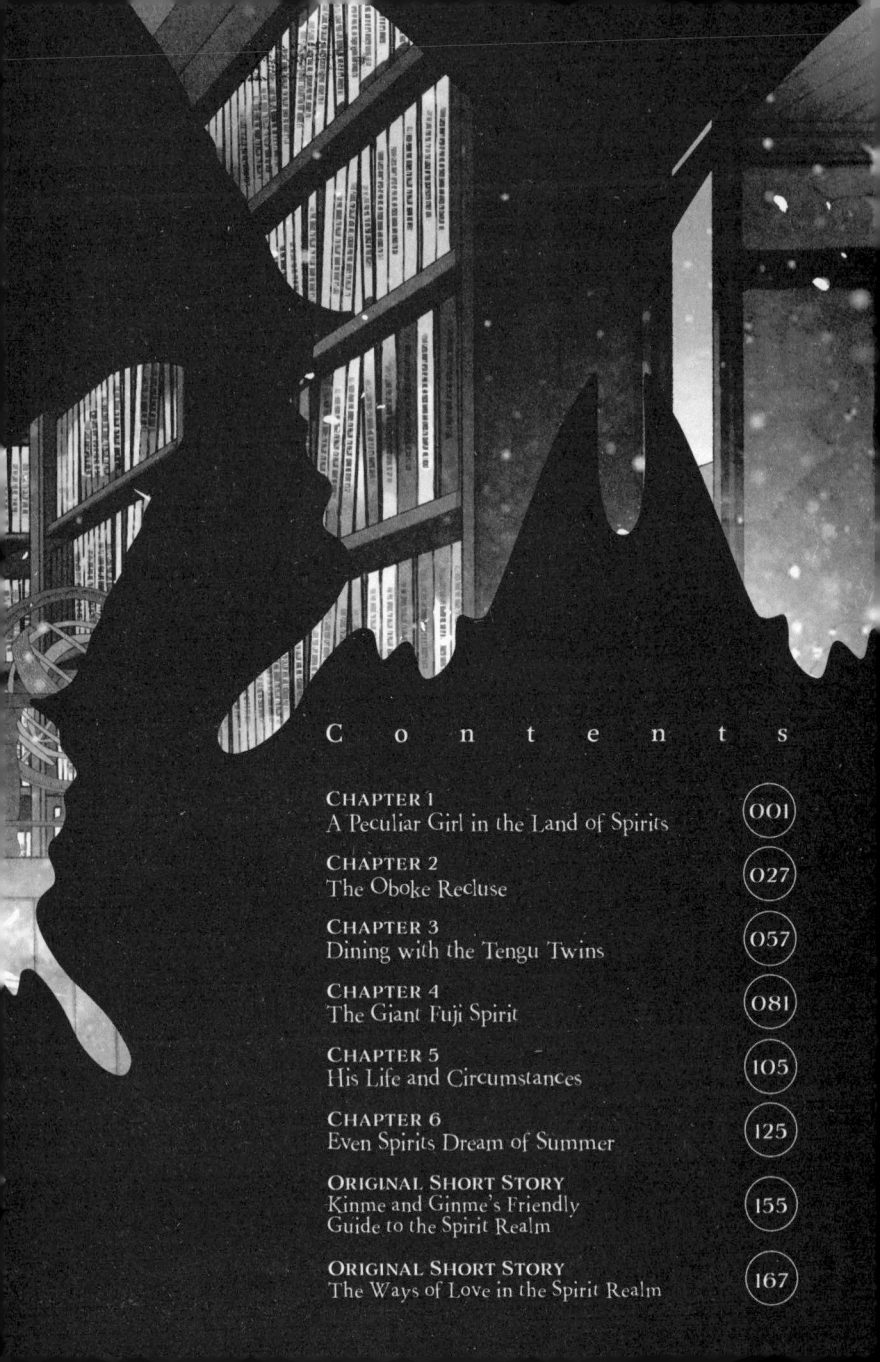

Contents

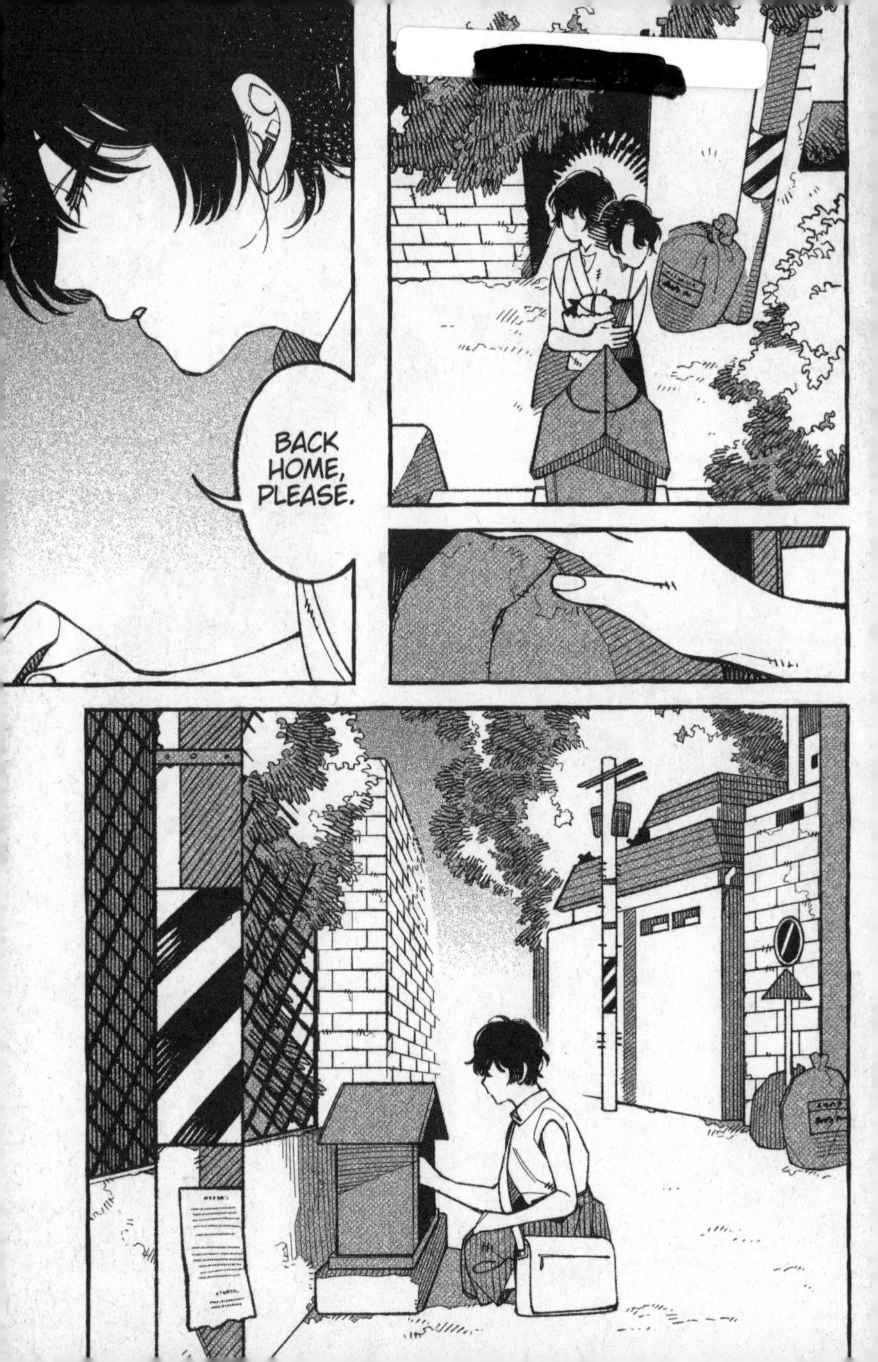
[redacted]
BACK HOME, PLEASE.

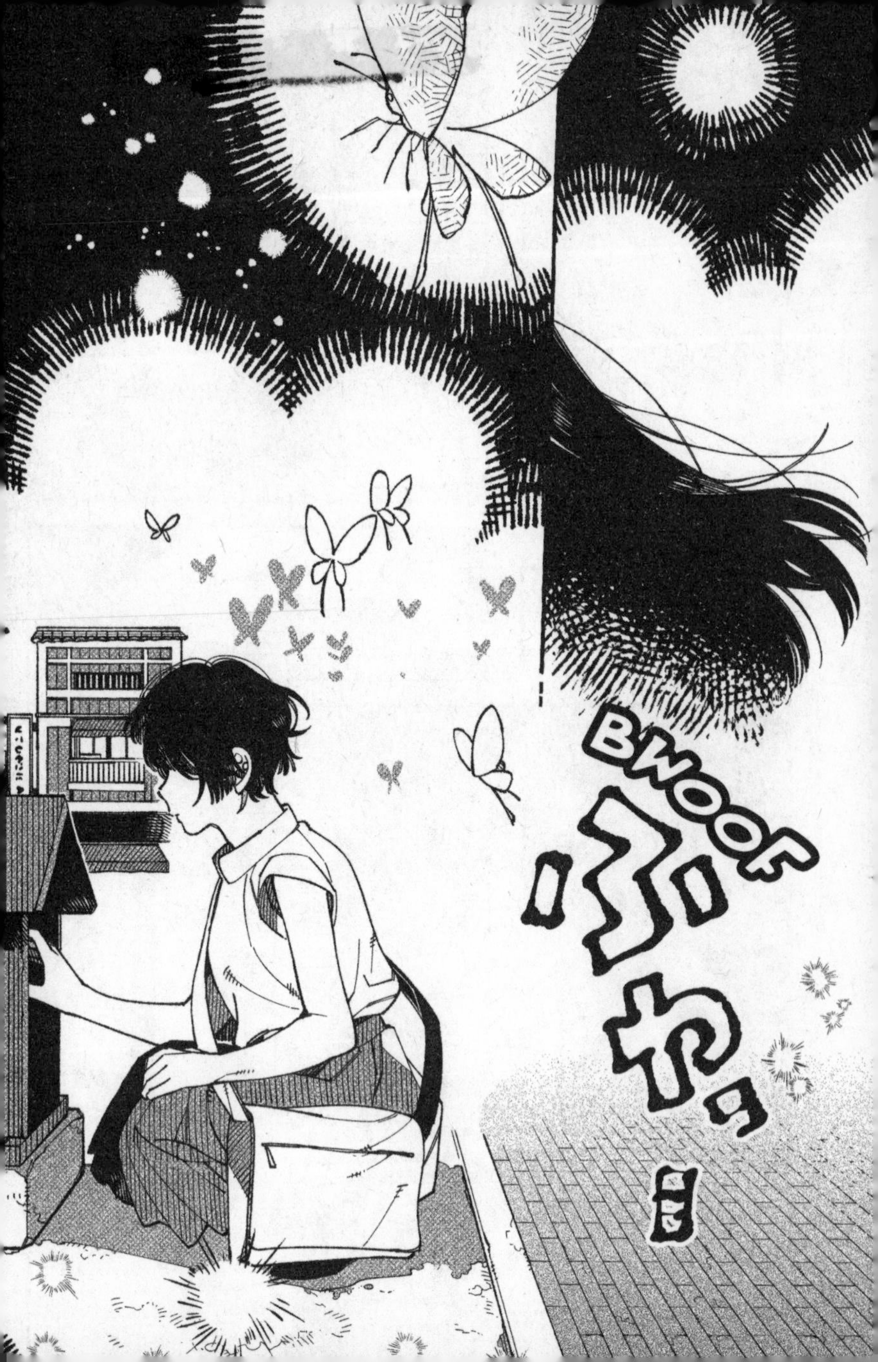
BWOOF

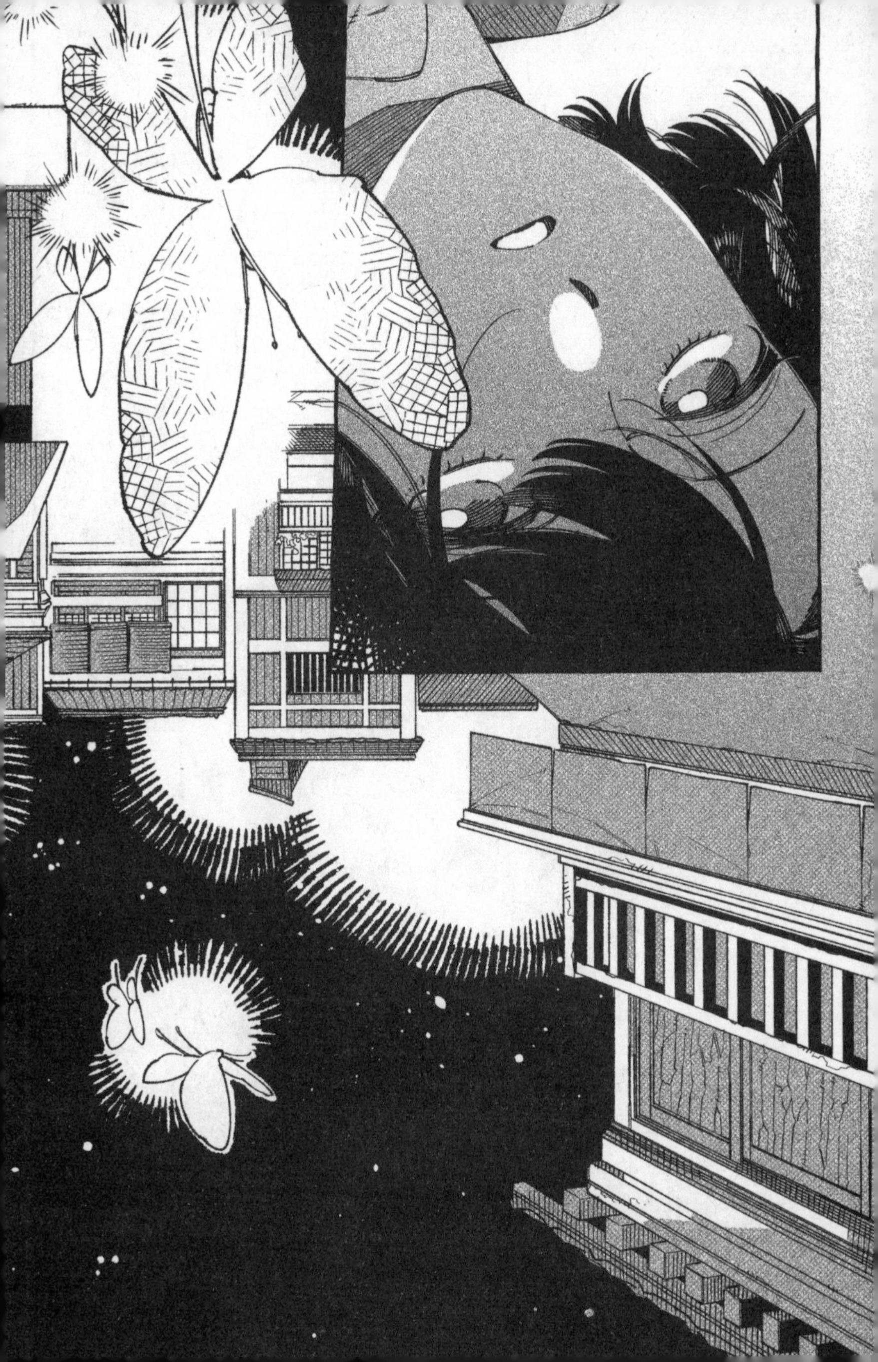

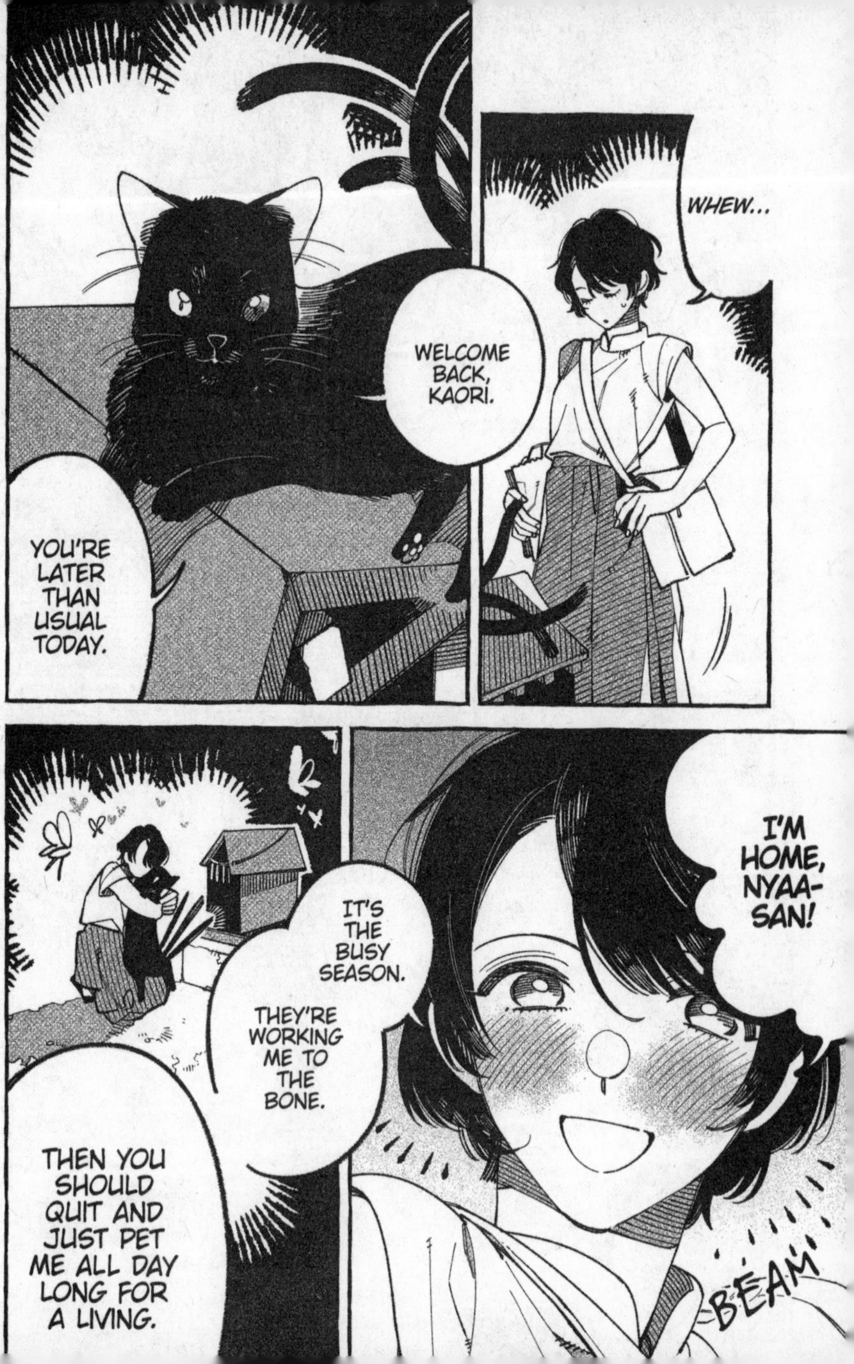
WHEW...
WELCOME BACK, KAORI.
YOU'RE LATER THAN USUAL TODAY.
I'M HOME, NYAA-SAN!
BEAM
IT'S THE BUSY SEASON.
THEY'RE WORKING ME TO THE BONE.
THEN YOU SHOULD QUIT AND JUST PET ME ALL DAY LONG FOR A LIVING.

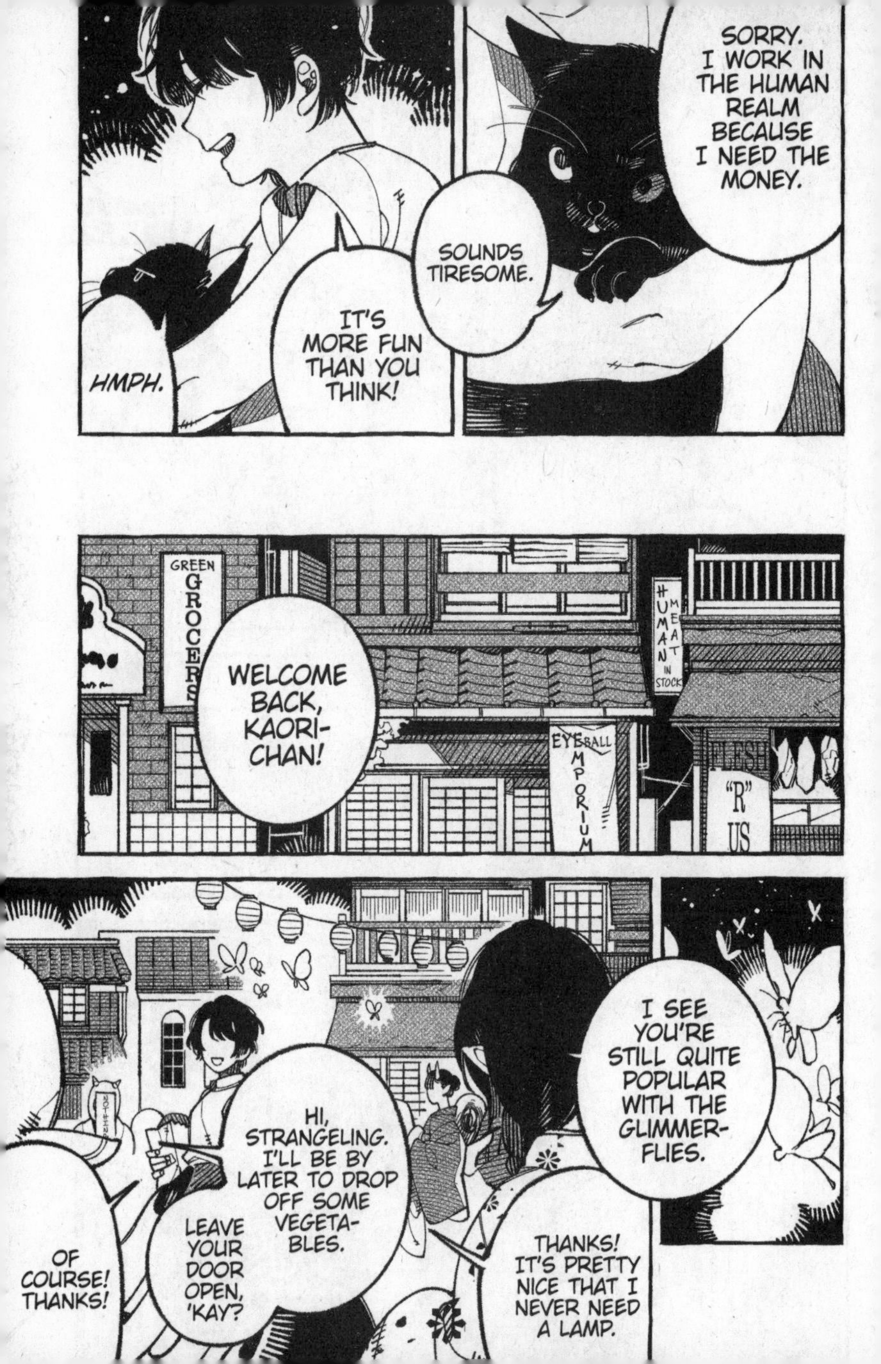
SORRY. I WORK IN THE HUMAN REALM BECAUSE I NEED THE MONEY.
SOUNDS TIRESOME.
IT'S MORE FUN THAN YOU THINK!
HMPH.
WELCOME BACK, KAORI-CHAN!
GREEN GROCERS
HUMAN MEAT IN STOCK
EYEBALL EMPORIUM
FLESH "R" US
I SEE YOU'RE STILL QUITE POPULAR WITH THE GLIMMER-FLIES.
THANKS! IT'S PRETTY NICE THAT I NEVER NEED A LAMP.
HI, STRANGELING. I'LL BE BY LATER TO DROP OFF SOME VEGETA-BLES.
LEAVE YOUR DOOR OPEN, 'KAY?
OF COURSE! THANKS!

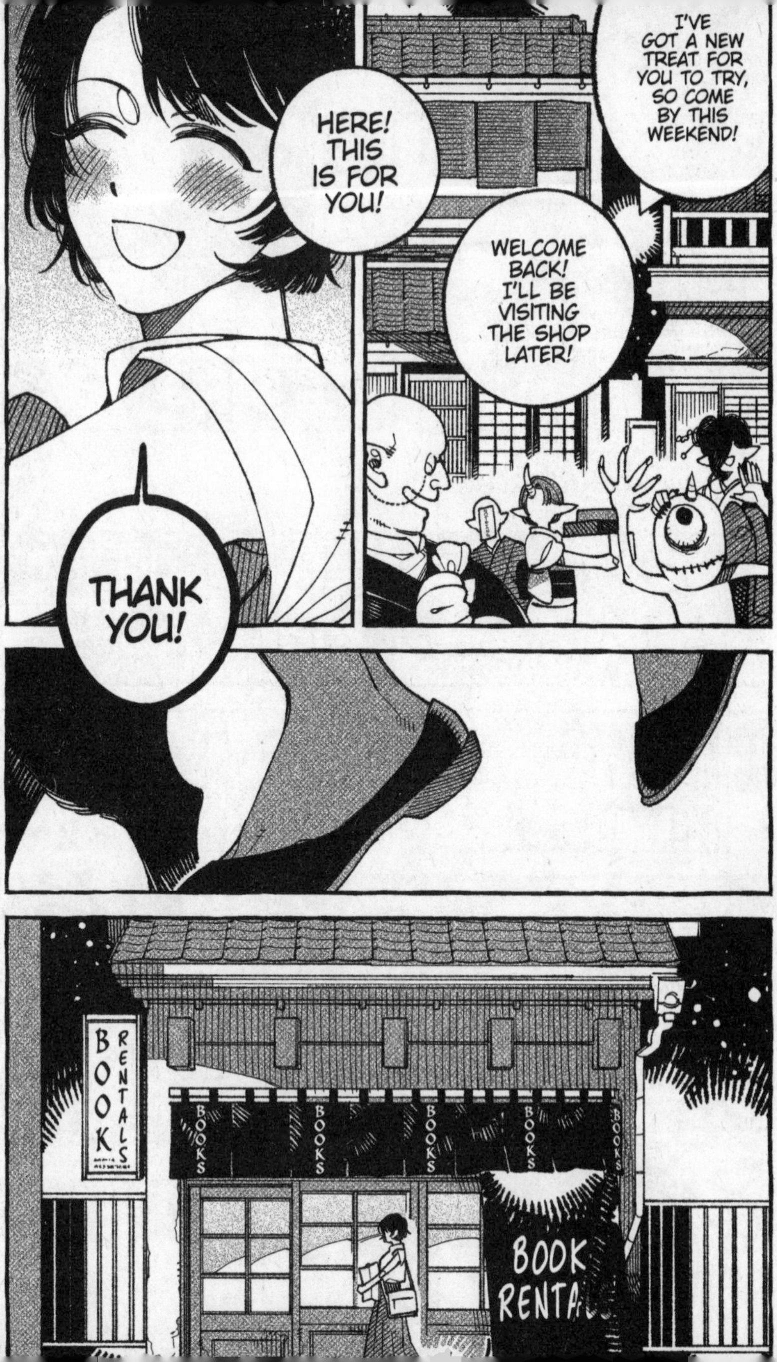
I'VE GOT A NEW TREAT FOR YOU TO TRY, SO COME BY THIS WEEKEND!
WELCOME BACK! I'LL BE VISITING THE SHOP LATER!
HERE! THIS IS FOR YOU!
THANK YOU!
BOOK RENTA
BOOKS
BOOKS
BOOKS
BOOKS
BOOKS
BOOK RENTALS

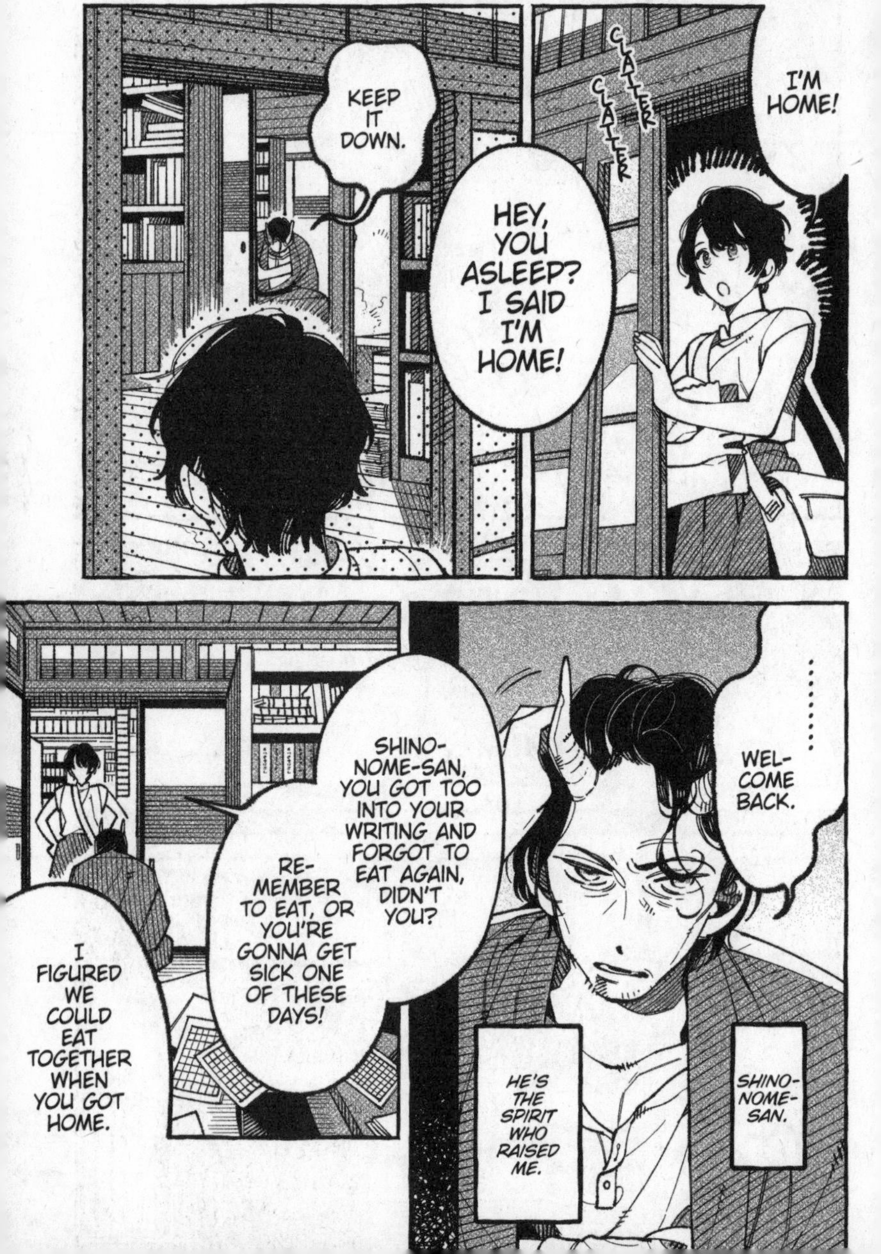
I'M HOME!
CLATTER CLATTER
HEY, YOU ASLEEP? I SAID I'M HOME!
KEEP IT DOWN.
......
WEL-COME BACK.
SHINO-NOME-SAN.
HE'S THE SPIRIT WHO RAISED ME.
SHINO-NOME-SAN, YOU GOT TOO INTO YOUR WRITING AND FORGOT TO EAT AGAIN, DIDN'T YOU?
RE-MEMBER TO EAT, OR YOU'RE GONNA GET SICK ONE OF THESE DAYS!
I FIGURED WE COULD EAT TOGETHER WHEN YOU GOT HOME.

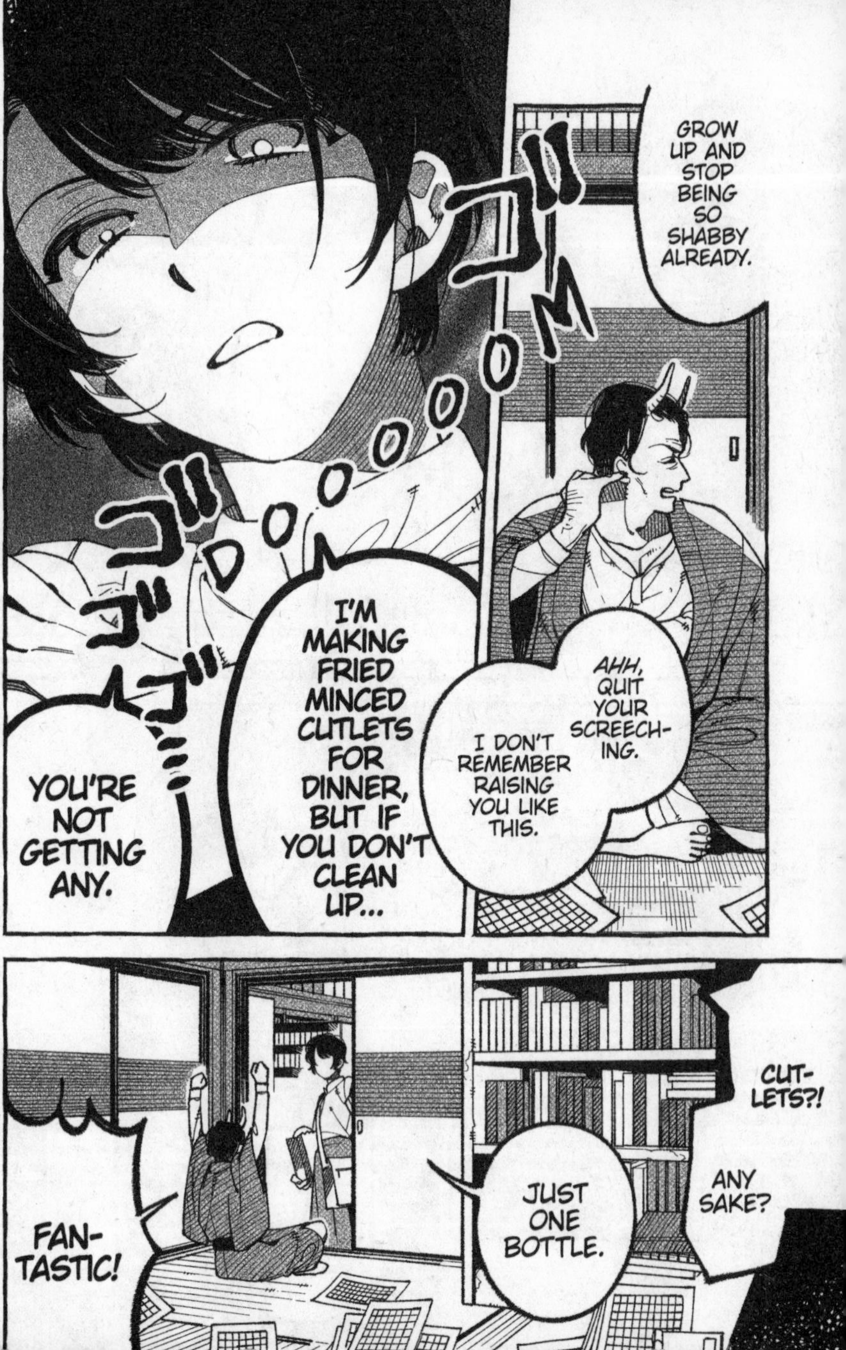
GROW UP AND STOP BEING SO SHABBY ALREADY.
AHH, QUIT YOUR SCREECH-ING.
I DON'T REMEMBER RAISING YOU LIKE THIS.
DOOOOOOM
I'M MAKING FRIED MINCED CUTLETS FOR DINNER, BUT IF YOU DON'T CLEAN UP...
YOU'RE NOT GETTING ANY.
CUT-LETS?!
ANY SAKE?
JUST ONE BOTTLE.
FAN-TASTIC!

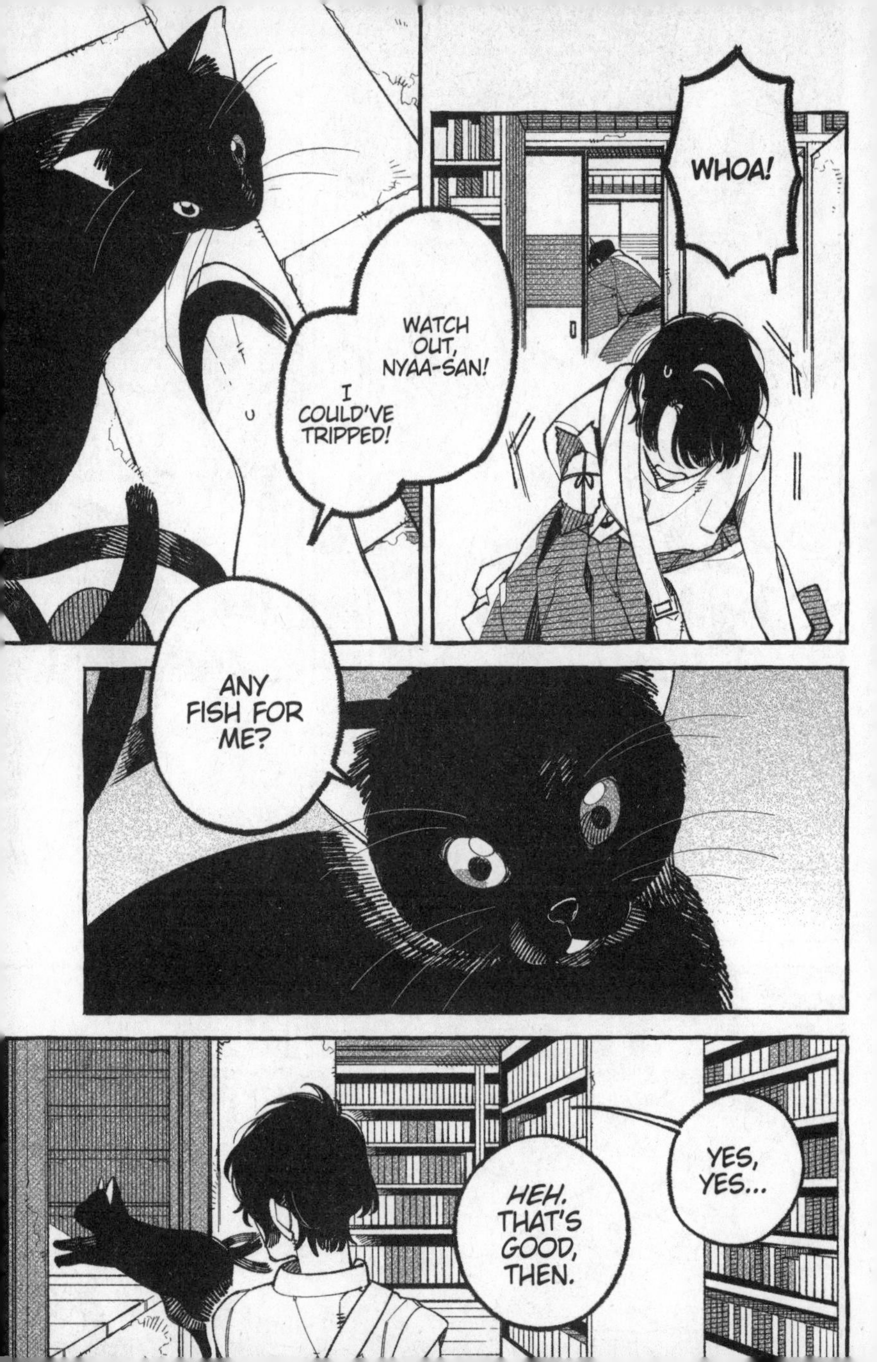
WHOA!
WATCH OUT, NYAA-SAN!
I COULD'VE TRIPPED!
ANY FISH FOR ME?
YES, YES...
HEH. THAT'S GOOD, THEN.

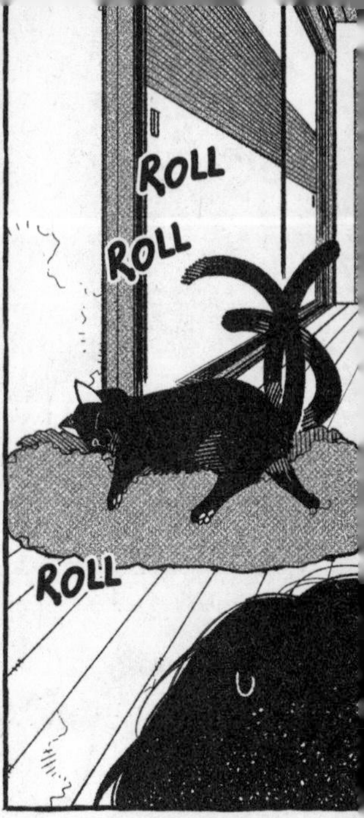
ROLL
ROLL
ROLL
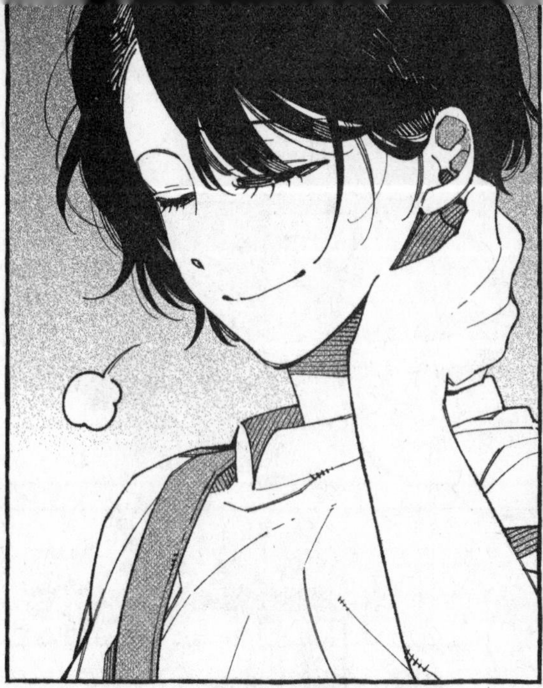
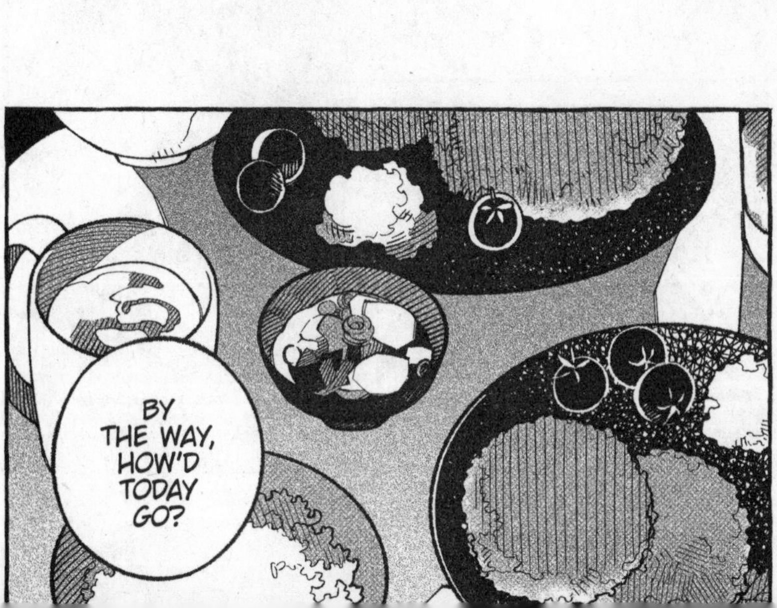
BY THE WAY, HOW'D TODAY GO?

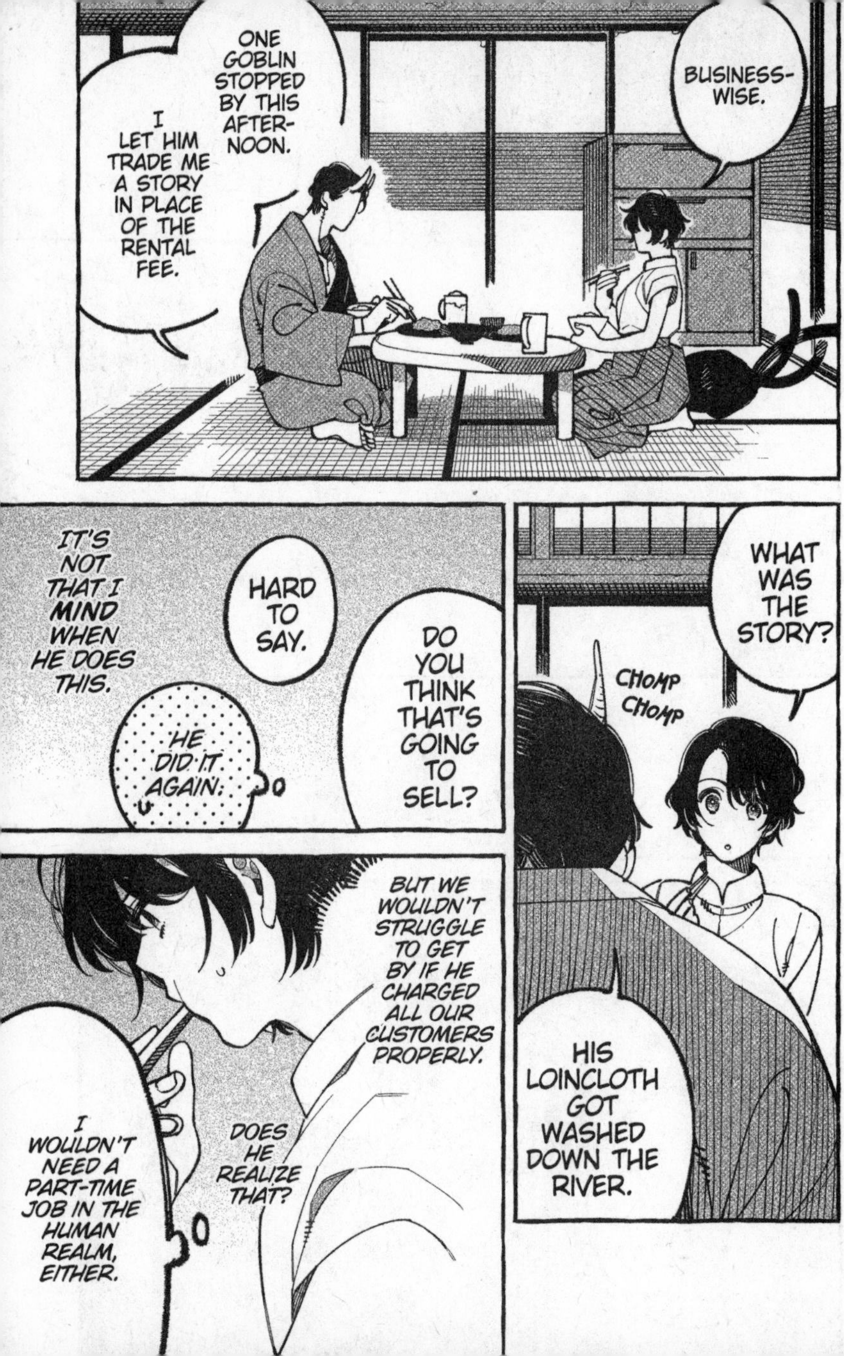
BUSINESS-WISE.
ONE GOBLIN STOPPED BY THIS AFTERNOON.
I LET HIM TRADE ME A STORY IN PLACE OF THE RENTAL FEE.
WHAT WAS THE STORY?
CHOMP CHOMP
HIS LOINCLOTH GOT WASHED DOWN THE RIVER.
DO YOU THINK THAT'S GOING TO SELL?
HARD TO SAY.
IT'S NOT THAT I MIND WHEN HE DOES THIS.
HE DID IT AGAIN.
BUT WE WOULDN'T STRUGGLE TO GET BY IF HE CHARGED ALL OUR CUSTOMERS PROPERLY.
DOES HE REALIZE THAT?
I WOULDN'T NEED A PART-TIME JOB IN THE HUMAN REALM, EITHER.

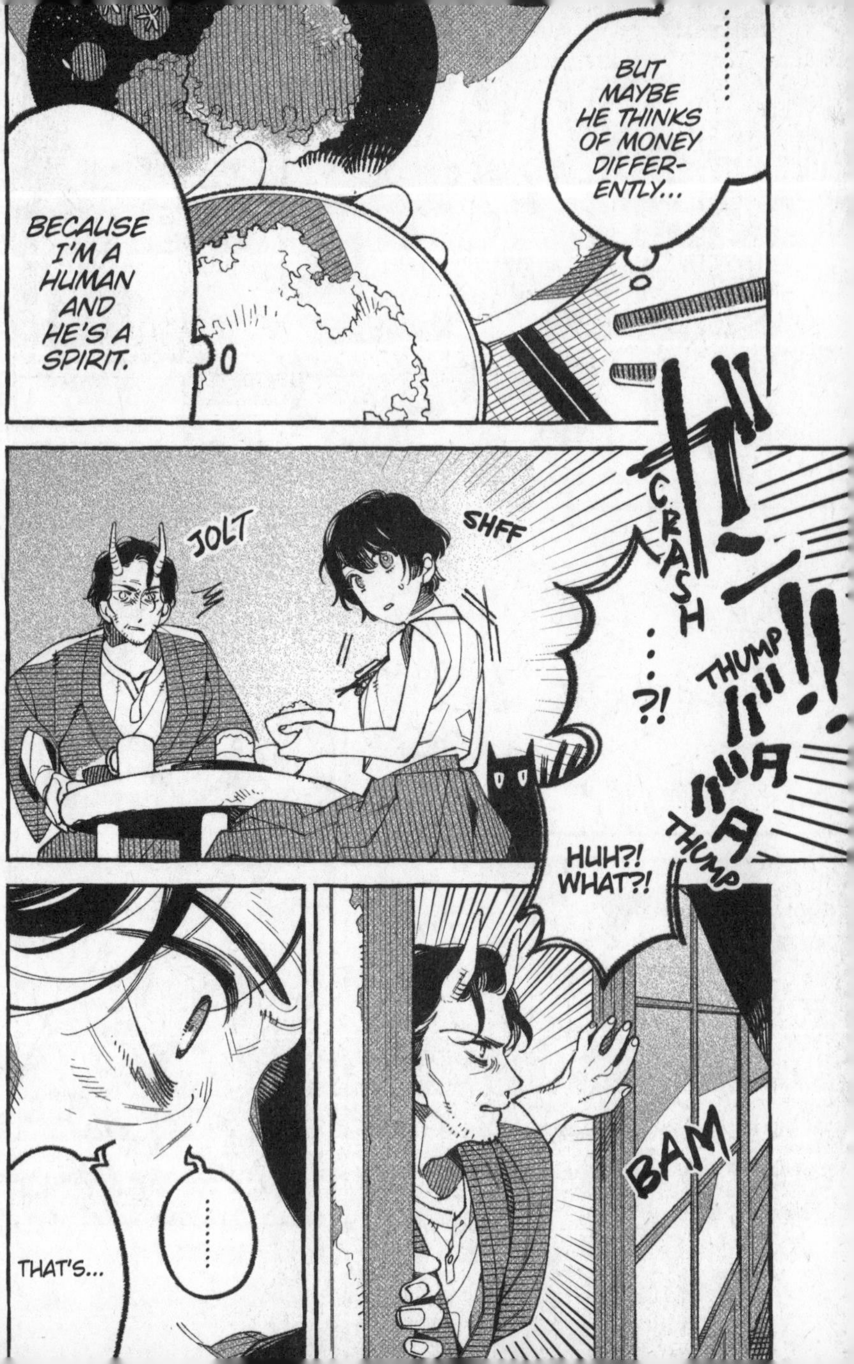
......
BUT MAYBE HE THINKS OF MONEY DIFFER-ENTLY...
BECAUSE I'M A HUMAN AND HE'S A SPIRIT.
CRASH
...?!
THUMP THUMP
SHFF
JOLT
HUH?! WHAT?!
BAM
......
THAT'S...

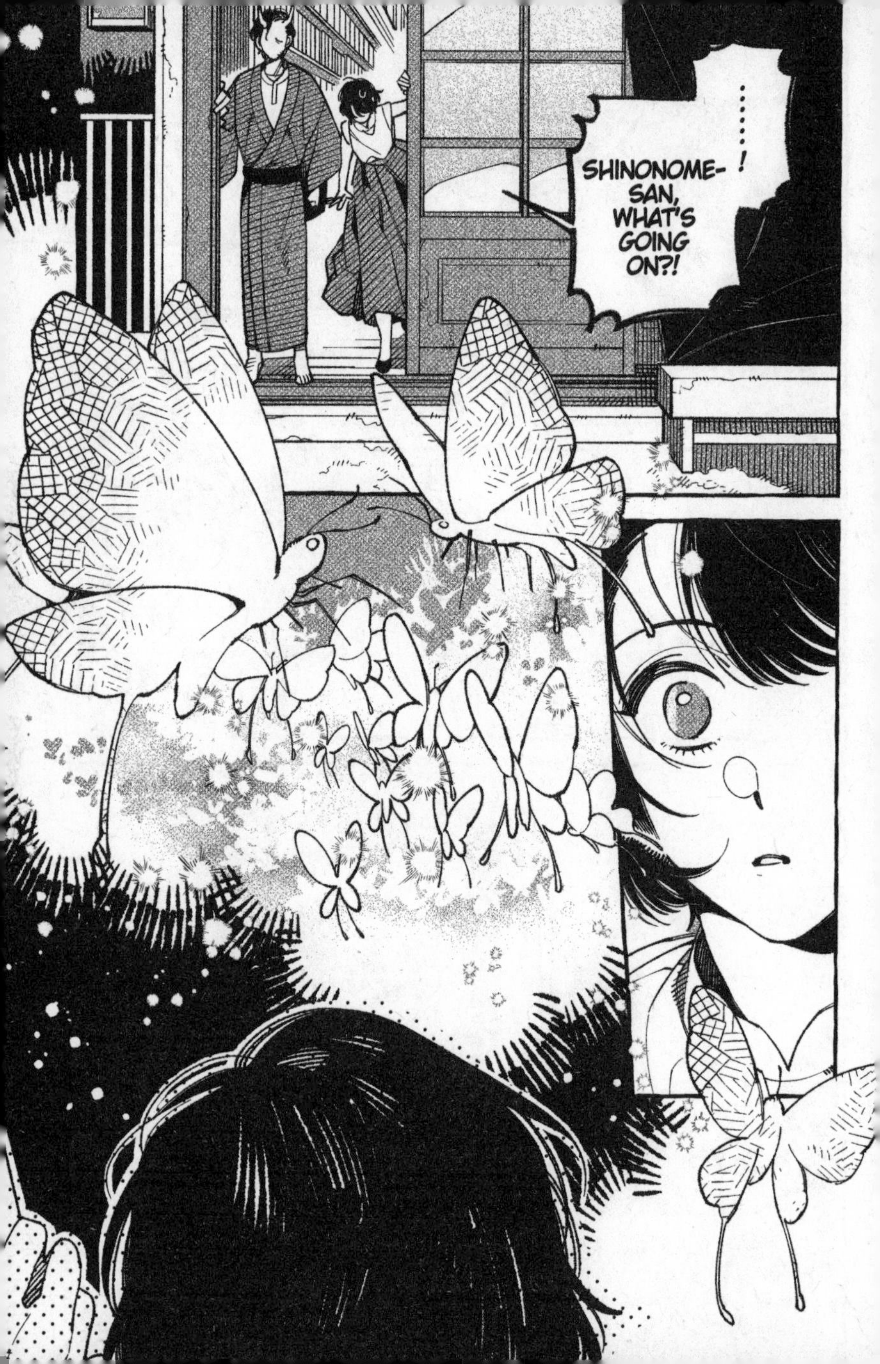
......!
SHINONOME-SAN, WHAT'S GOING ON?!

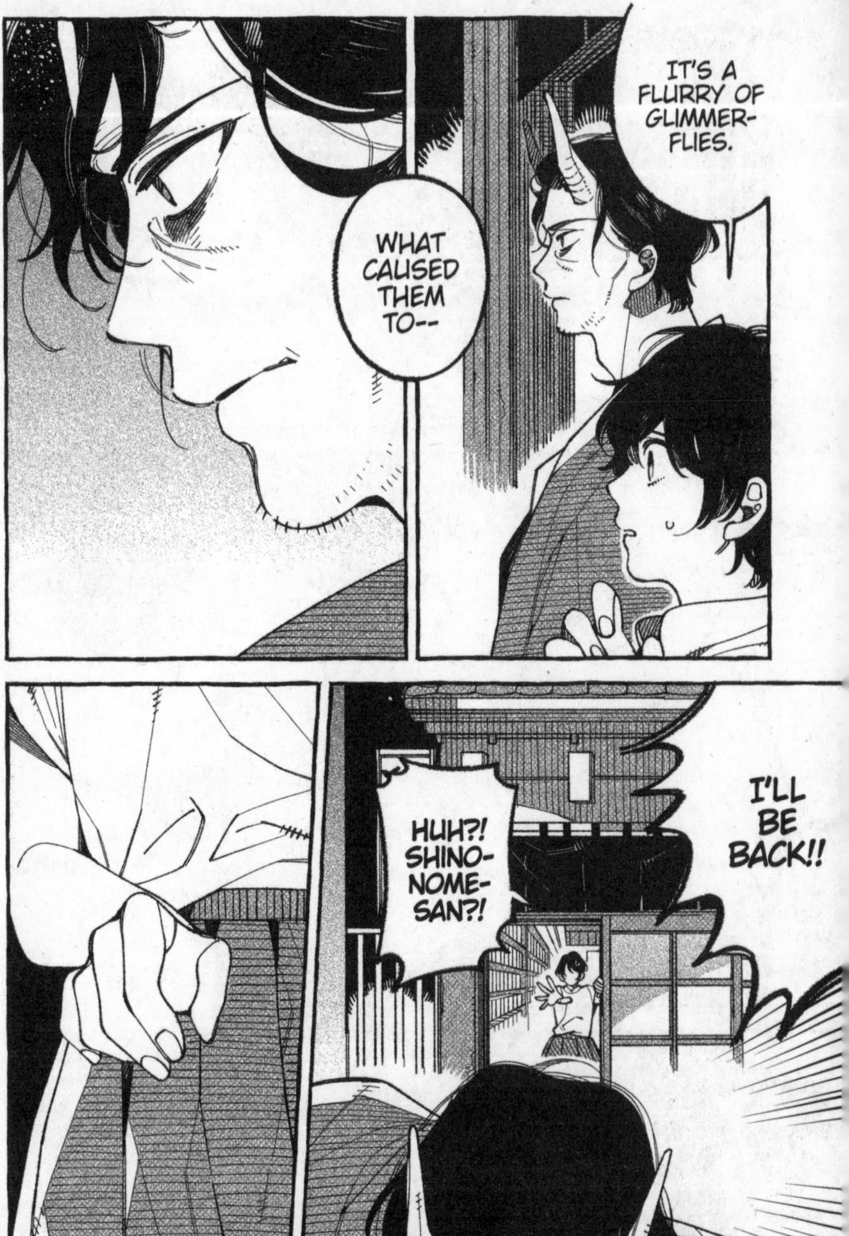
IT'S A FLURRY OF GLIMMER-FLIES.
WHAT CAUSED THEM TO--
I'LL BE BACK!!
HUH?! SHINO-NOME-SAN?!

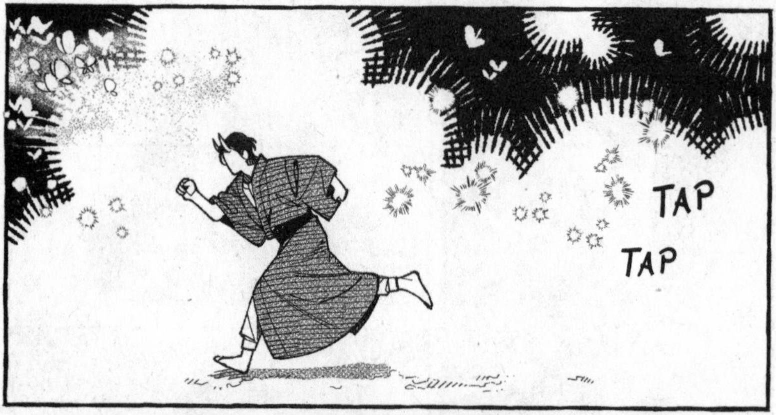
TAP
TAP

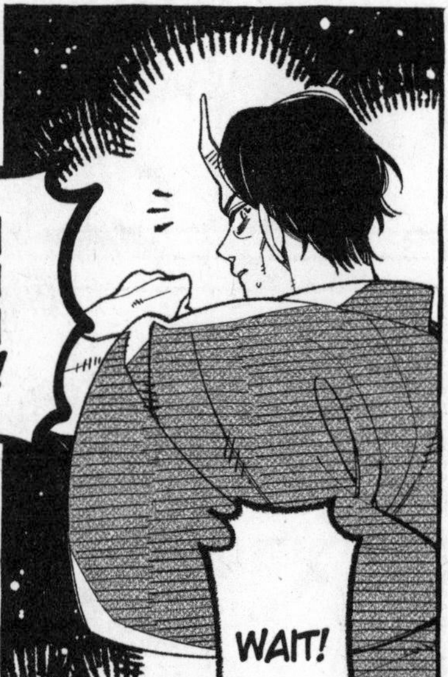
HUH?!
WAIT!

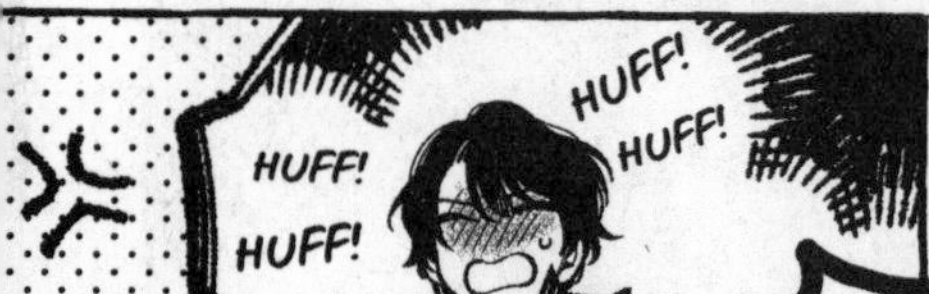
HUFF!
HUFF!
HUFF!
HUFF!
KAORI!
YOU'RE SUPPOSED TO WAIT AT HOME! STOP FOLLOWING ME!
NO WAY!

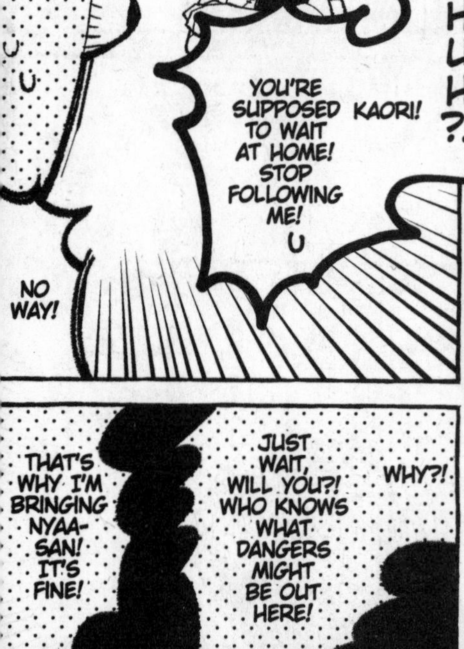
WHY?!
JUST WAIT, WILL YOU?! WHO KNOWS WHAT DANGERS MIGHT BE OUT HERE!
THAT'S WHY I'M BRINGING NYAA-SAN! IT'S FINE!

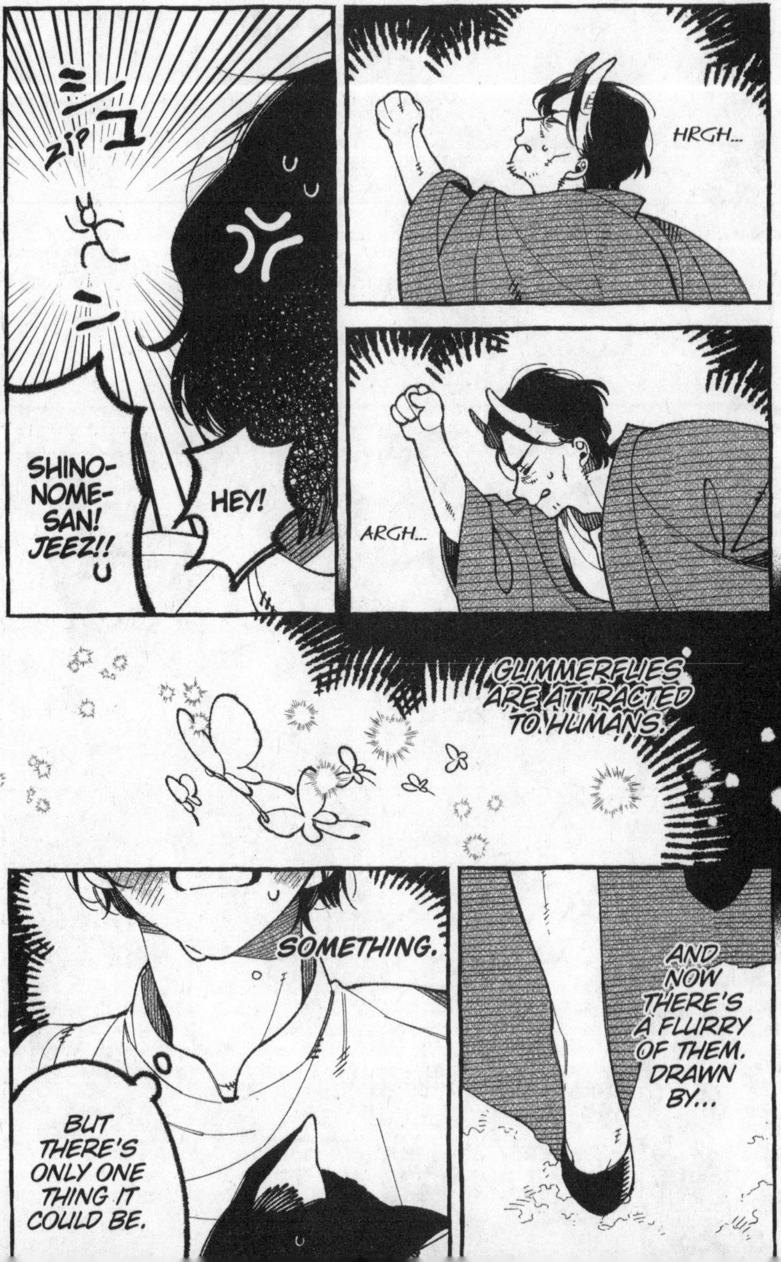
HRGH...
ARGH...
ズ
ZIP
HEY!
SHINO-NOME-SAN! JEEZ!!
GLIMMERFLIES ARE ATTRACTED TO HUMANS.
AND NOW THERE'S A FLURRY OF THEM. DRAWN BY...
SOMETHING.
BUT THERE'S ONLY ONE THING IT COULD BE.

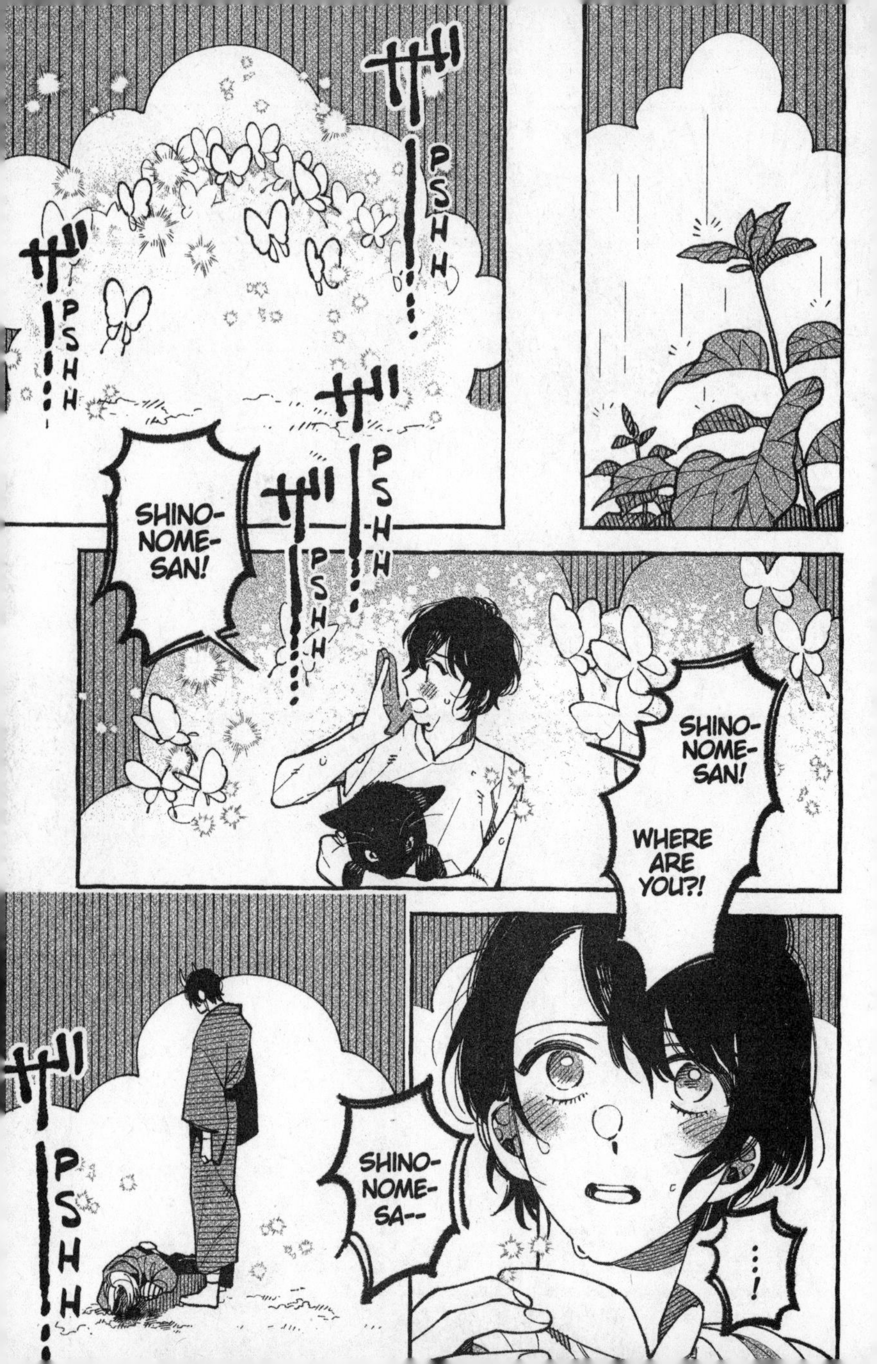
PSHH...
PSHH...
PSHH...
SHINO-NOME-SAN!
PSHH...
SHINO-NOME-SAN!
WHERE ARE YOU?!
...!
SHINO-NOME-SA--
PSHH...

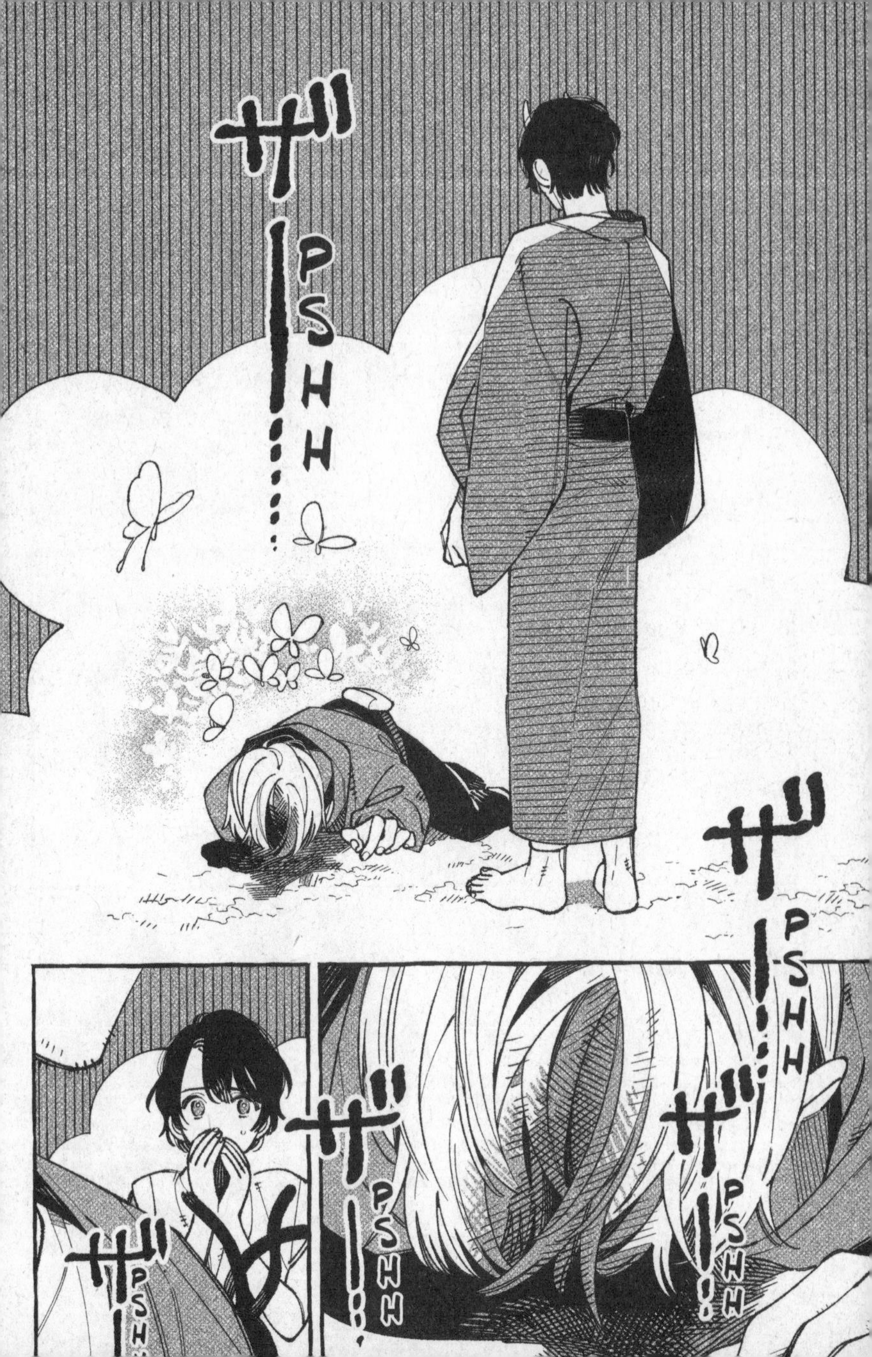
PSHH
PSHH
PSHH
PSHH
PSH

THE HAUNTED BOOKSTORE
Gateway to a Parallel Universe

THE
HAUNTED
BOOKSTORE
Gateway to a
Parallel Universe

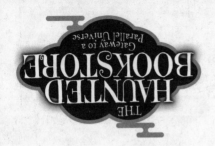

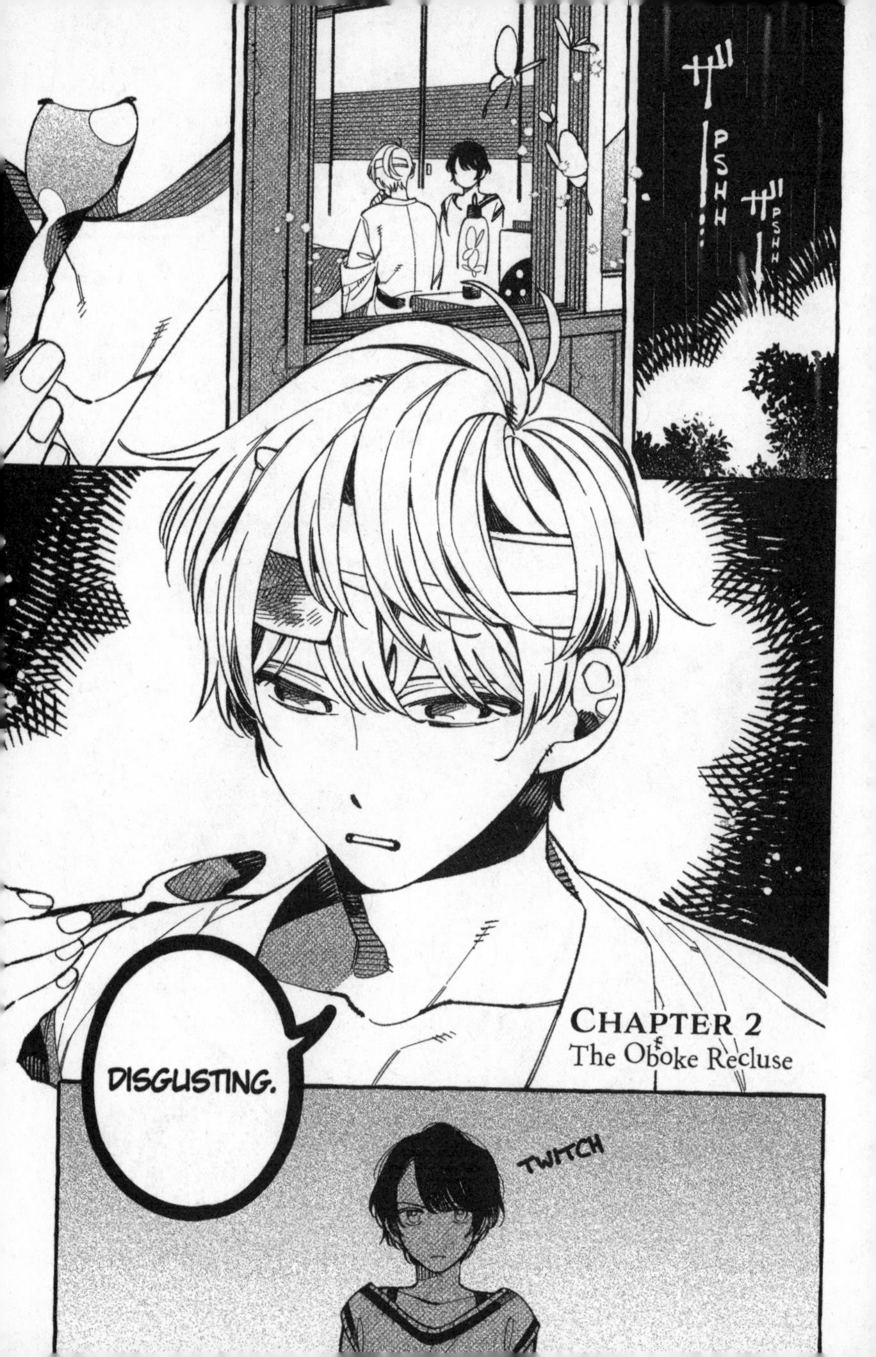
PSHH
PSHH
CHAPTER 2
The Oboke Recluse
DISGUSTING.
TWITCH

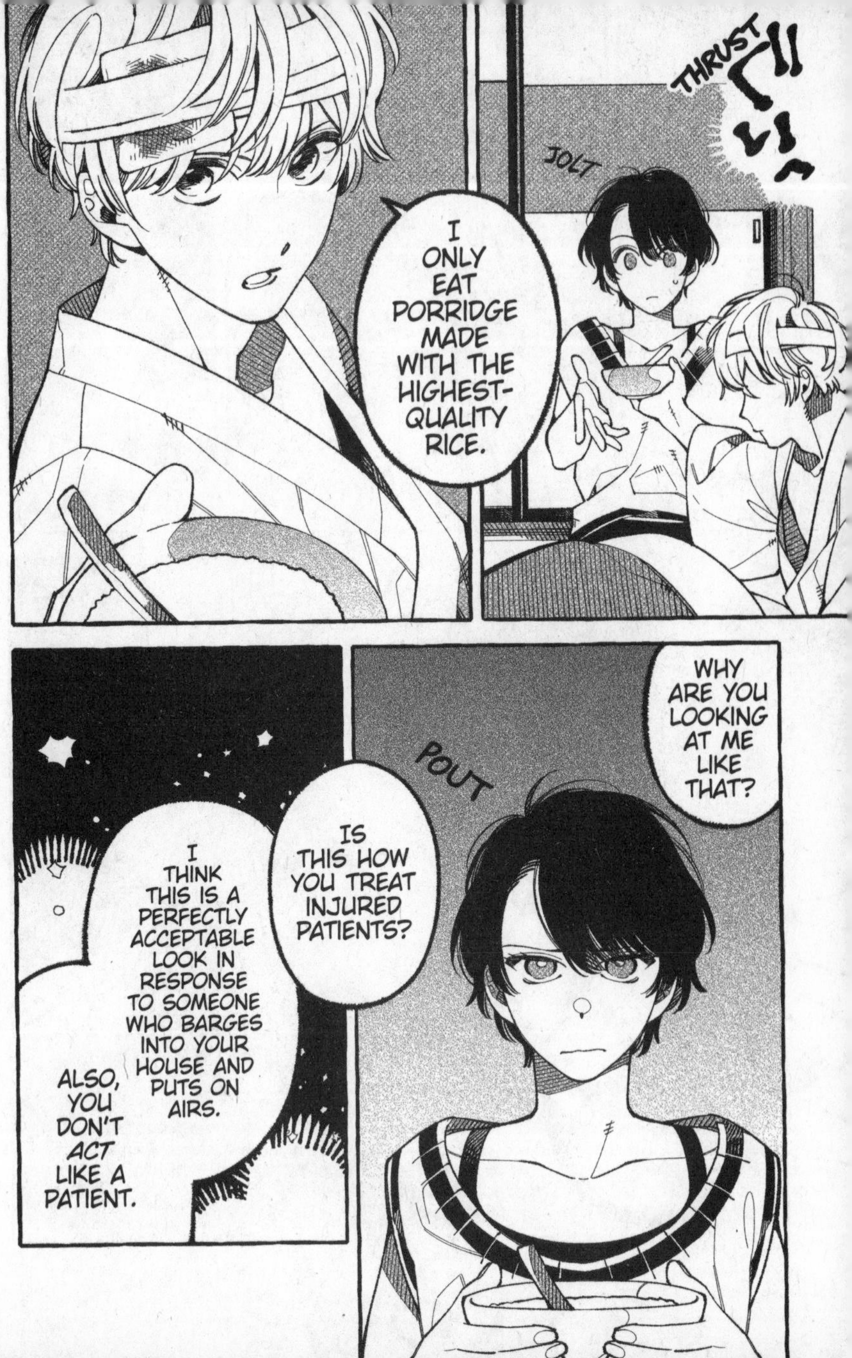
THRUST
JOLT
I ONLY EAT PORRIDGE MADE WITH THE HIGHEST-QUALITY RICE.
WHY ARE YOU LOOKING AT ME LIKE THAT?
POUT
IS THIS HOW YOU TREAT INJURED PATIENTS?
I THINK THIS IS A PERFECTLY ACCEPTABLE LOOK IN RESPONSE TO SOMEONE WHO BARGES INTO YOUR HOUSE AND PUTS ON AIRS.
ALSO, YOU DON'T *ACT* LIKE A PATIENT.

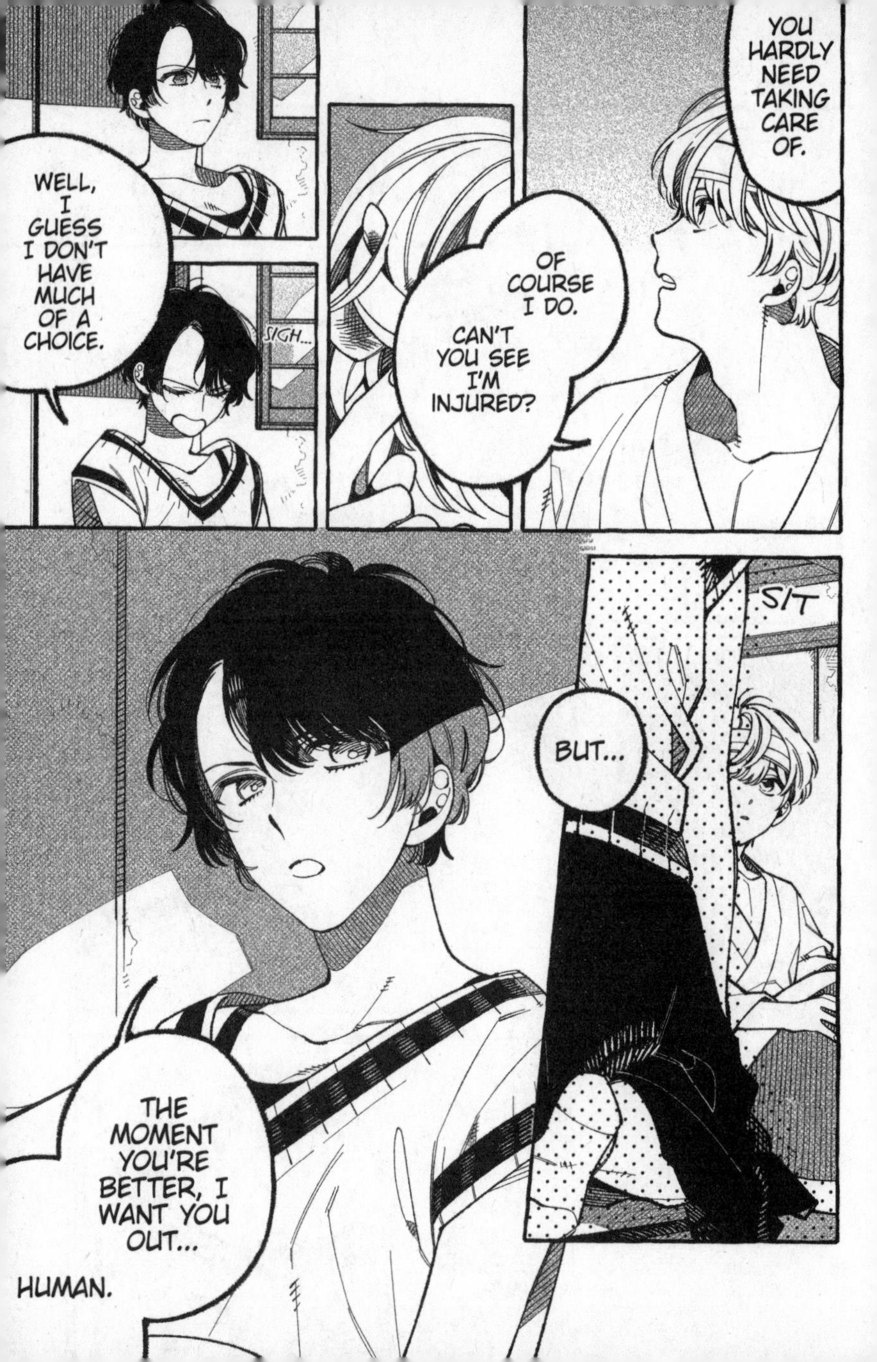
YOU HARDLY NEED TAKING CARE OF.
OF COURSE I DO.
CAN'T YOU SEE I'M INJURED?
WELL, I GUESS I DON'T HAVE MUCH OF A CHOICE.
SIGH...
SIT
BUT...
THE MOMENT YOU'RE BETTER, I WANT YOU OUT...
HUMAN.

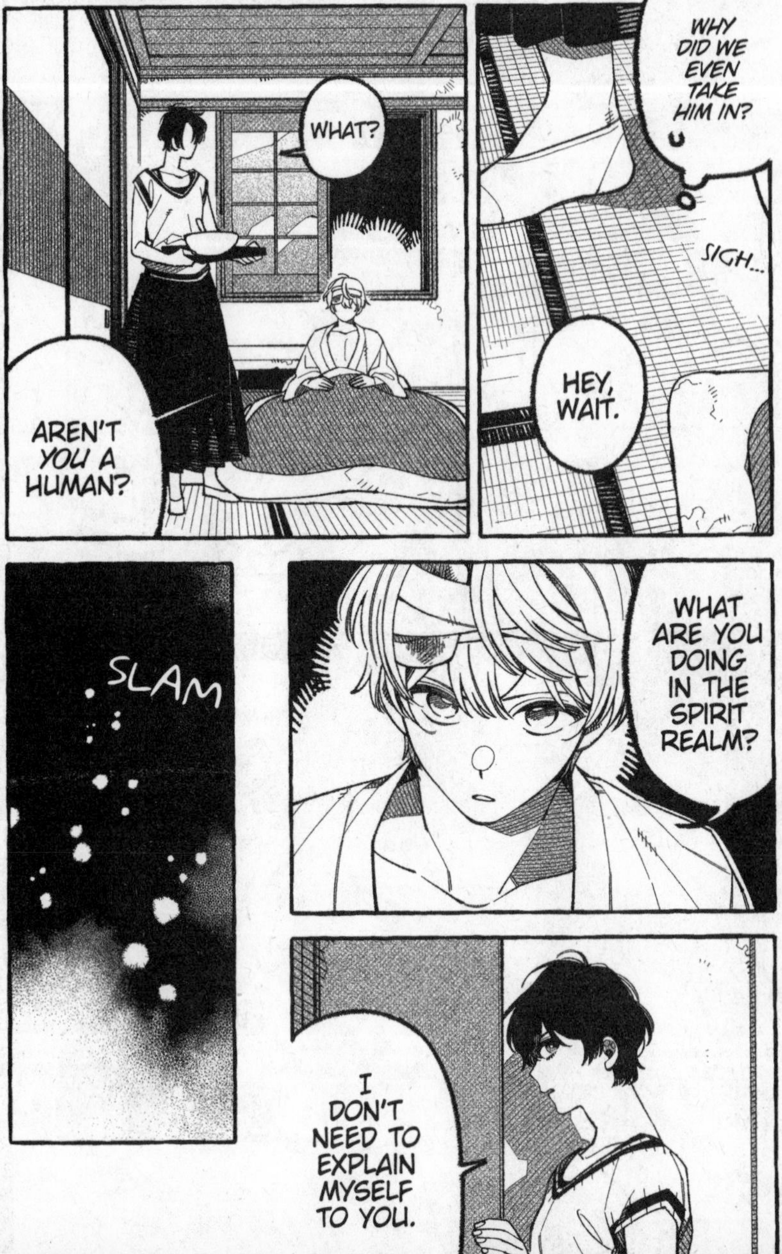
WHY DID WE EVEN TAKE HIM IN?
SIGH...
HEY, WAIT.
WHAT?
AREN'T YOU A HUMAN?
WHAT ARE YOU DOING IN THE SPIRIT REALM?
I DON'T NEED TO EXPLAIN MYSELF TO YOU.
SLAM

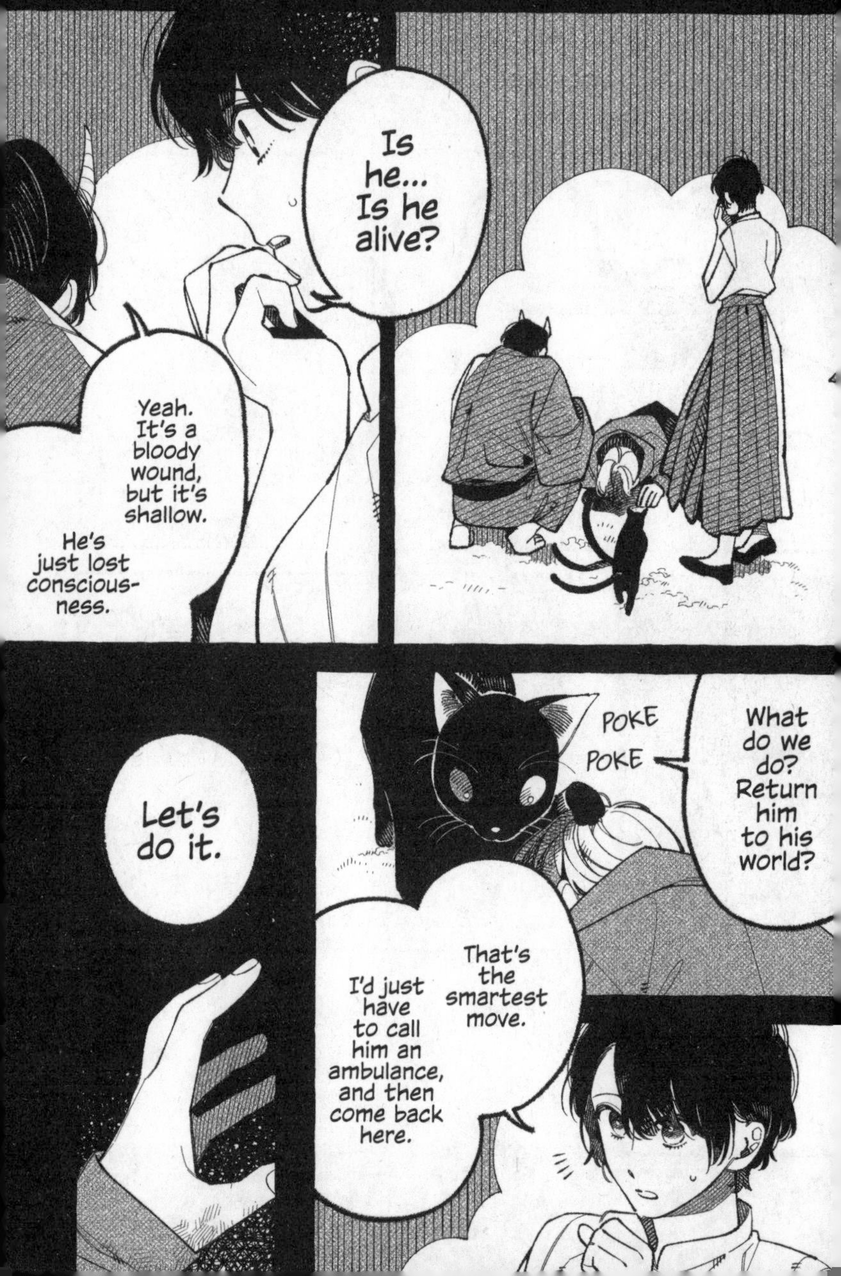
Is he... Is he alive?
Yeah. It's a bloody wound, but it's shallow.
He's just lost conscious-ness.
POKE
POKE
What do we do? Return him to his world?
That's the smartest move.
I'd just have to call him an ambulance, and then come back here.
Let's do it.

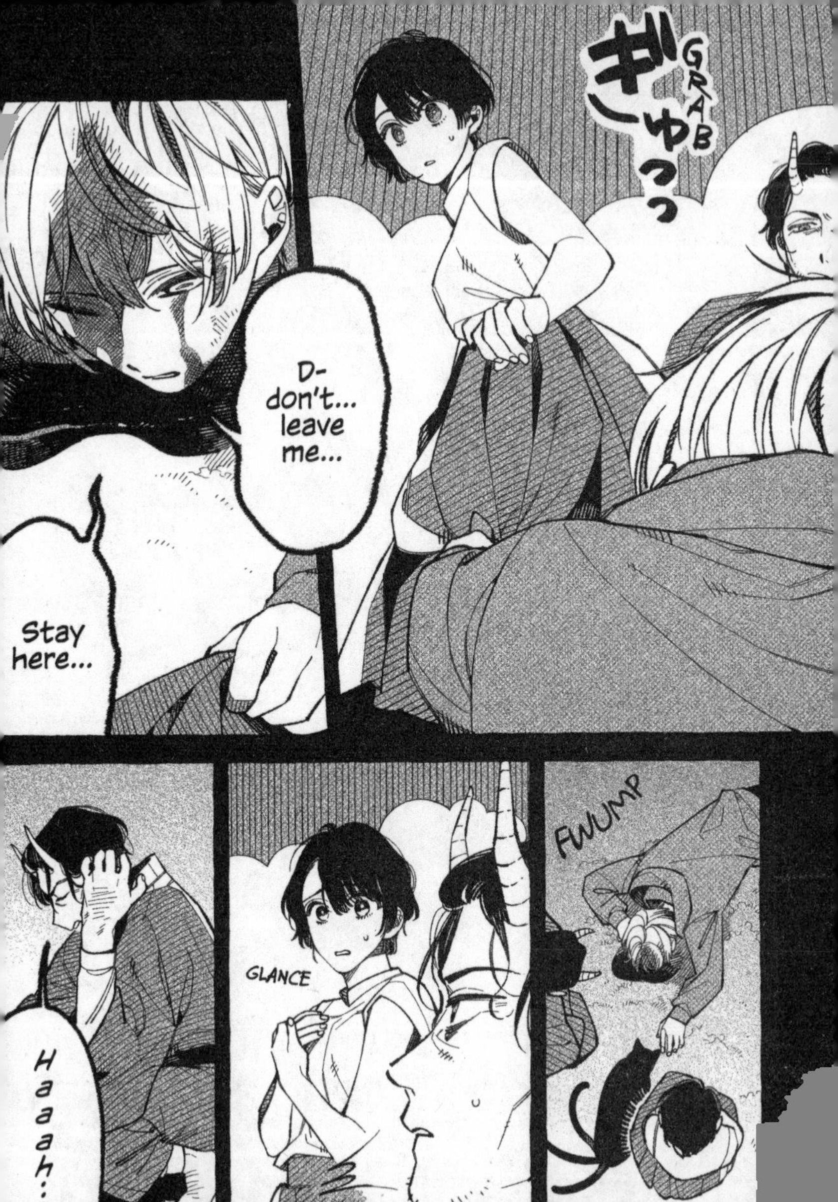
GRAB
D-
don't...
leave
me...
Stay
here...
FWUMP
GLANCE
Haaah...

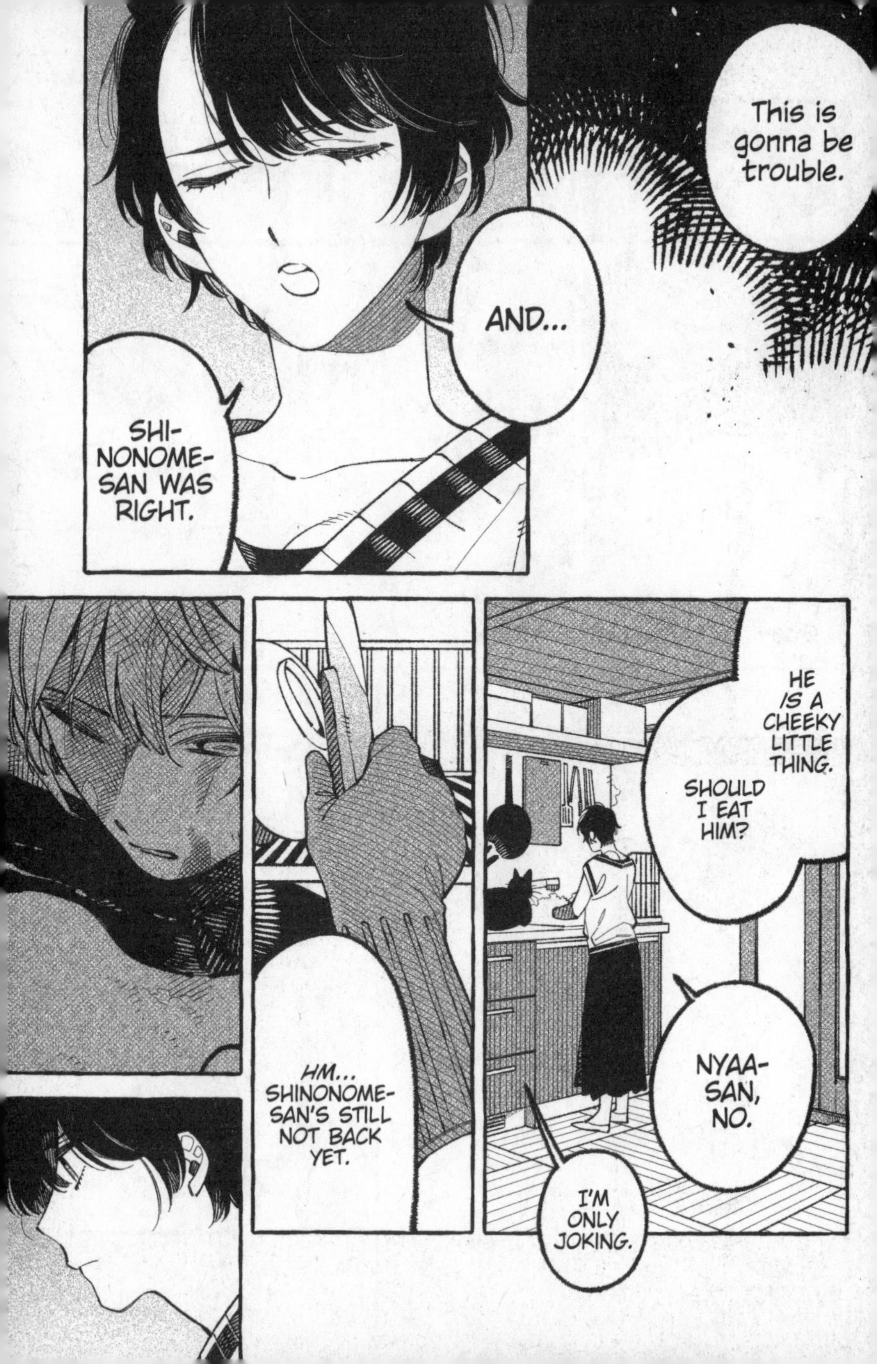
SHI-NONOME-SAN WAS RIGHT.
AND...
This is gonna be trouble.
HE IS A CHEEKY LITTLE THING.
SHOULD I EAT HIM?
NYAA-SAN, NO.
I'M ONLY JOKING.
HM... SHINONOME-SAN'S STILL NOT BACK YET.

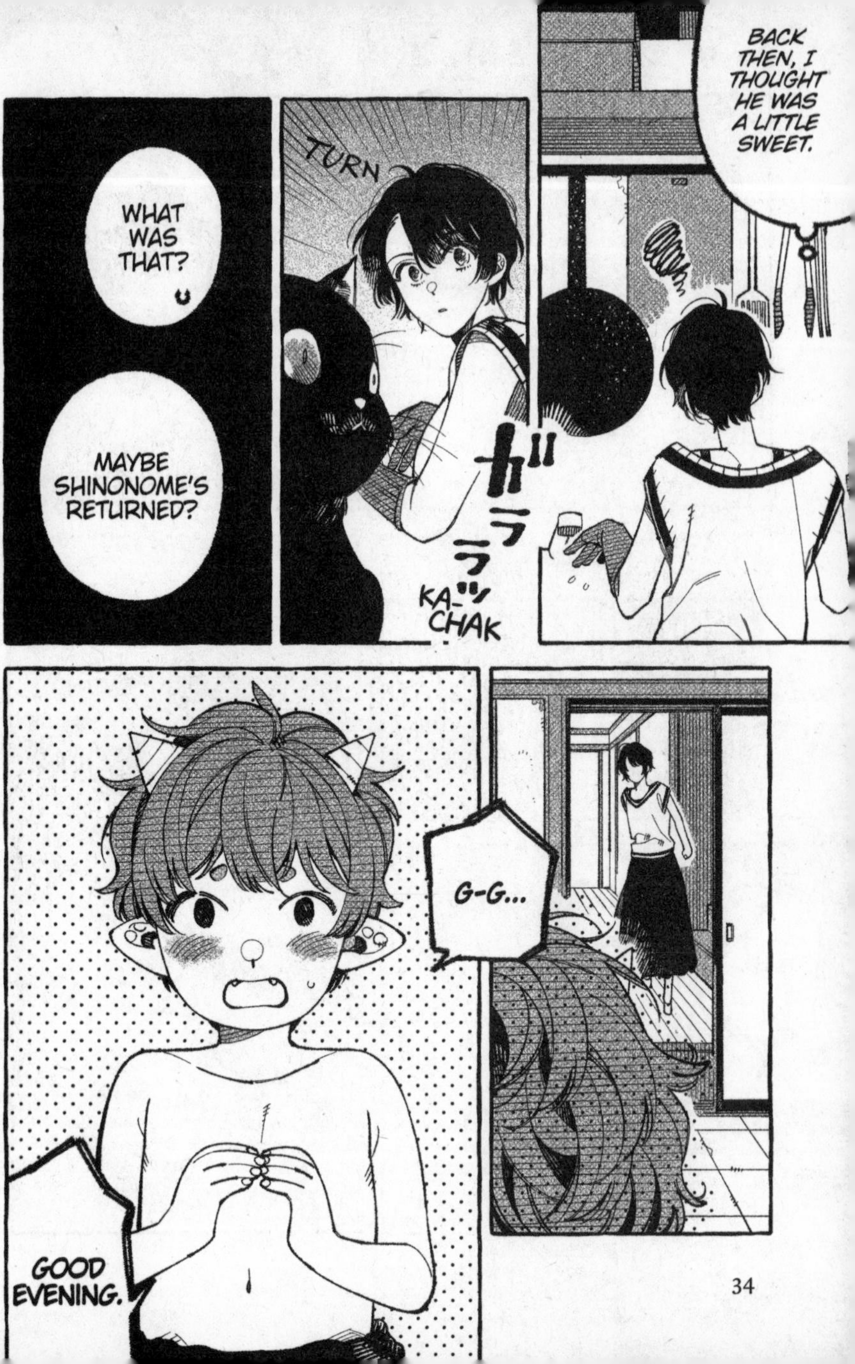
BACK THEN, I THOUGHT HE WAS A LITTLE SWEET.
ガラララッ
KA-CHAK
TURN
WHAT WAS THAT?
MAYBE SHINONOME'S RETURNED?
G-G...
GOOD EVENING.

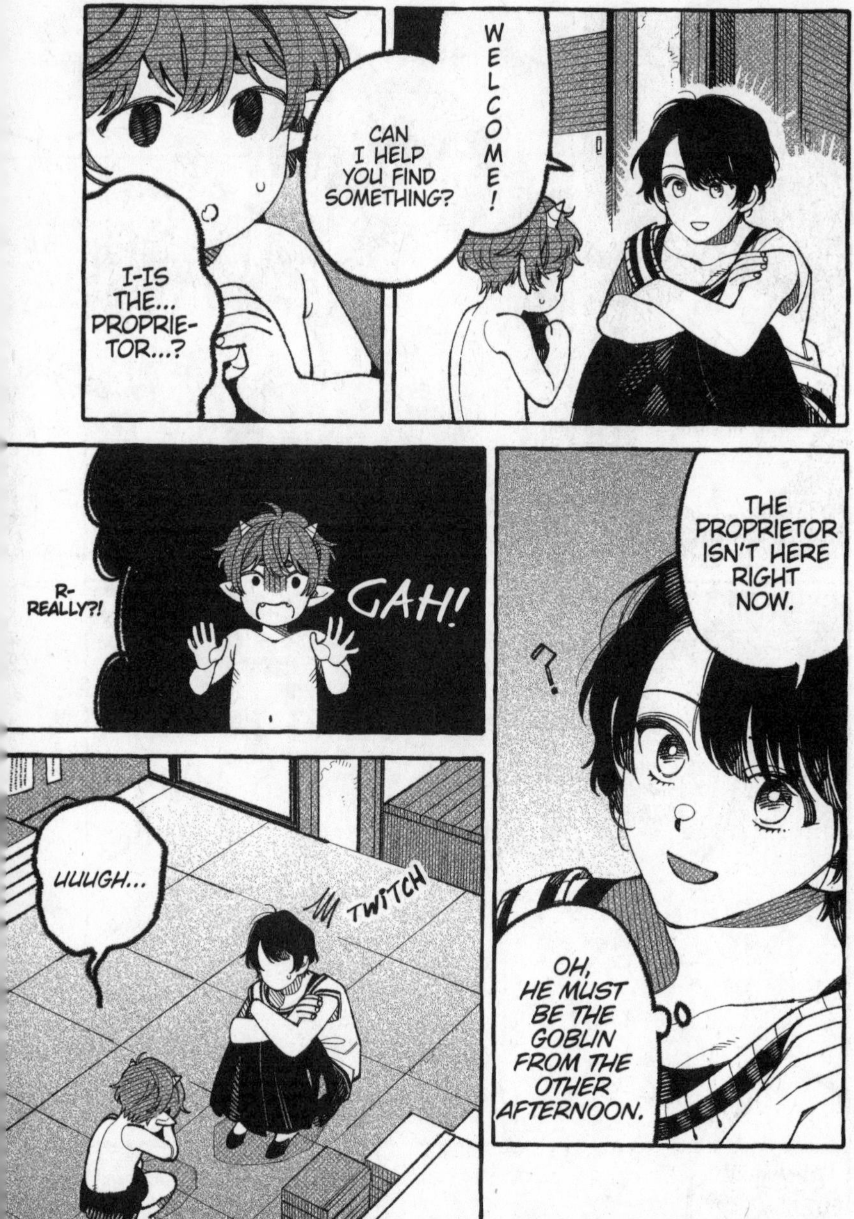
WELCOME!
CAN I HELP YOU FIND SOMETHING?
I-IS THE... PROPRIETOR...?
THE PROPRIETOR ISN'T HERE RIGHT NOW.
?
OH, HE MUST BE THE GOBLIN FROM THE OTHER AFTERNOON.
GAH!
R-REALLY?!
UUUGH...
TWITCH

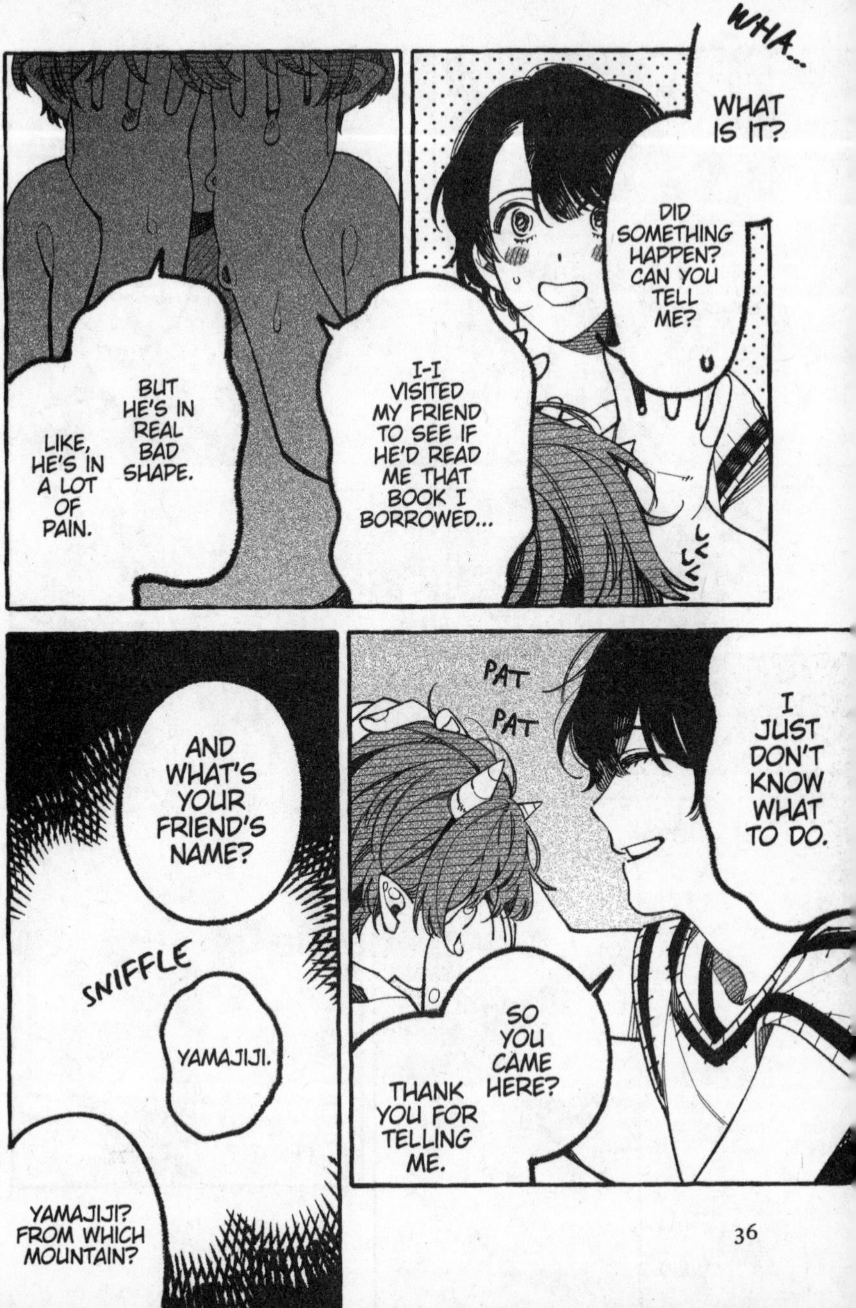
WHA...
WHAT IS IT?
DID SOMETHING HAPPEN? CAN YOU TELL ME?
I-I VISITED MY FRIEND TO SEE IF HE'D READ ME THAT BOOK I BORROWED...
BUT HE'S IN REAL BAD SHAPE.
LIKE, HE'S IN A LOT OF PAIN.
PAT
PAT
I JUST DON'T KNOW WHAT TO DO.
SO YOU CAME HERE?
THANK YOU FOR TELLING ME.
AND WHAT'S YOUR FRIEND'S NAME?
SNIFFLE
YAMAJIJI.
YAMAJIJI? FROM WHICH MOUNTAIN?

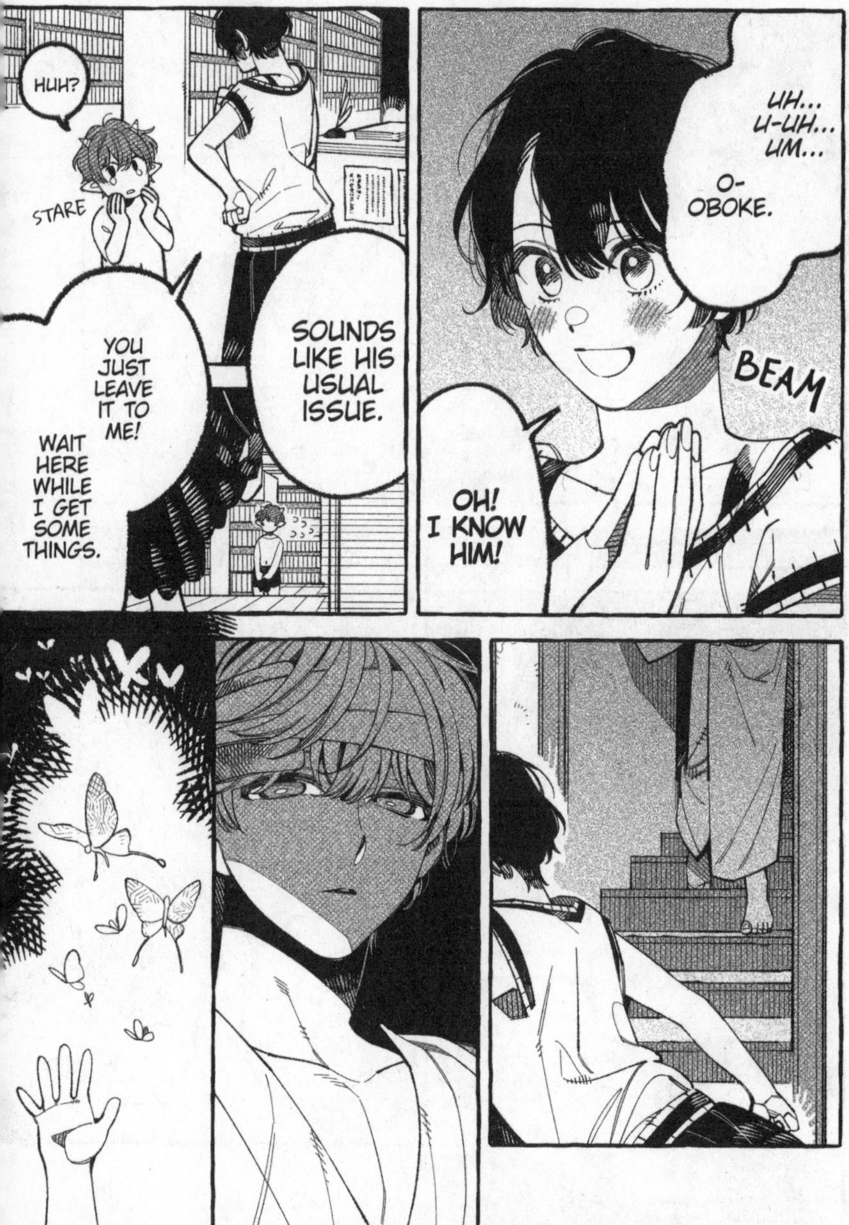
UH... U-UH... UM...
O-OBOKE.
BEAM
OH! I KNOW HIM!
SOUNDS LIKE HIS USUAL ISSUE.
HUH?
STARE
YOU JUST LEAVE IT TO ME!
WAIT HERE WHILE I GET SOME THINGS.

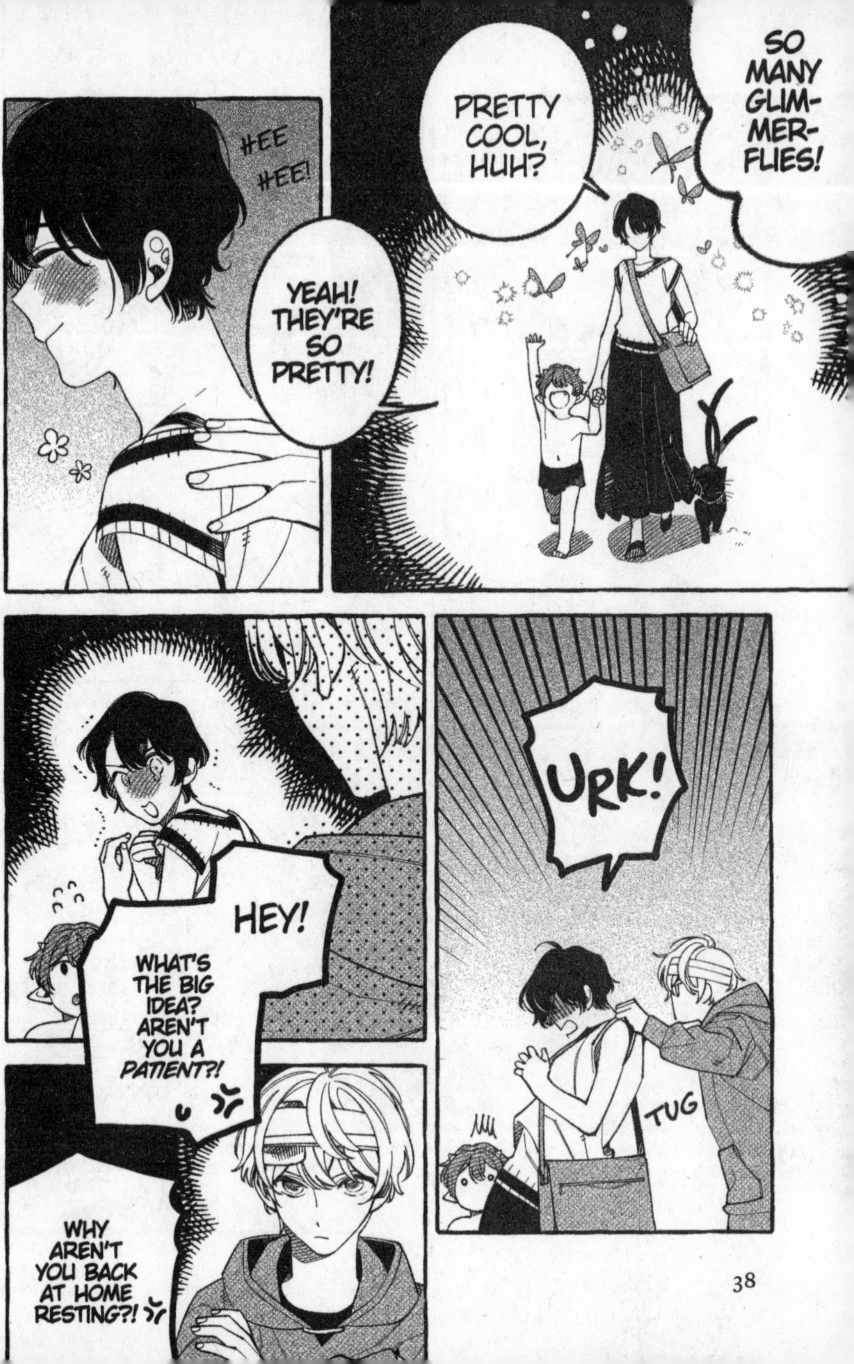
SO MANY GLIM-MER-FLIES!
PRETTY COOL, HUH?
YEAH! THEY'RE SO PRETTY!
HEE HEE!
URK!
TUG
HEY!
WHAT'S THE BIG IDEA? AREN'T YOU A PATIENT?!
WHY AREN'T YOU BACK AT HOME RESTING?!

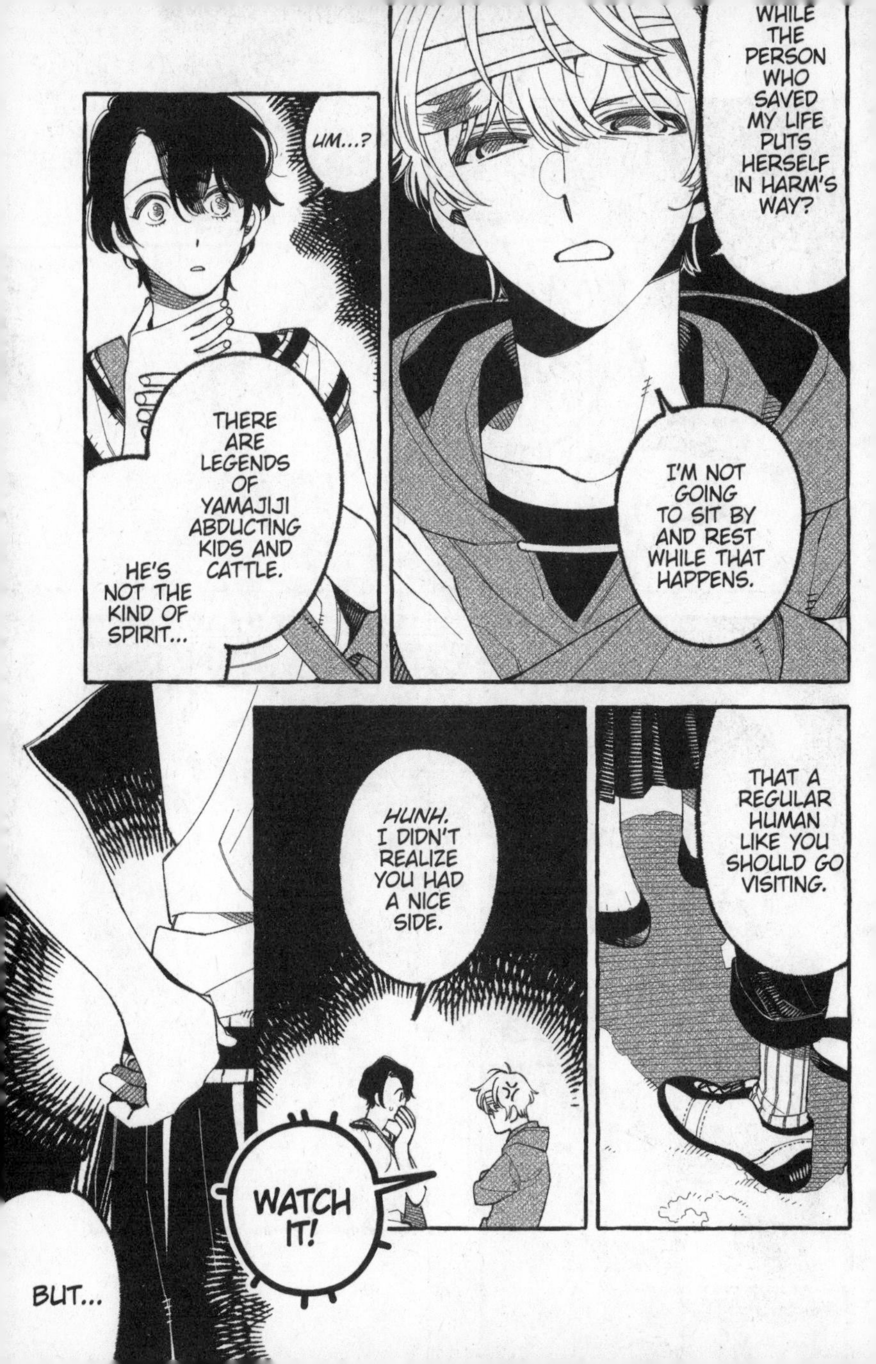
WHILE THE PERSON WHO SAVED MY LIFE PUTS HERSELF IN HARM'S WAY?
I'M NOT GOING TO SIT BY AND REST WHILE THAT HAPPENS.
UM...?
THERE ARE LEGENDS OF YAMAJIJI ABDUCTING KIDS AND CATTLE.
HE'S NOT THE KIND OF SPIRIT...
THAT A REGULAR HUMAN LIKE YOU SHOULD GO VISITING.
HUNH. I DIDN'T REALIZE YOU HAD A NICE SIDE.
WATCH IT!
BUT...

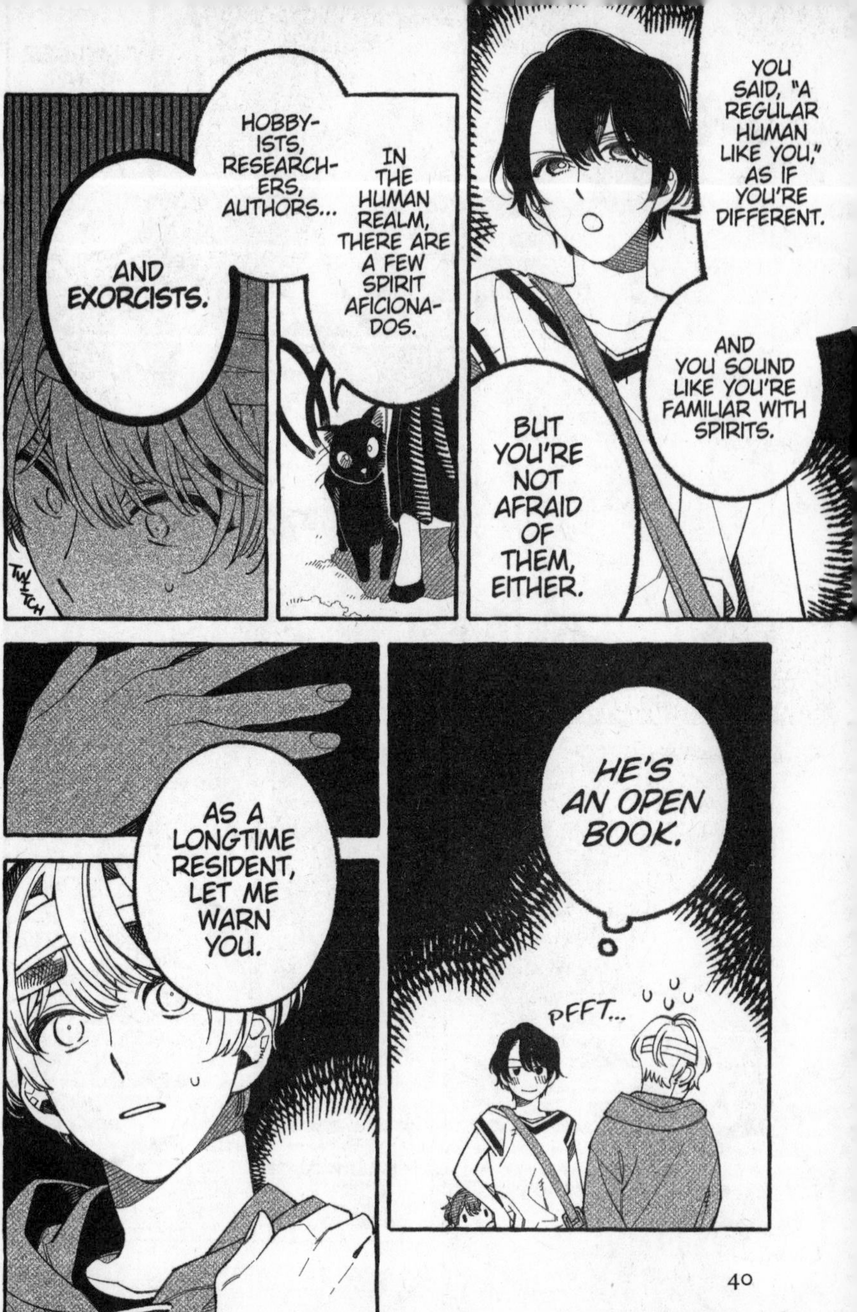
YOU SAID, "A REGULAR HUMAN LIKE YOU," AS IF YOU'RE DIFFERENT.
AND YOU SOUND LIKE YOU'RE FAMILIAR WITH SPIRITS.
BUT YOU'RE NOT AFRAID OF THEM, EITHER.
IN THE HUMAN REALM, THERE ARE A FEW SPIRIT AFICIONADOS.
HOBBYISTS, RESEARCHERS, AUTHORS...
AND EXORCISTS.
TWITCH
HE'S AN OPEN BOOK.
PFFT...
AS A LONGTIME RESIDENT, LET ME WARN YOU.

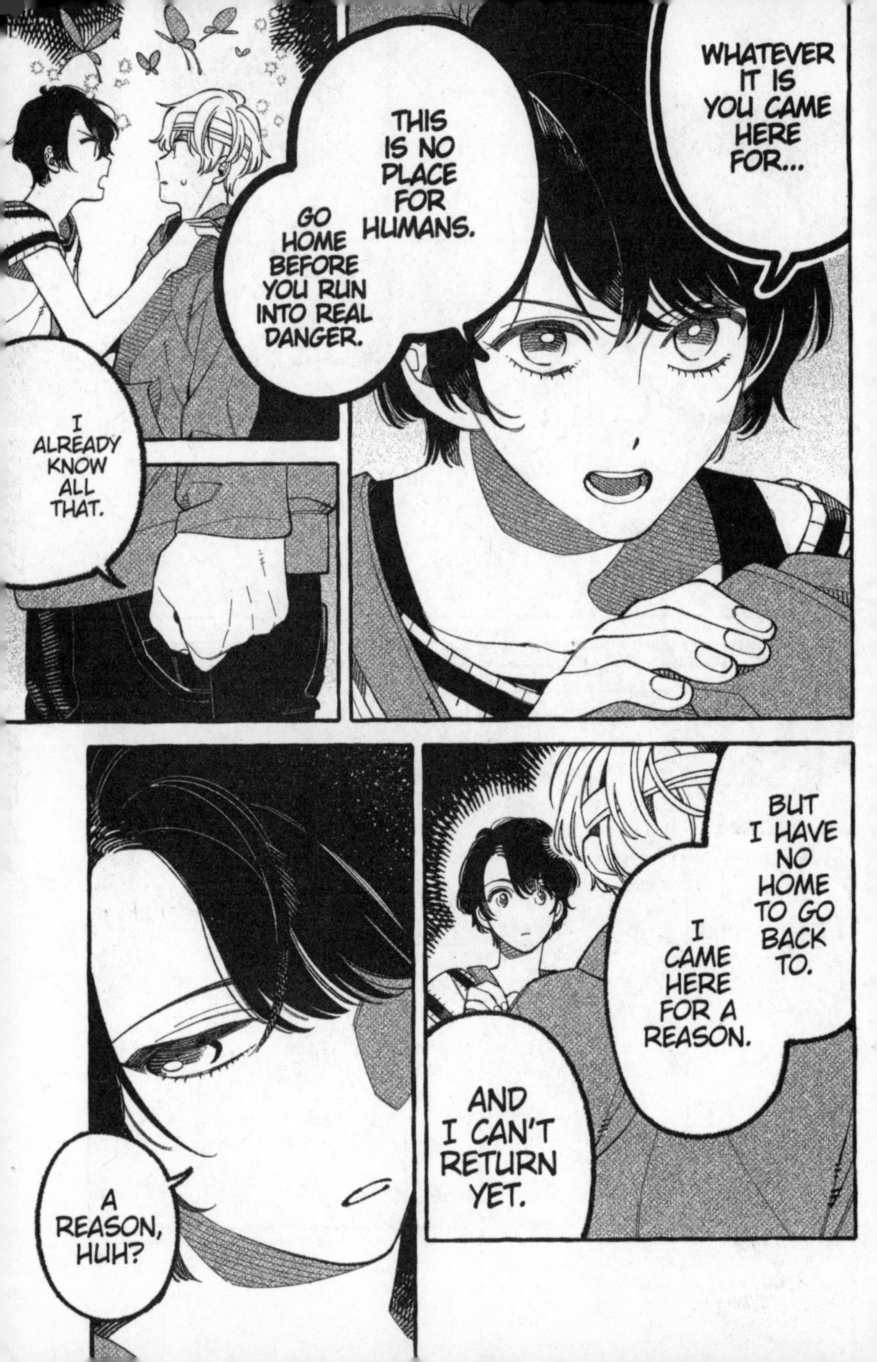
WHATEVER IT IS YOU CAME HERE FOR...
THIS IS NO PLACE FOR HUMANS.
GO HOME BEFORE YOU RUN INTO REAL DANGER.
I ALREADY KNOW ALL THAT.
BUT I HAVE NO HOME TO GO BACK TO.
I CAME HERE FOR A REASON.
AND I CAN'T RETURN YET.
A REASON, HUH?

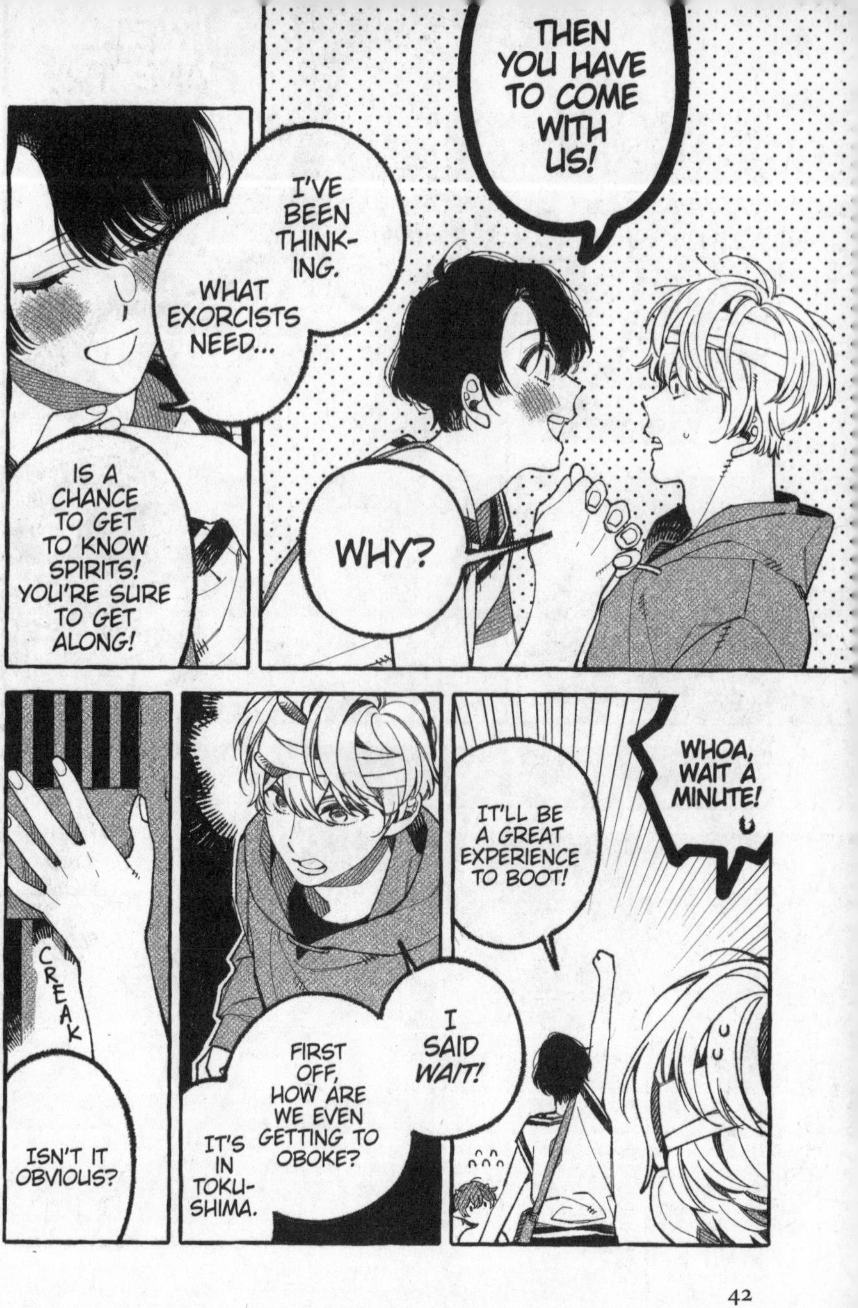
THEN YOU HAVE TO COME WITH US!
WHY?
I'VE BEEN THINK-ING.
WHAT EXORCISTS NEED...
IS A CHANCE TO GET TO KNOW SPIRITS! YOU'RE SURE TO GET ALONG!
WHOA, WAIT A MINUTE!
IT'LL BE A GREAT EXPERIENCE TO BOOT!
I SAID WAIT!
FIRST OFF, HOW ARE WE EVEN GETTING TO OBOKE?
IT'S IN TOKU-SHIMA.
CREAK
ISN'T IT OBVIOUS?

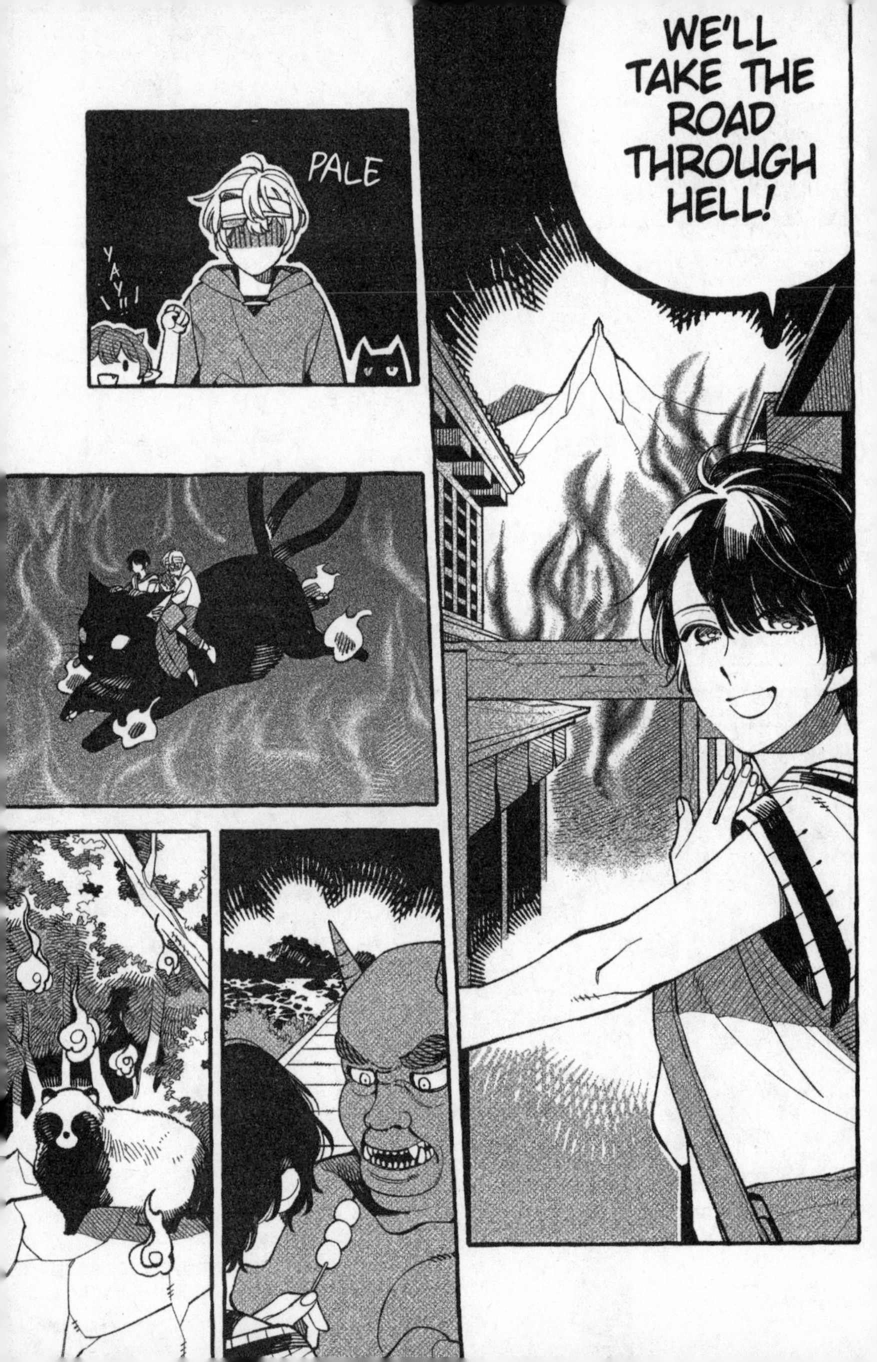
WE'LL TAKE THE ROAD THROUGH HELL!
PALE
YAY!!

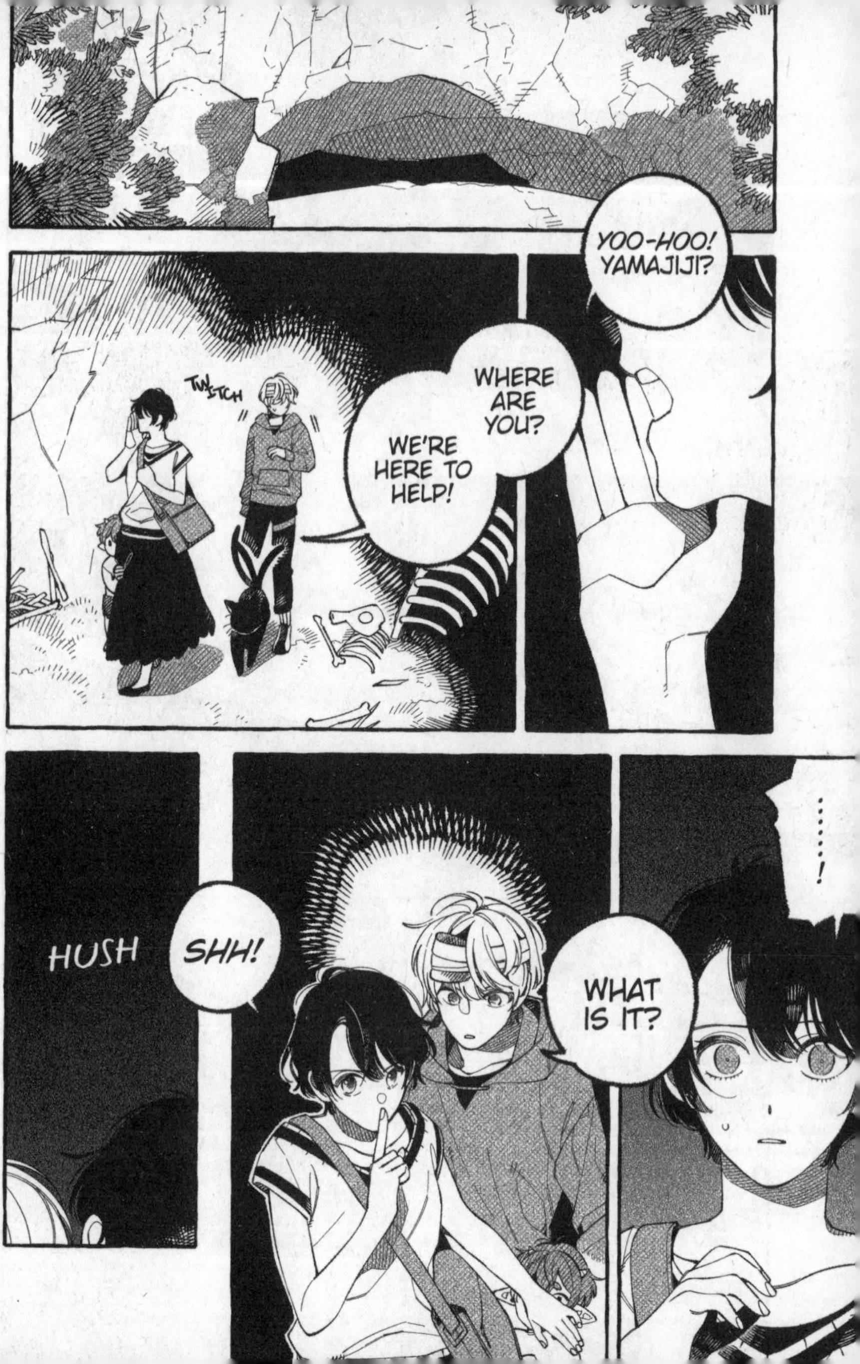
YOO-HOO! YAMAJIJI?
WHERE ARE YOU?
WE'RE HERE TO HELP!
TWITCH
......!
WHAT IS IT?
SHH!
HUSH

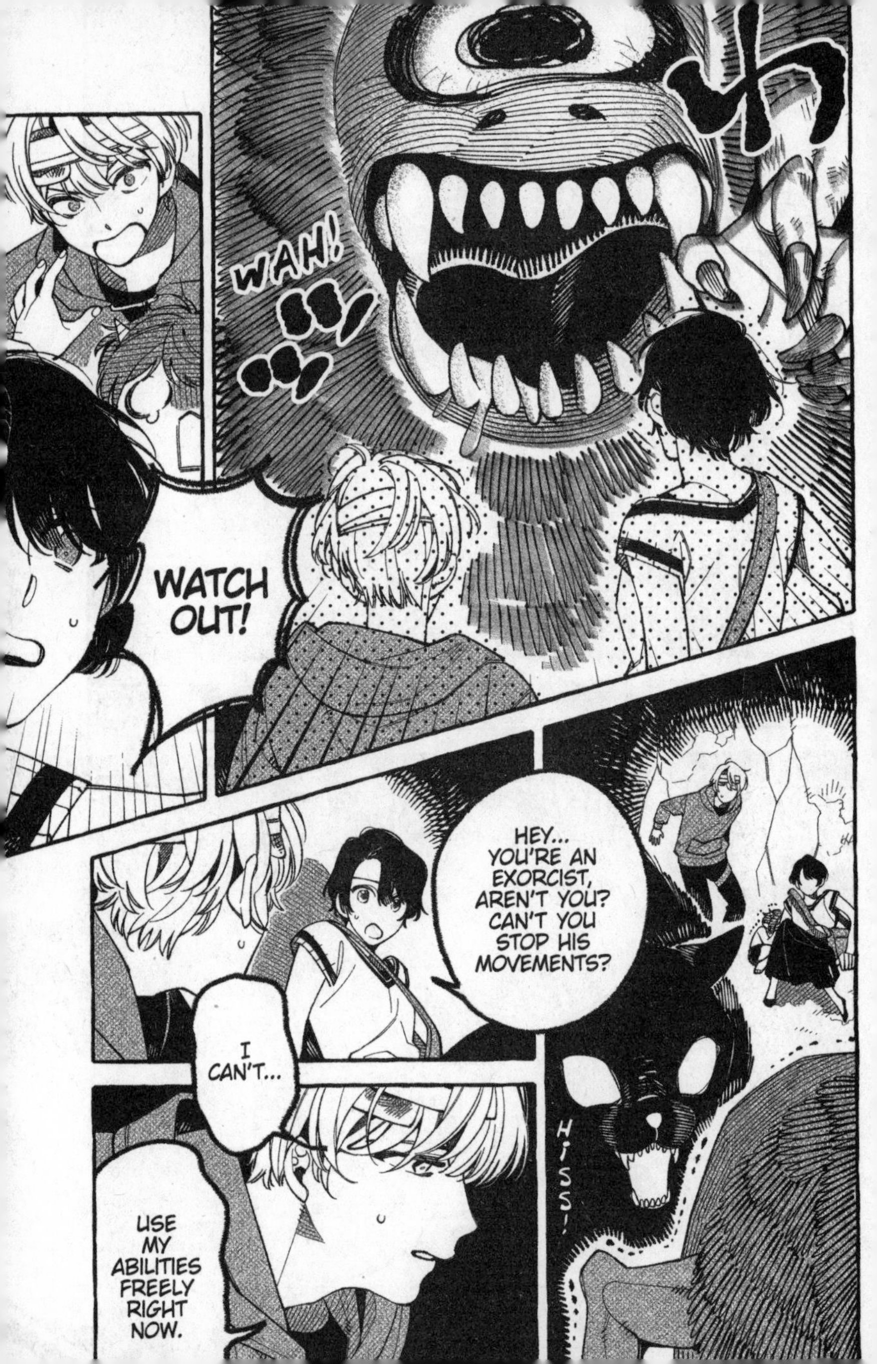
WAH!
WATCH OUT!
HISS!
HEY... YOU'RE AN EXORCIST, AREN'T YOU? CAN'T YOU STOP HIS MOVEMENTS?
I CAN'T...
USE MY ABILITIES FREELY RIGHT NOW.

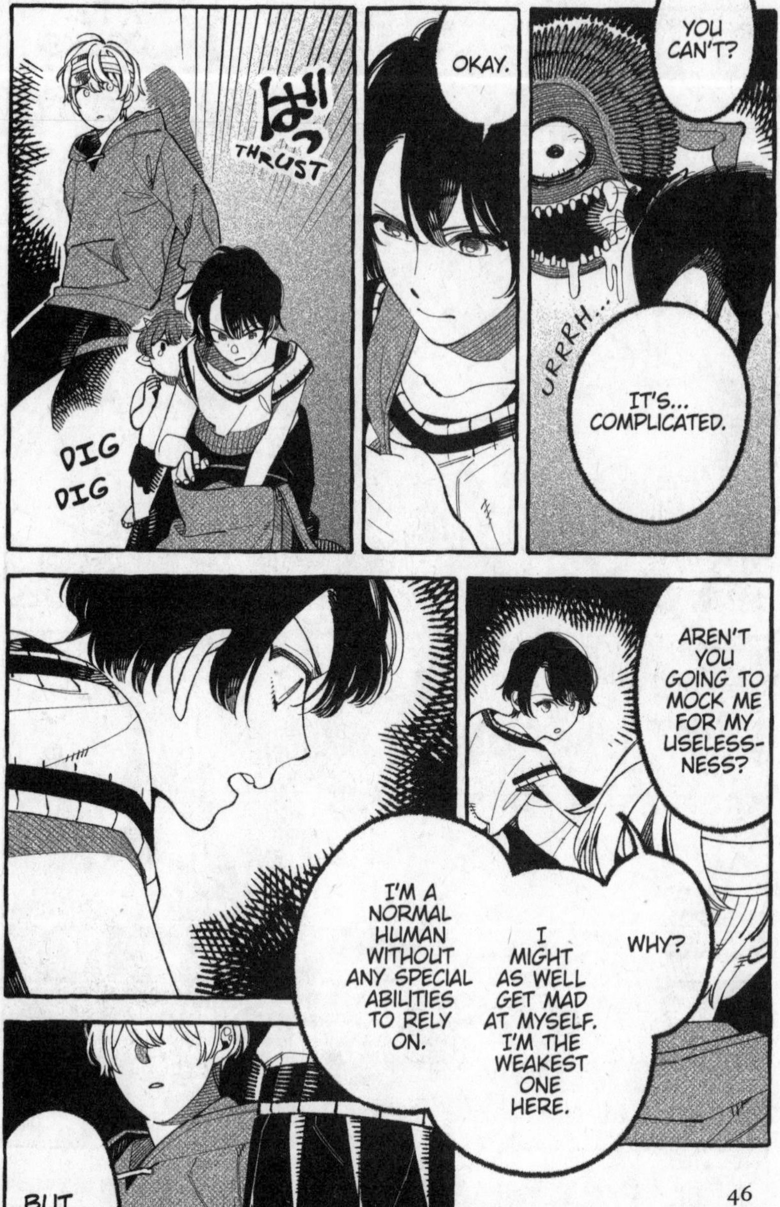
YOU CAN'T?
URRRH...
IT'S... COMPLICATED.
OKAY.
ぱっ THRUST
DIG DIG
AREN'T YOU GOING TO MOCK ME FOR MY USELESS-NESS?
WHY?
I MIGHT AS WELL GET MAD AT MYSELF. I'M THE WEAKEST ONE HERE.
I'M A NORMAL HUMAN WITHOUT ANY SPECIAL ABILITIES TO RELY ON.
BUT...

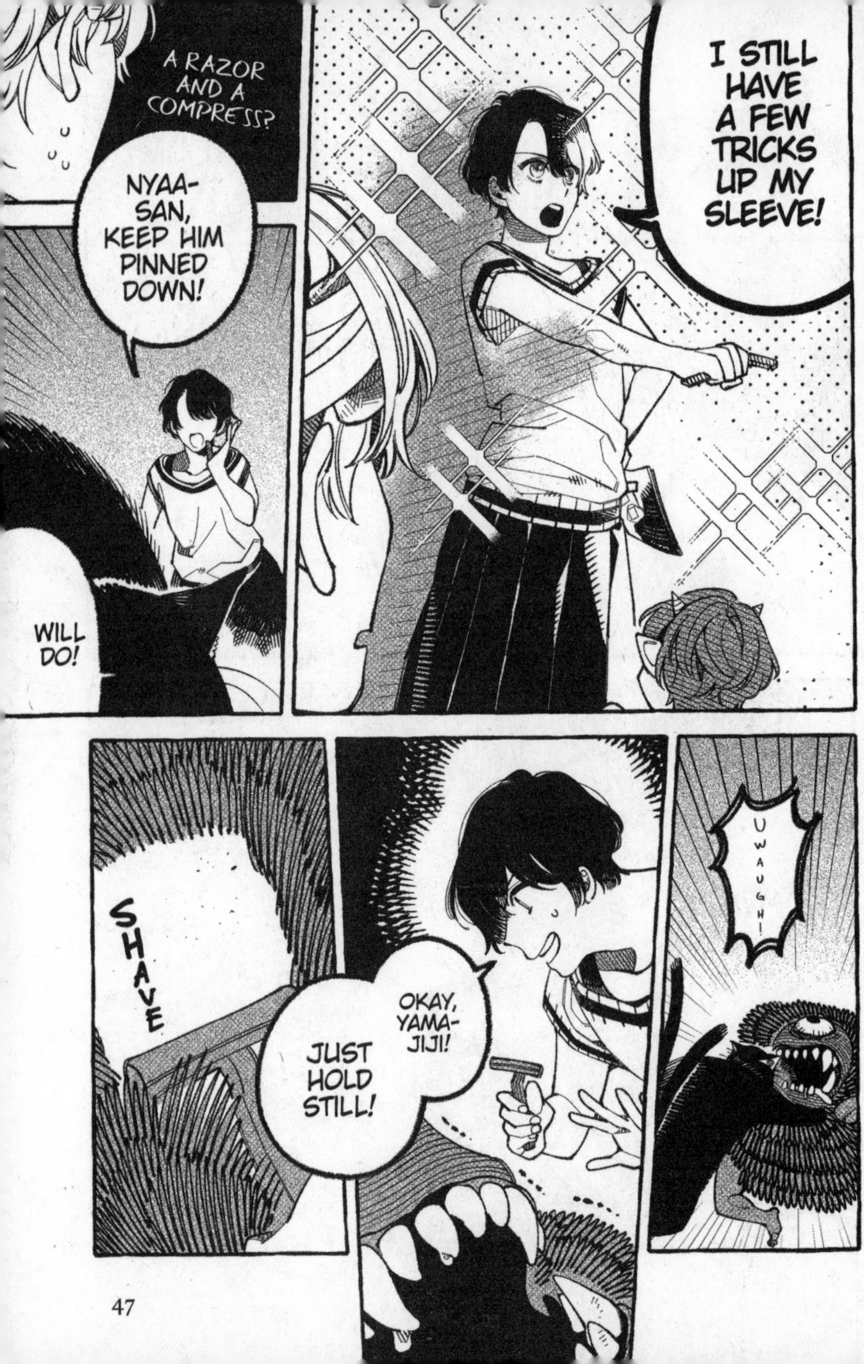
I STILL HAVE A FEW TRICKS UP MY SLEEVE!
A RAZOR AND A COMPRESS?
NYAA-SAN, KEEP HIM PINNED DOWN!
WILL DO!
UWAUGH!
OKAY, YAMAJIJI!
JUST HOLD STILL!
SHAVE

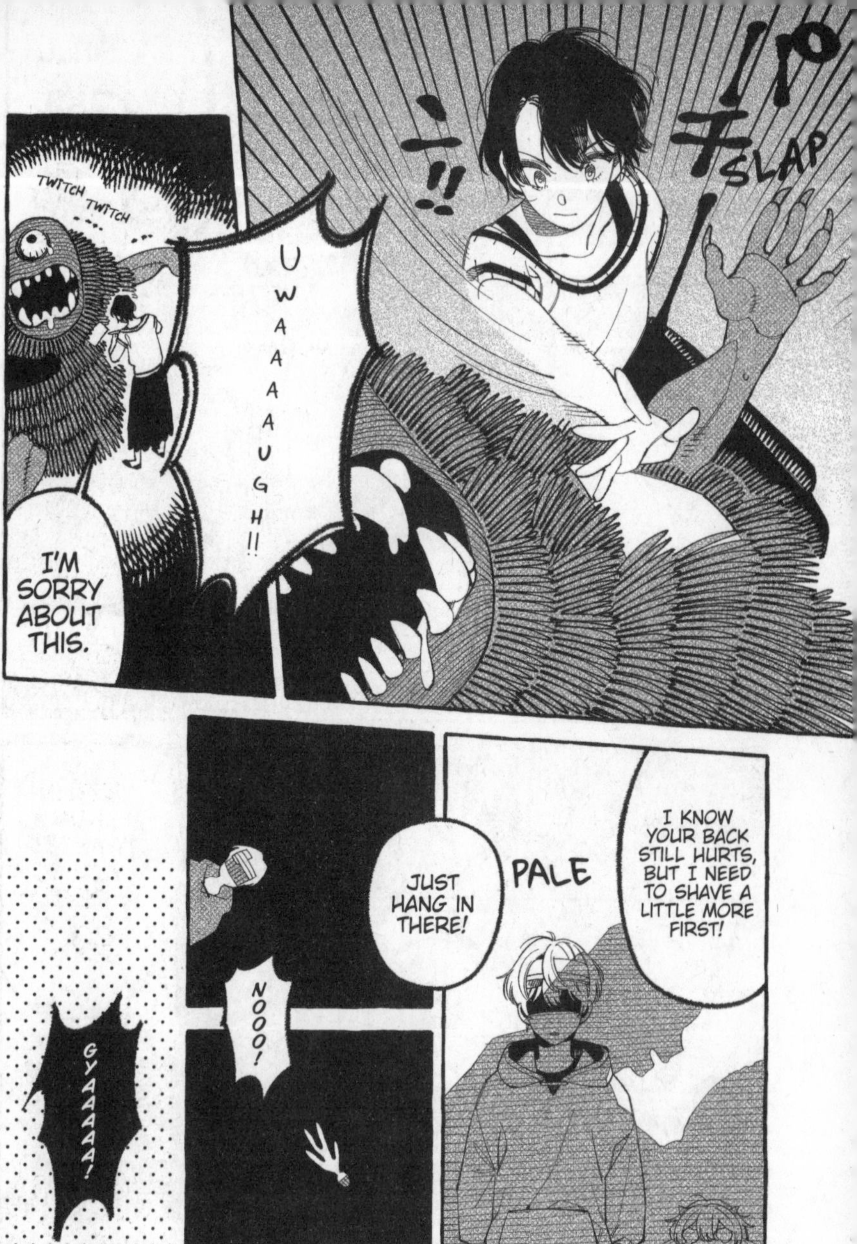
SLAP
!!
UWAAAAAUGH!!
TWITCH TWITCH
I'M SORRY ABOUT THIS.
I KNOW YOUR BACK STILL HURTS, BUT I NEED TO SHAVE A LITTLE MORE FIRST!
PALE
JUST HANG IN THERE!
NOOO!
GYAAAAA!

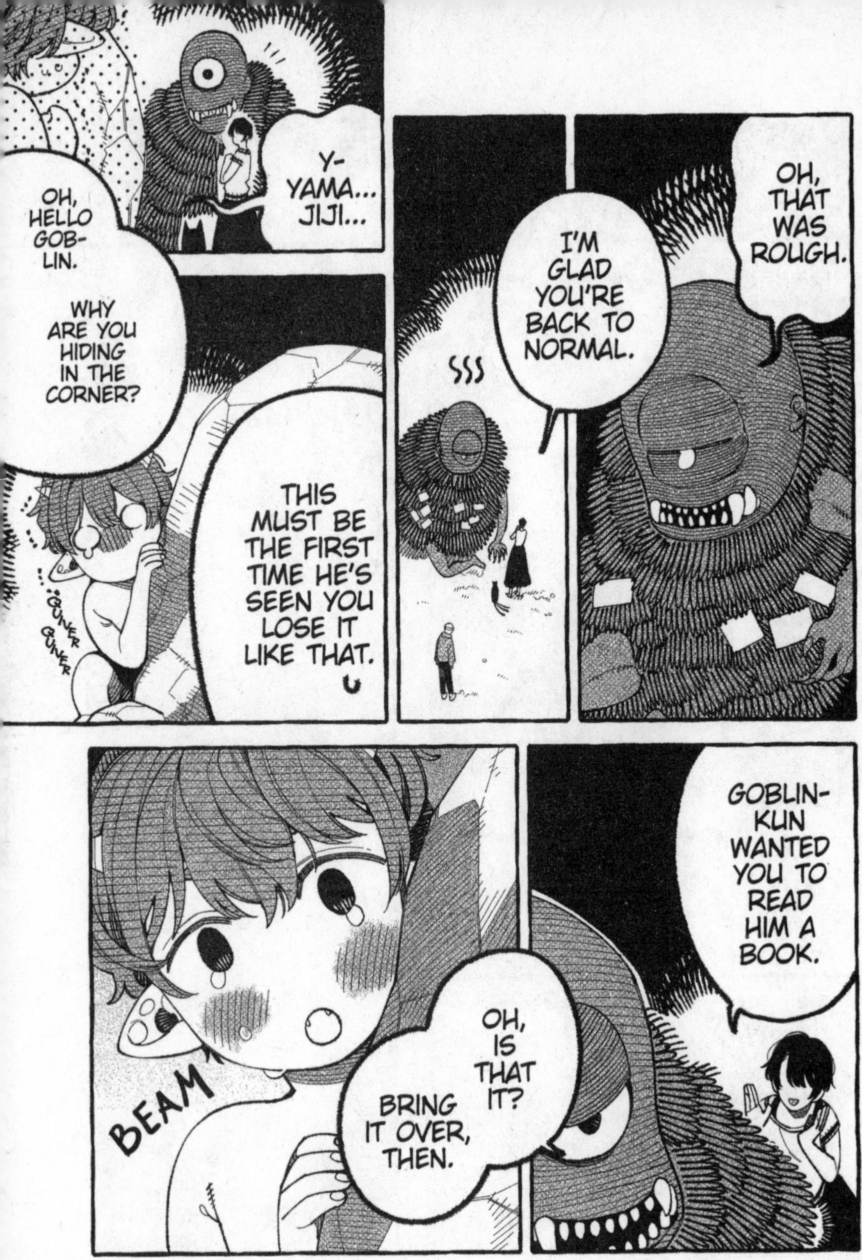
OH, THAT WAS ROUGH.
I'M GLAD YOU'RE BACK TO NORMAL.
Y-YAMA... JIJI...
OH, HELLO GOB-LIN.
WHY ARE YOU HIDING IN THE CORNER?
GUNER GUNER
THIS MUST BE THE FIRST TIME HE'S SEEN YOU LOSE IT LIKE THAT.
GOBLIN-KUN WANTED YOU TO READ HIM A BOOK.
OH, IS THAT IT?
BRING IT OVER, THEN.
BEAM

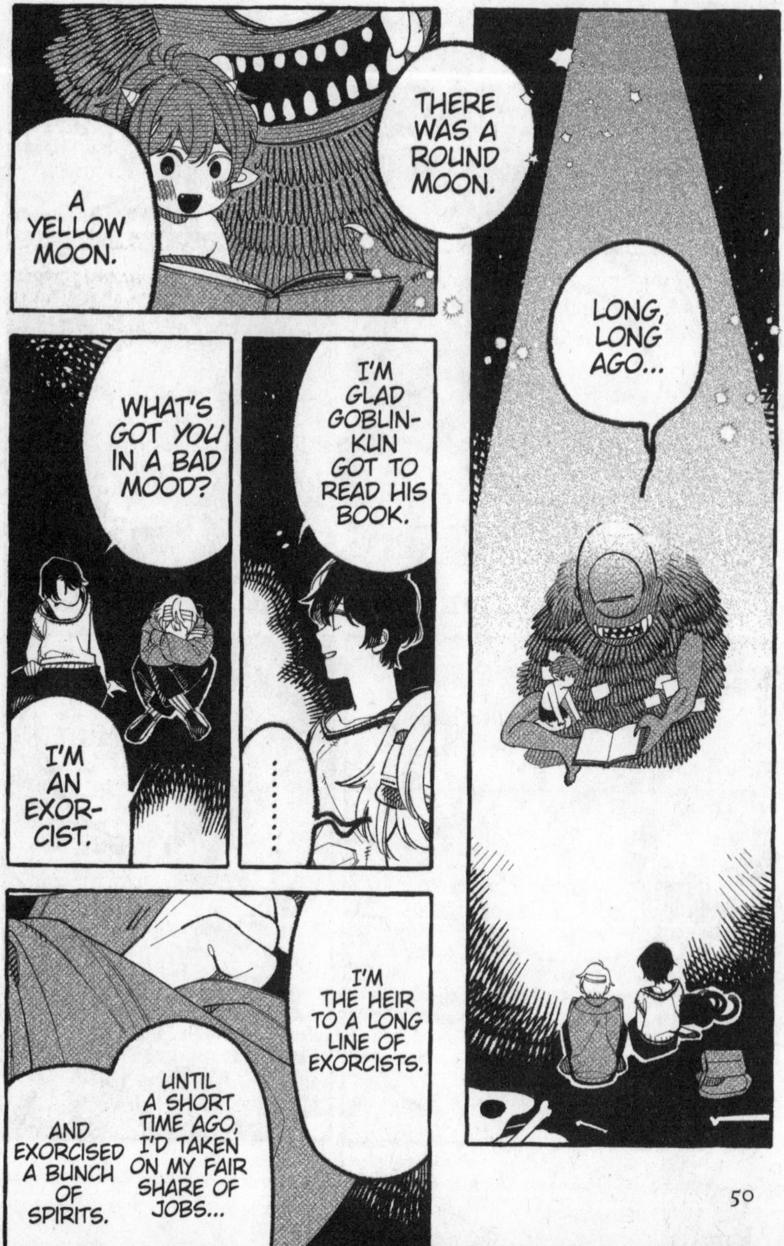
LONG, LONG AGO...
THERE WAS A ROUND MOON.
A YELLOW MOON.
I'M GLAD GOBLIN-KUN GOT TO READ HIS BOOK.
....
WHAT'S GOT YOU IN A BAD MOOD?
I'M AN EXOR-CIST.
I'M THE HEIR TO A LONG LINE OF EXORCISTS.
UNTIL A SHORT TIME AGO, I'D TAKEN ON MY FAIR SHARE OF JOBS...
AND EXORCISED A BUNCH OF SPIRITS.

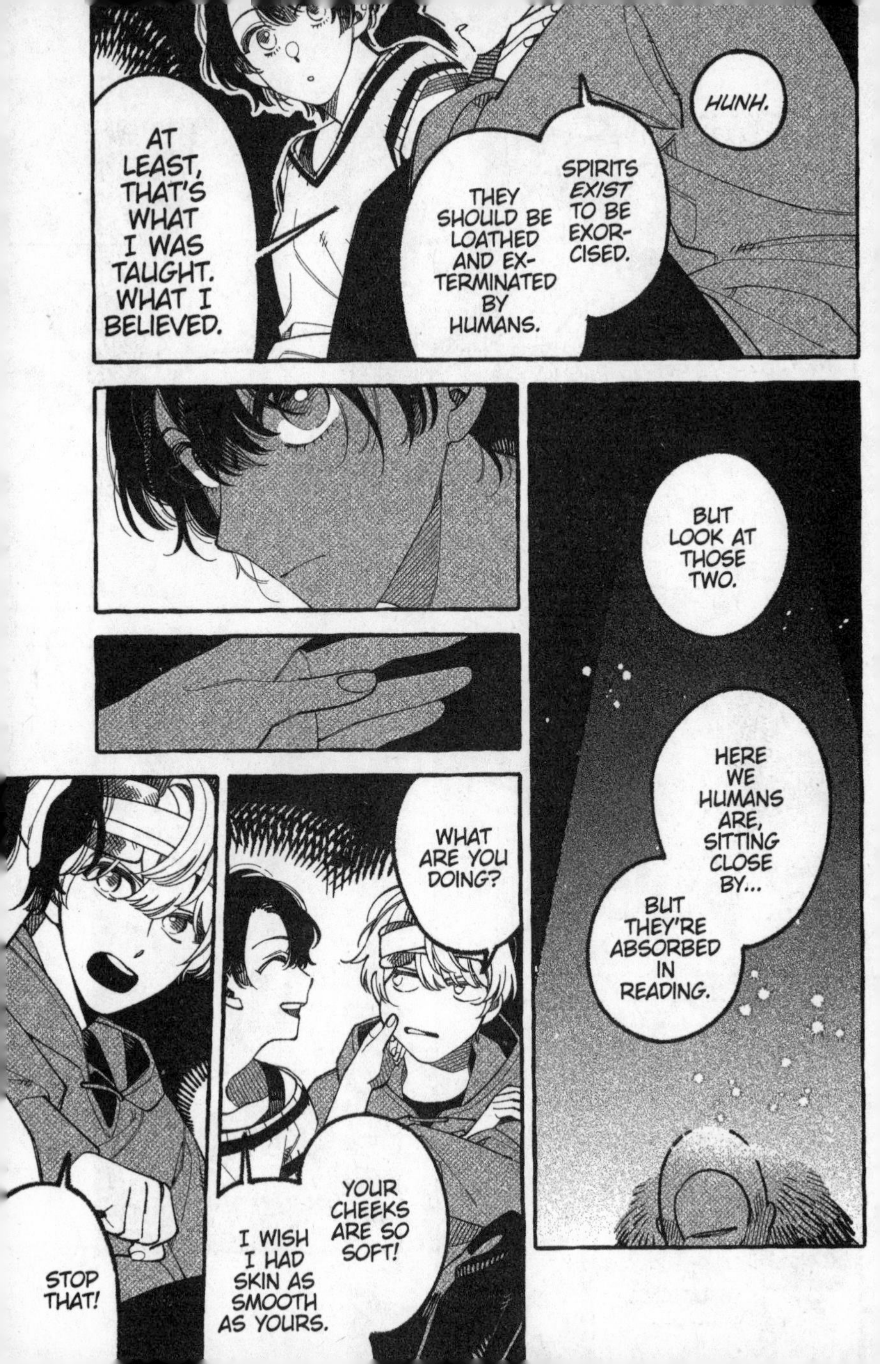
HUNH.
SPIRITS *EXIST* TO BE EXORCISED.
THEY SHOULD BE LOATHED AND EXTERMINATED BY HUMANS.
AT LEAST, THAT'S WHAT I WAS TAUGHT. WHAT I BELIEVED.
BUT LOOK AT THOSE TWO.
HERE WE HUMANS ARE, SITTING CLOSE BY...
BUT THEY'RE ABSORBED IN READING.
WHAT ARE YOU DOING?
YOUR CHEEKS ARE SO SOFT!
I WISH I HAD SKIN AS SMOOTH AS YOURS.
STOP THAT!

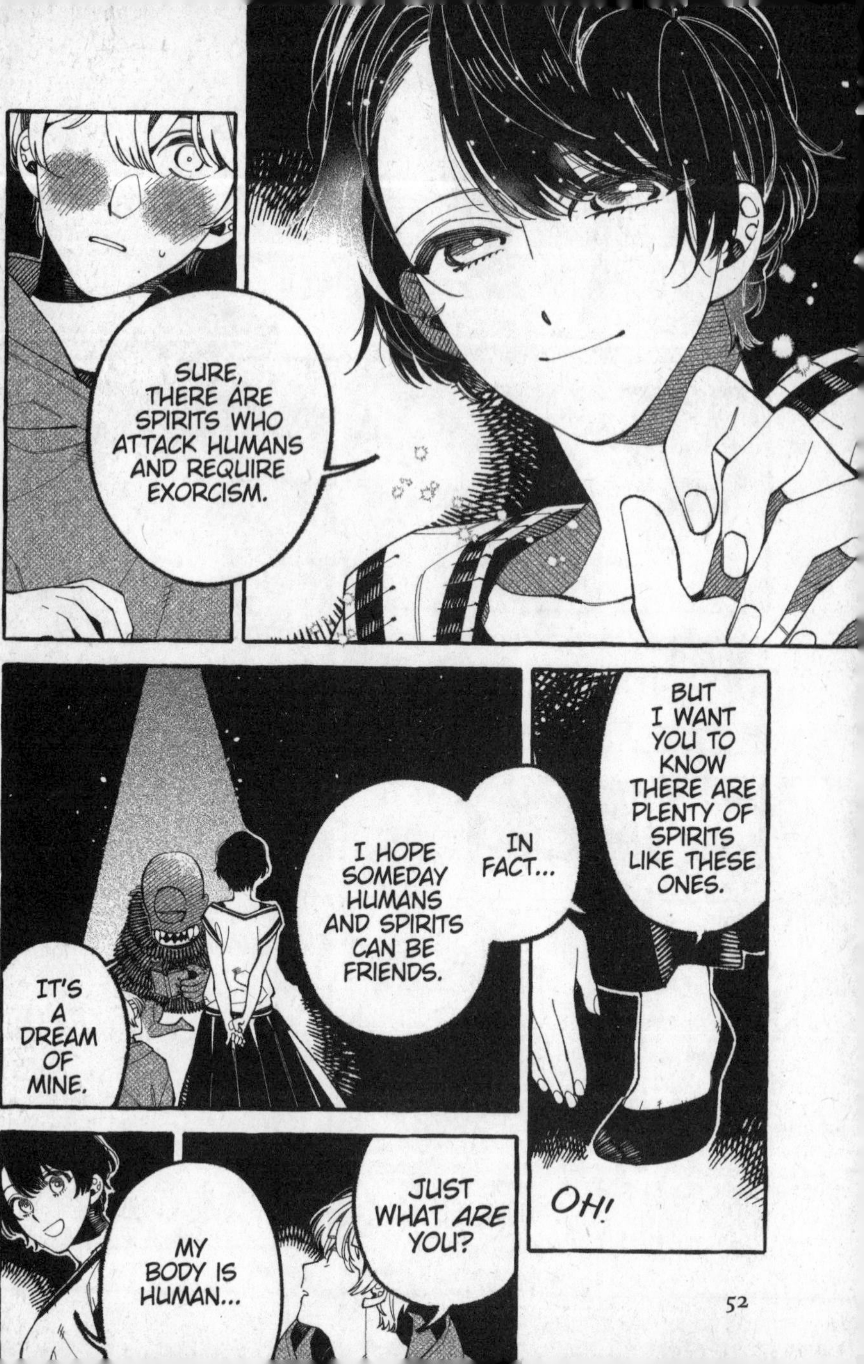
SURE, THERE ARE SPIRITS WHO ATTACK HUMANS AND REQUIRE EXORCISM.
BUT I WANT YOU TO KNOW THERE ARE PLENTY OF SPIRITS LIKE THESE ONES.
OH!
IN FACT...
I HOPE SOMEDAY HUMANS AND SPIRITS CAN BE FRIENDS.
IT'S A DREAM OF MINE.
JUST WHAT ARE YOU?
MY BODY IS HUMAN...

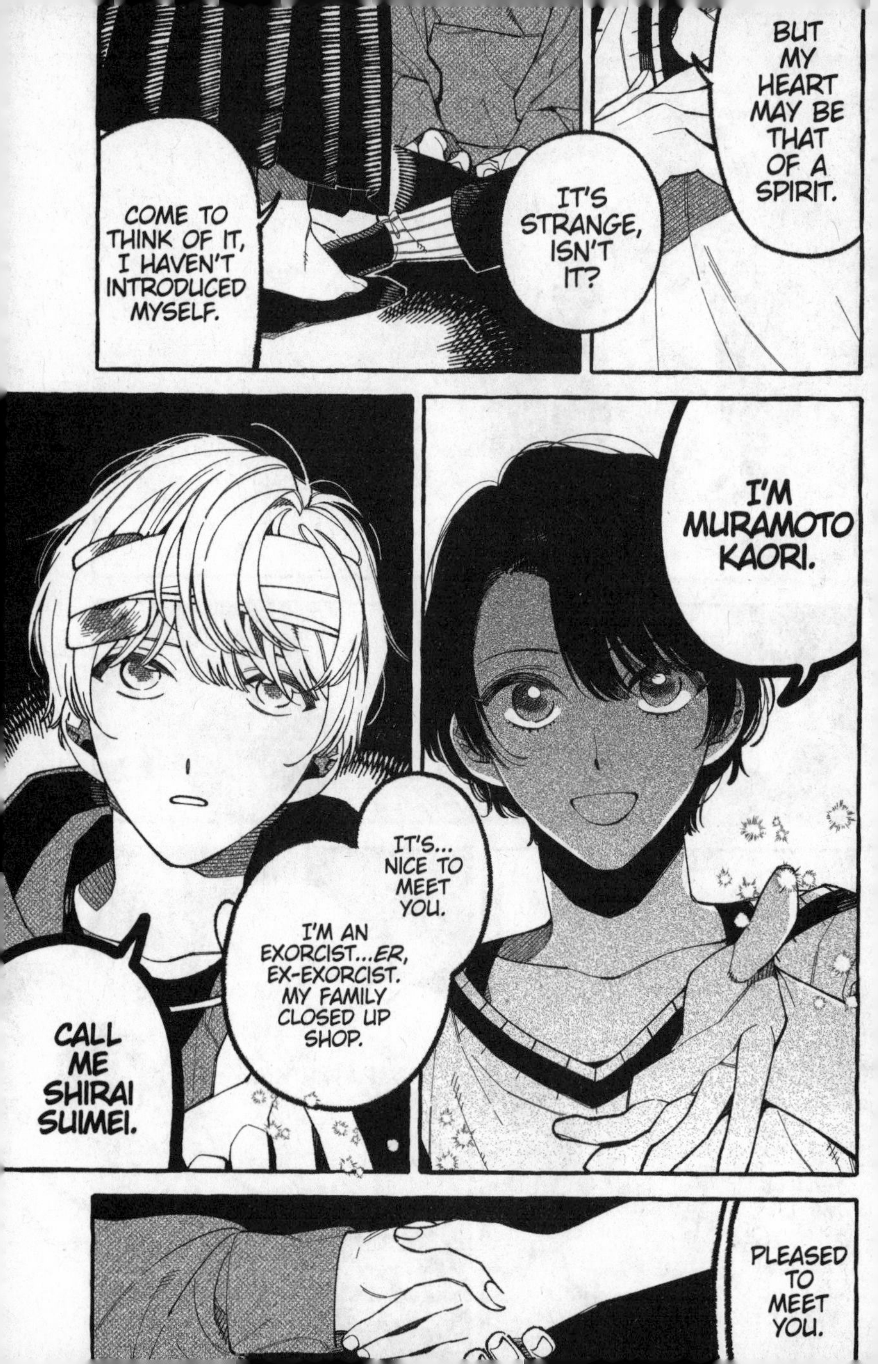
BUT MY HEART MAY BE THAT OF A SPIRIT.
IT'S STRANGE, ISN'T IT?
COME TO THINK OF IT, I HAVEN'T INTRODUCED MYSELF.
I'M MURAMOTO KAORI.
IT'S... NICE TO MEET YOU.
I'M AN EXORCIST...ER, EX-EXORCIST. MY FAMILY CLOSED UP SHOP.
CALL ME SHIRAI SUIMEI.
PLEASED TO MEET YOU.

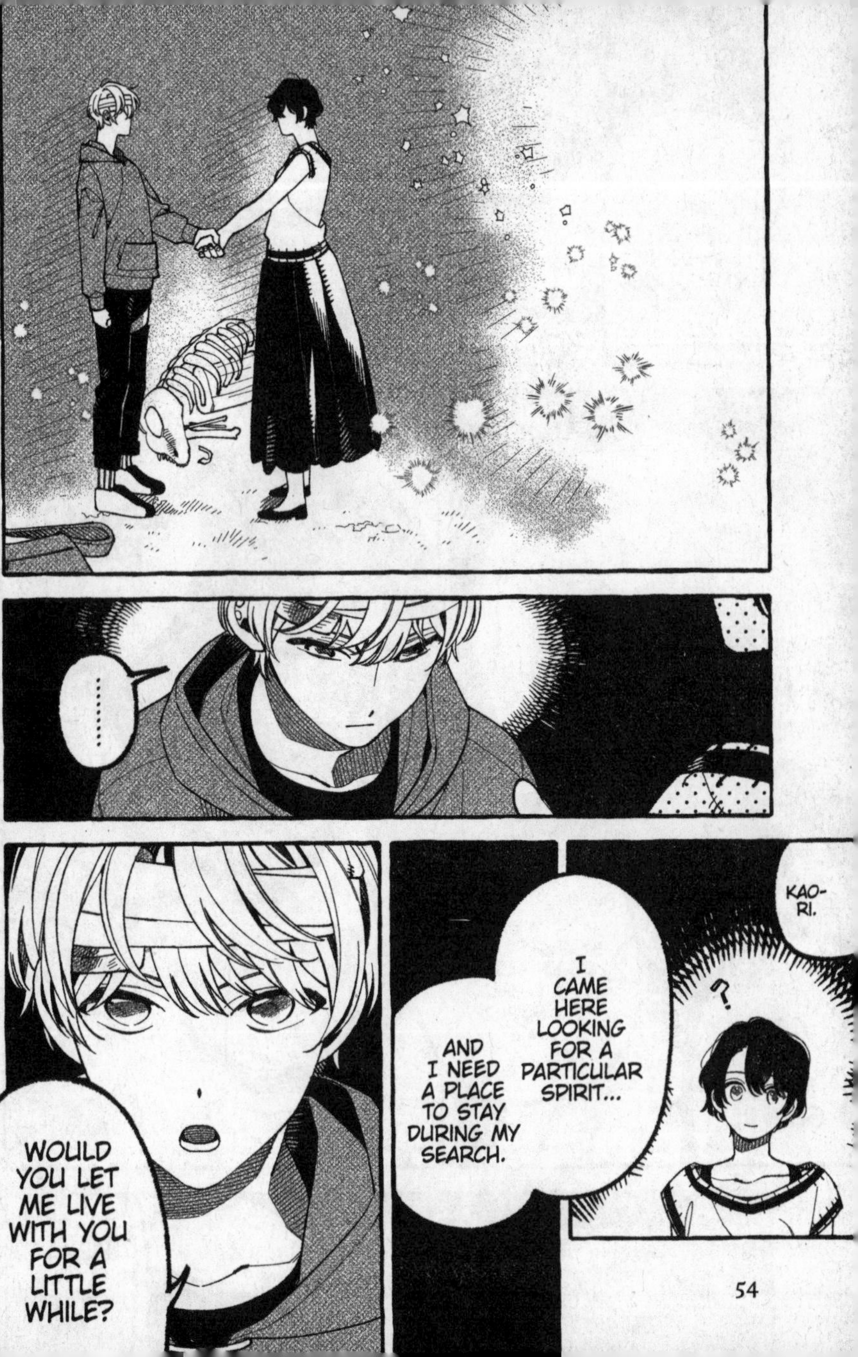
......
KAO-RI.
?
I CAME HERE LOOKING FOR A PARTICULAR SPIRIT...
AND I NEED A PLACE TO STAY DURING MY SEARCH.
WOULD YOU LET ME LIVE WITH YOU FOR A LITTLE WHILE?

THE HAUNTED BOOKSTORE

Gateway to a
Parallel Universe

THE HAUNTED BOOKSTORE

Gateway to a Parallel Universe

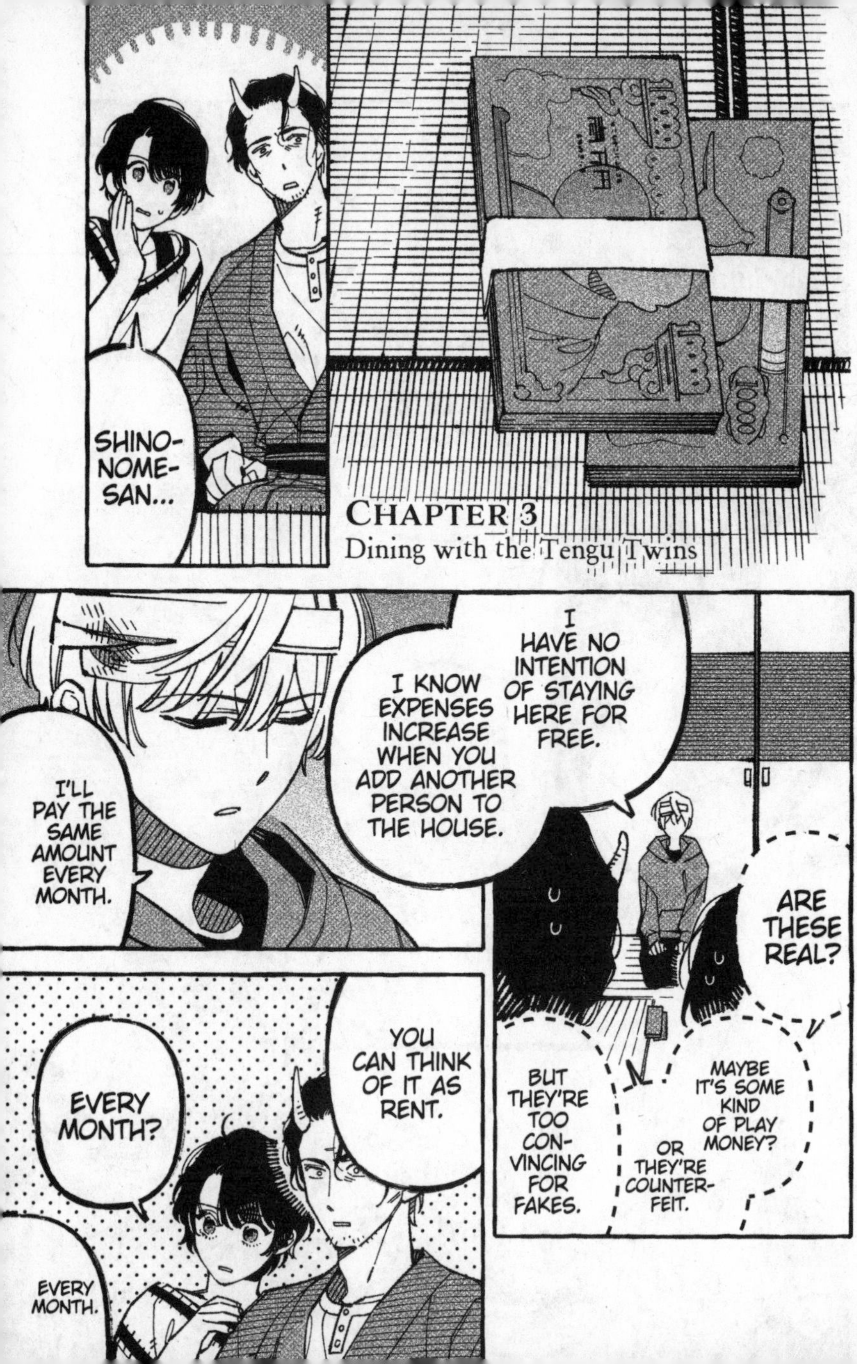

CHAPTER 3
Dining with the Tengu Twins
SHINO-NOME-SAN...
ARE THESE REAL?
MAYBE IT'S SOME KIND OF PLAY MONEY?
OR THEY'RE COUNTER-FEIT.
BUT THEY'RE TOO CON-VINCING FOR FAKES.
I HAVE NO INTENTION OF STAYING HERE FOR FREE.
I KNOW EXPENSES INCREASE WHEN YOU ADD ANOTHER PERSON TO THE HOUSE.
I'LL PAY THE SAME AMOUNT EVERY MONTH.
YOU CAN THINK OF IT AS RENT.
EVERY MONTH?
EVERY MONTH.

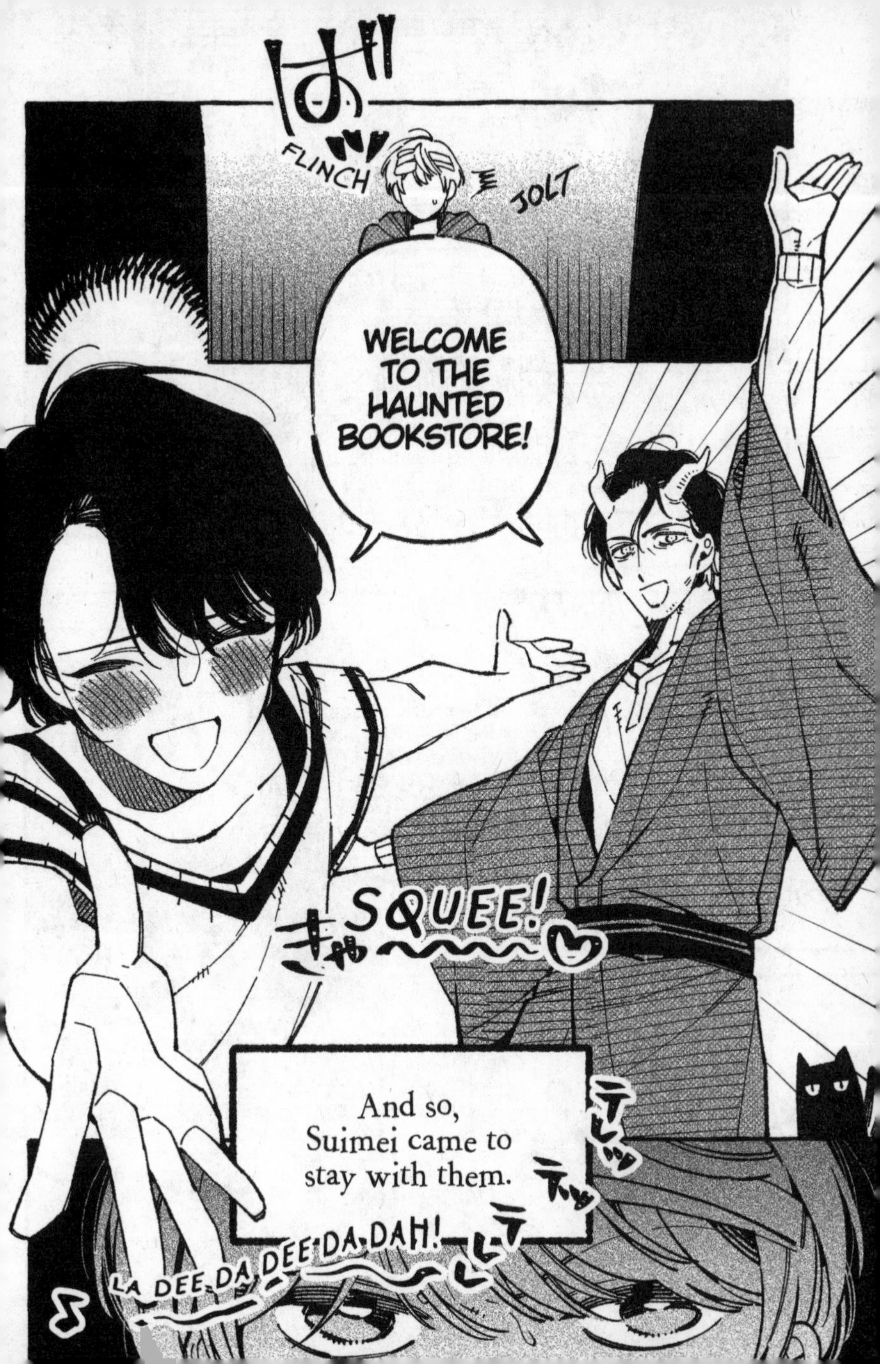
はっ
FLINCH
JOLT
WELCOME TO THE HAUNTED BOOKSTORE!
SQUEE!
きゃ
And so, Suimei came to stay with them.
LA DEE DA DEE DA DAH!

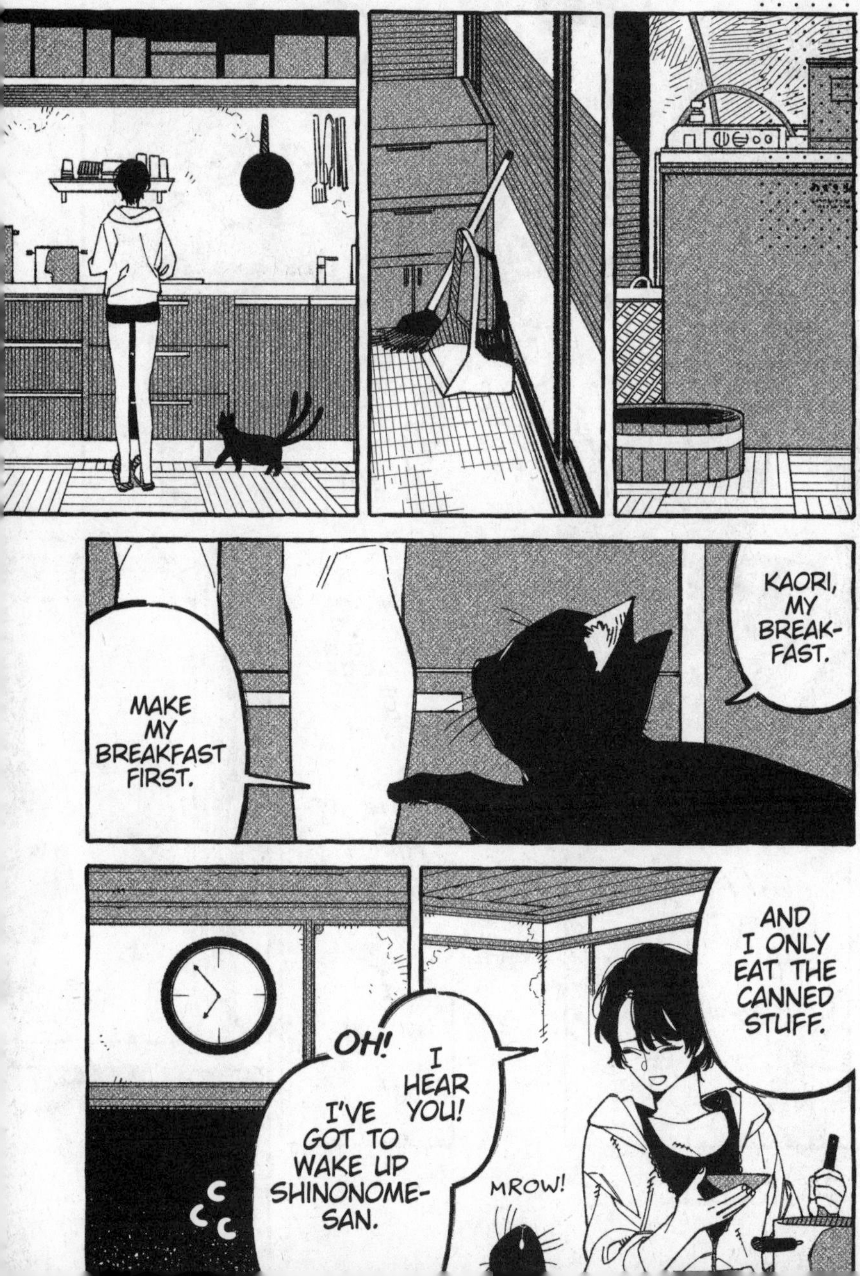
KAORI, MY BREAK-FAST.
MAKE MY BREAKFAST FIRST.
AND I ONLY EAT THE CANNED STUFF.
OH!
I HEAR YOU!
I'VE GOT TO WAKE UP SHINONOME-SAN.
MROW!

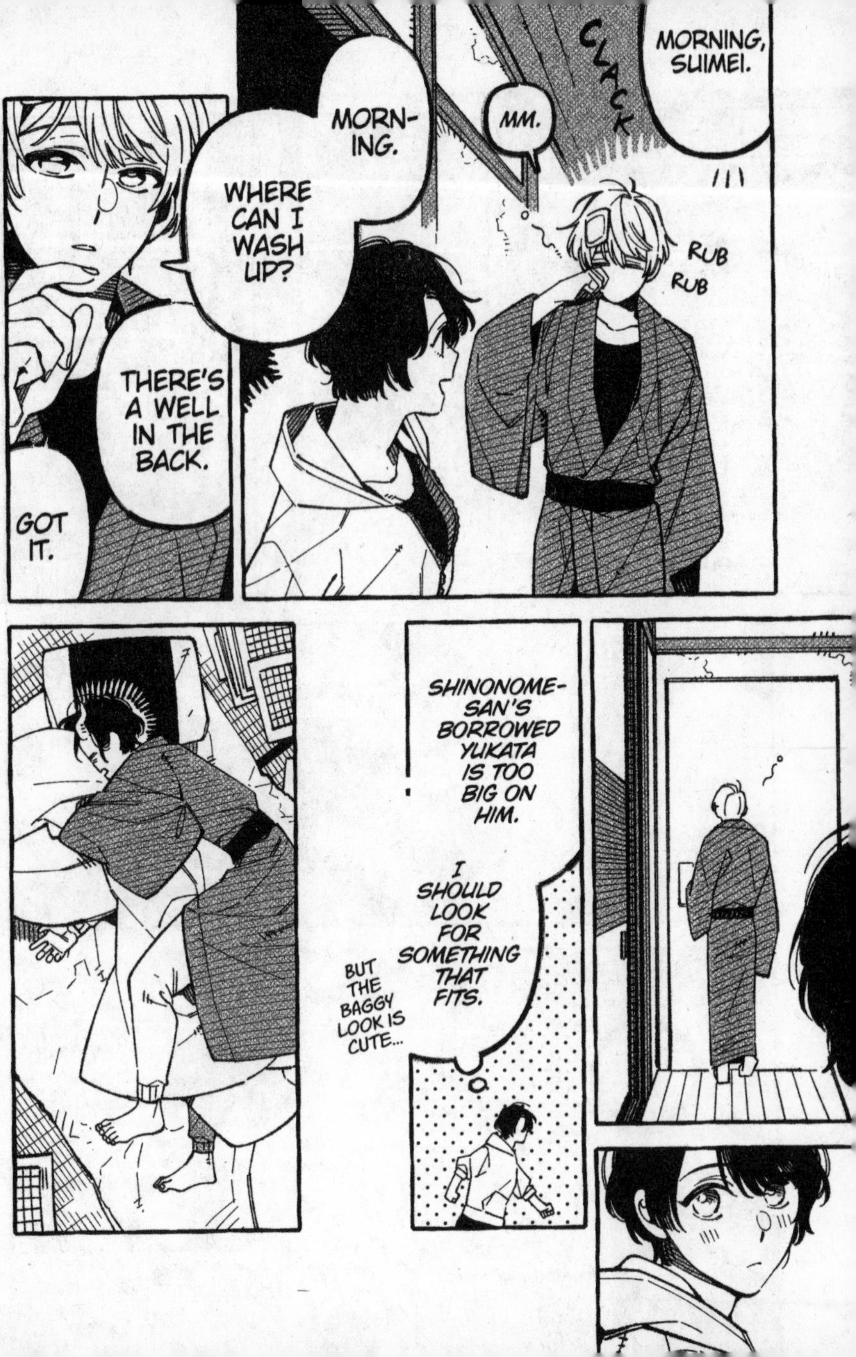
MORNING, SUIMEI.
CLACK
MM.
RUB RUB
MORN-ING.
WHERE CAN I WASH UP?
THERE'S A WELL IN THE BACK.
GOT IT.
SHINONOME-SAN'S BORROWED YUKATA IS TOO BIG ON HIM.
I SHOULD LOOK FOR SOMETHING THAT FITS.
BUT THE BAGGY LOOK IS CUTE...

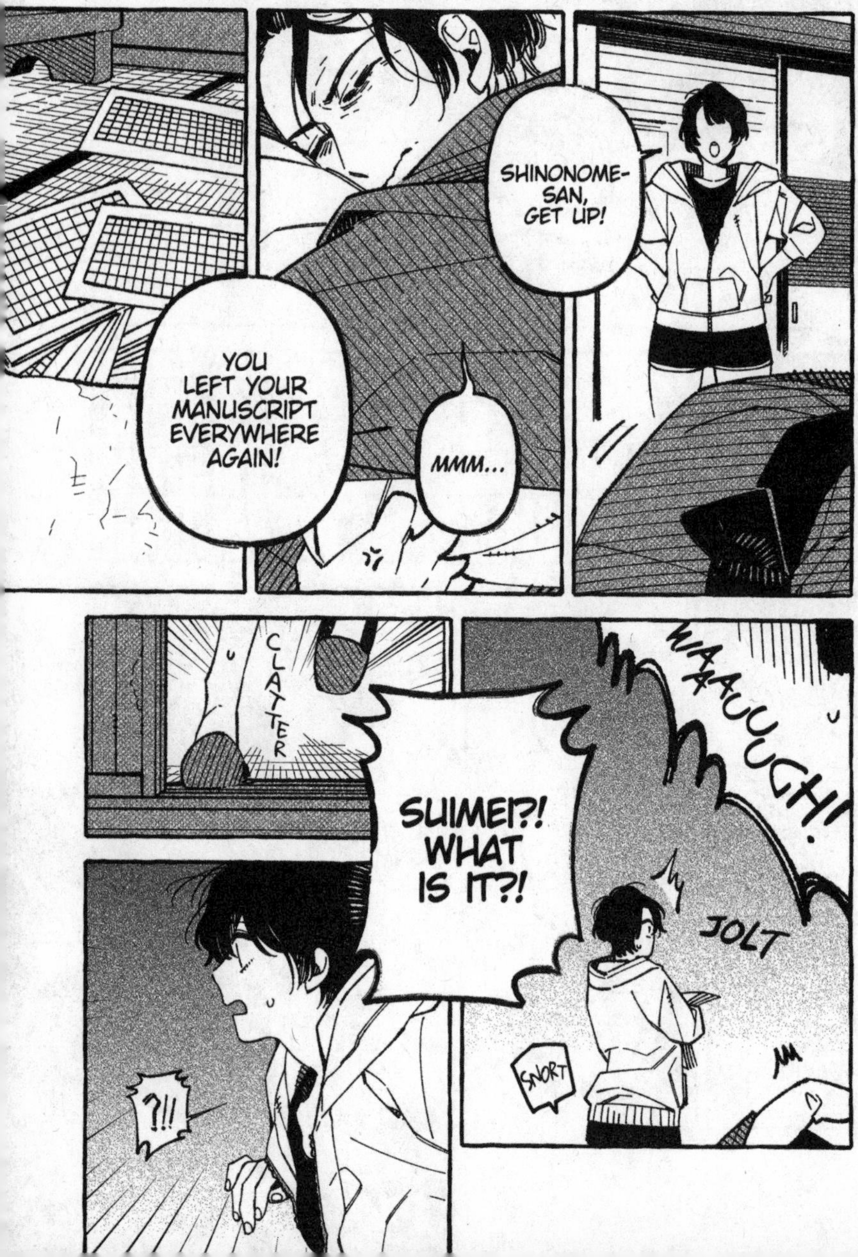
SHINONOME-SAN, GET UP!
MMM...
YOU LEFT YOUR MANUSCRIPT EVERYWHERE AGAIN!
WAAAUUGH!
JOLT
SNORT
CLATTER
SUIMEI?! WHAT IS IT?!
?!!

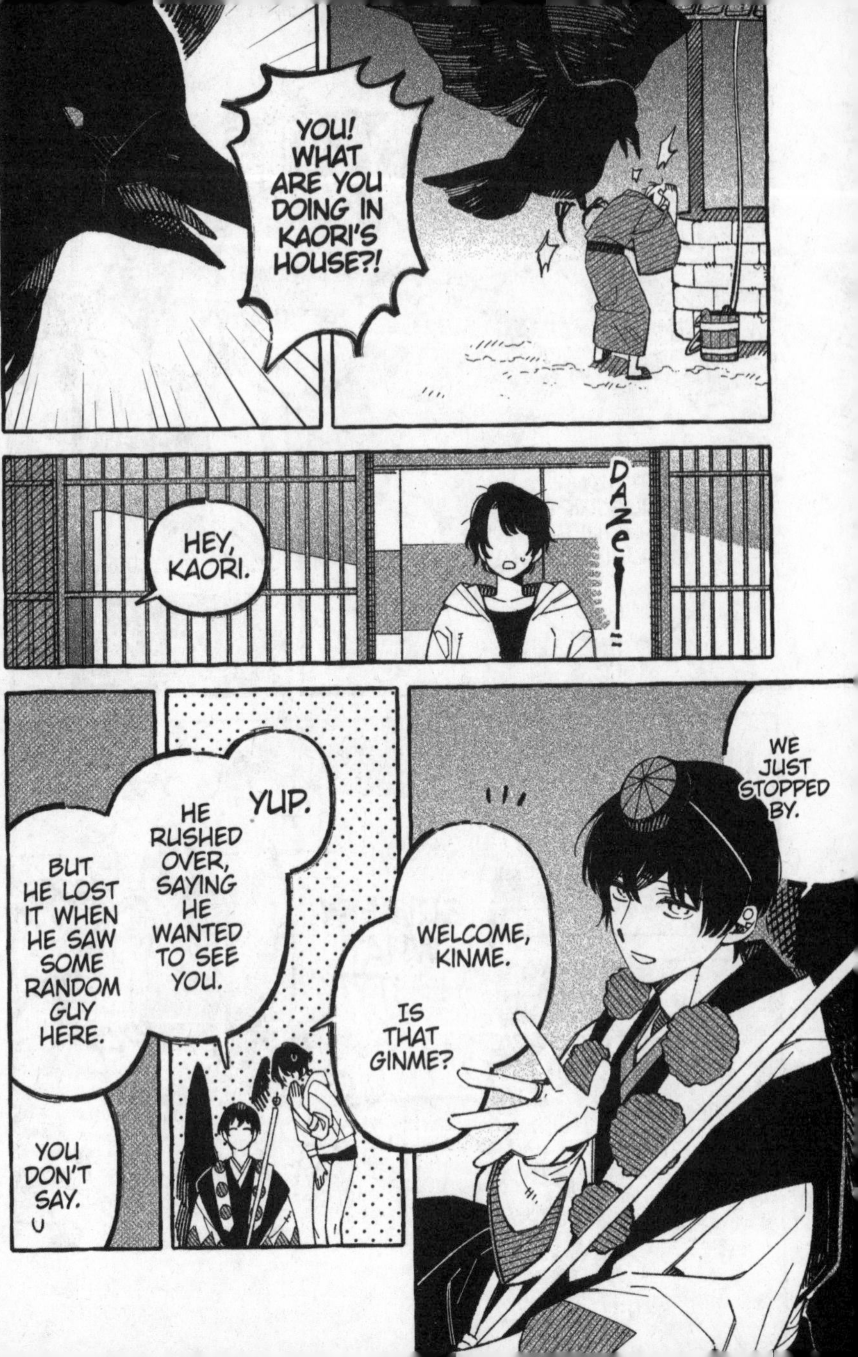
YOU! WHAT ARE YOU DOING IN KAORI'S HOUSE?!
DAZE...!!
HEY, KAORI.
WE JUST STOPPED BY.
WELCOME, KINME.
IS THAT GINME?
YUP.
HE RUSHED OVER, SAYING HE WANTED TO SEE YOU.
BUT HE LOST IT WHEN HE SAW SOME RANDOM GUY HERE.
YOU DON'T SAY.

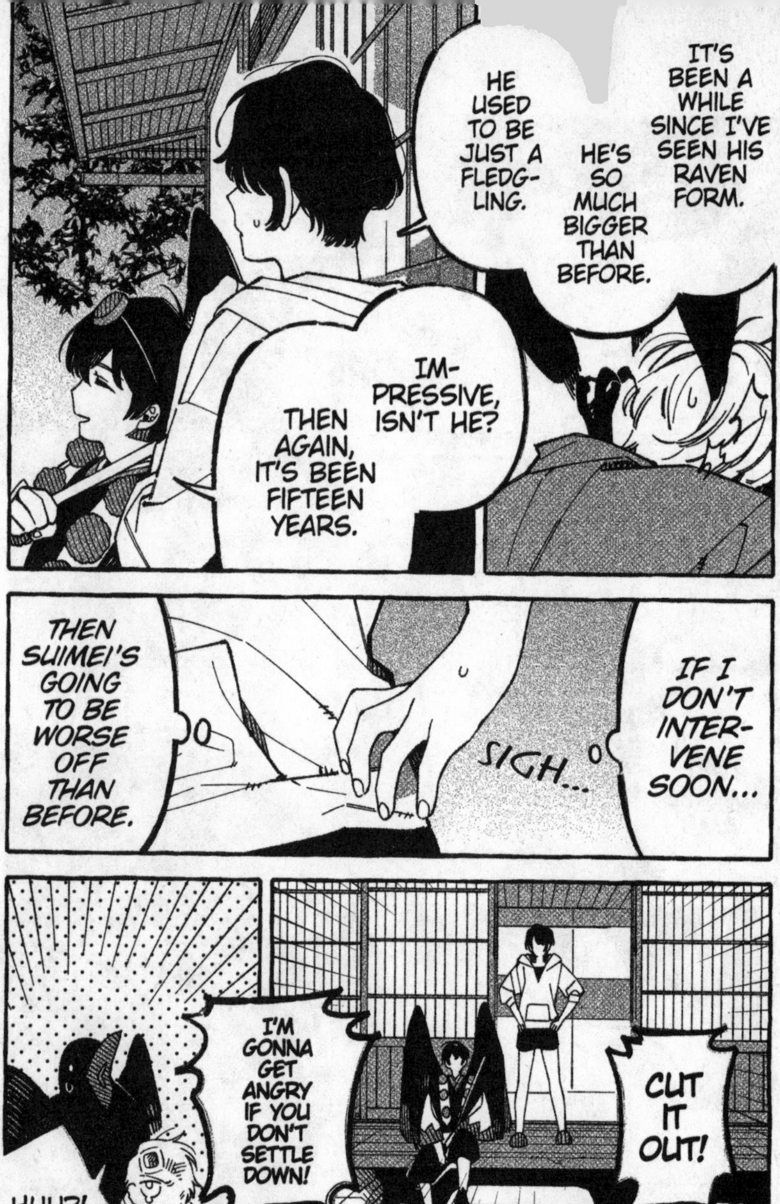
IT'S BEEN A WHILE SINCE I'VE SEEN HIS RAVEN FORM.
HE'S SO MUCH BIGGER THAN BEFORE.
HE USED TO BE JUST A FLEDG-LING.
IM-PRESSIVE, ISN'T HE?
THEN AGAIN, IT'S BEEN FIFTEEN YEARS.
IF I DON'T INTER-VENE SOON...
SIGH...
THEN SUIMEI'S GOING TO BE WORSE OFF THAN BEFORE.
CUT IT OUT!
I'M GONNA GET ANGRY IF YOU DON'T SETTLE DOWN!
HUH?!

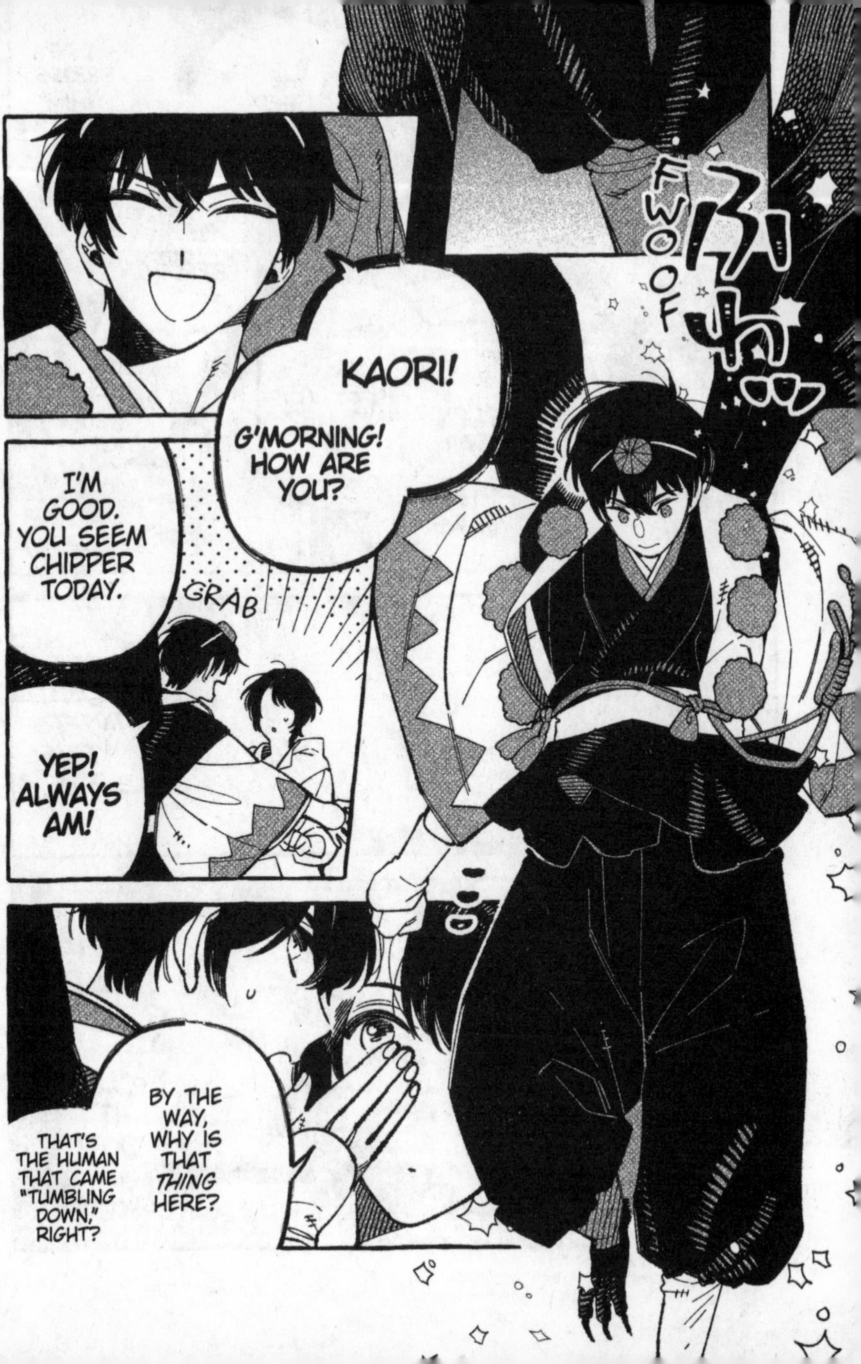
ふわ
FWOOF
KAORI!
G'MORNING! HOW ARE YOU?
I'M GOOD. YOU SEEM CHIPPER TODAY.
GRAB
YEP! ALWAYS AM!
BY THE WAY, WHY IS THAT *THING* HERE?
THAT'S THE HUMAN THAT CAME "TUMBLING DOWN," RIGHT?

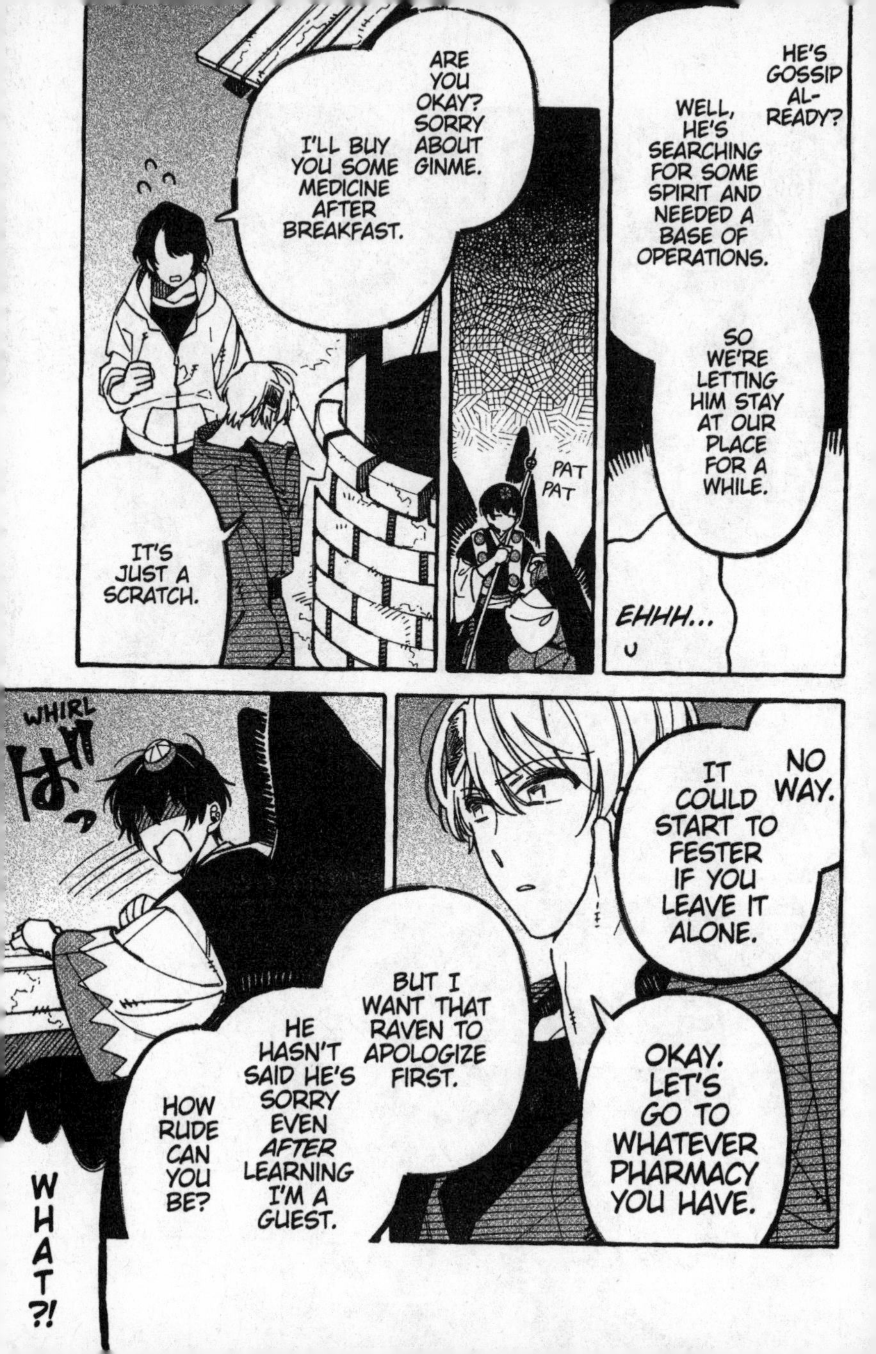
HE'S GOSSIP AL-READY?
WELL, HE'S SEARCHING FOR SOME SPIRIT AND NEEDED A BASE OF OPERATIONS.
SO WE'RE LETTING HIM STAY AT OUR PLACE FOR A WHILE.
EHHH...
PAT PAT
ARE YOU OKAY? SORRY ABOUT GINME.
I'LL BUY YOU SOME MEDICINE AFTER BREAKFAST.
IT'S JUST A SCRATCH.
NO WAY.
IT COULD START TO FESTER IF YOU LEAVE IT ALONE.
OKAY. LET'S GO TO WHATEVER PHARMACY YOU HAVE.
BUT I WANT THAT RAVEN TO APOLOGIZE FIRST.
HE HASN'T SAID HE'S SORRY EVEN *AFTER* LEARNING I'M A GUEST.
HOW RUDE CAN YOU BE?
WHIRL
WHAT?!

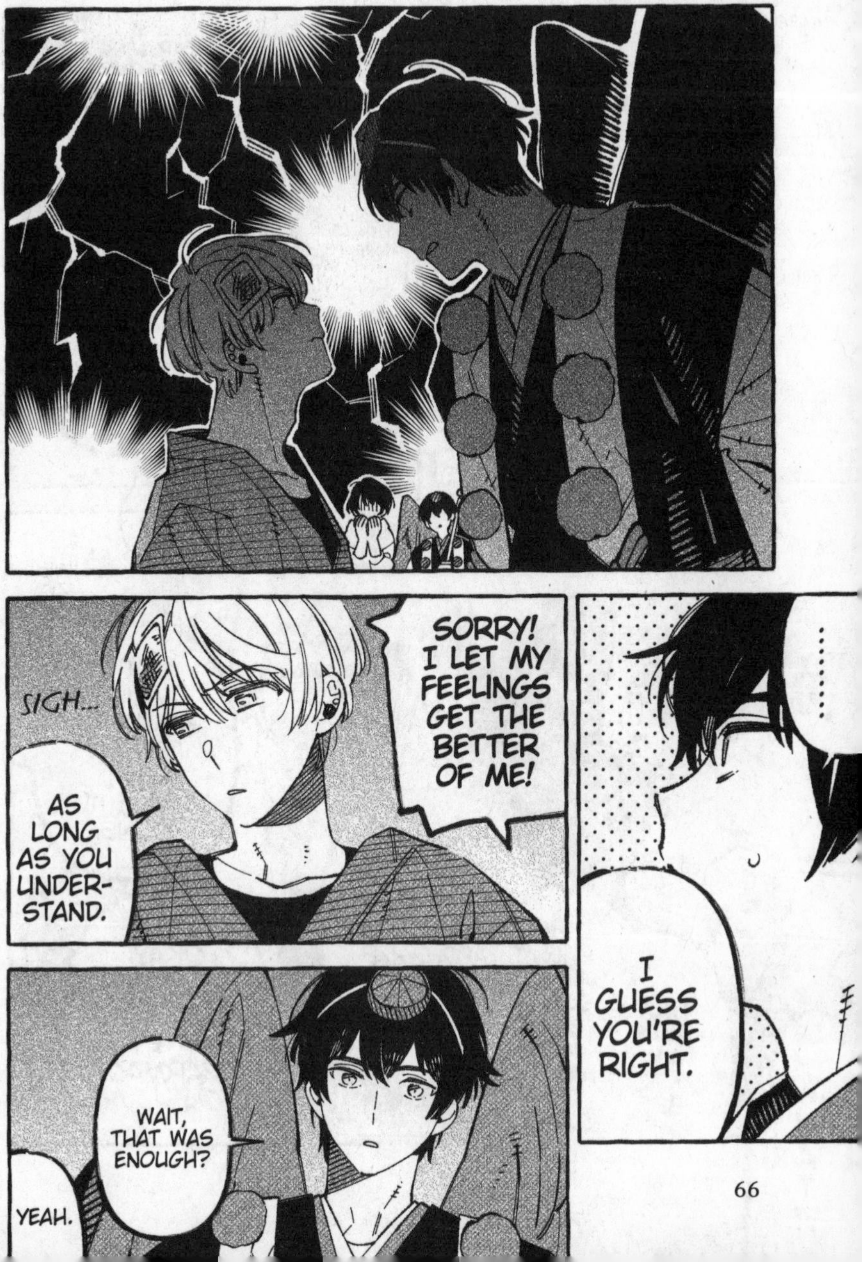
......
I GUESS YOU'RE RIGHT.
SORRY! I LET MY FEELINGS GET THE BETTER OF ME!
SIGH...
AS LONG AS YOU UNDER-STAND.
WAIT, THAT WAS ENOUGH?
YEAH.

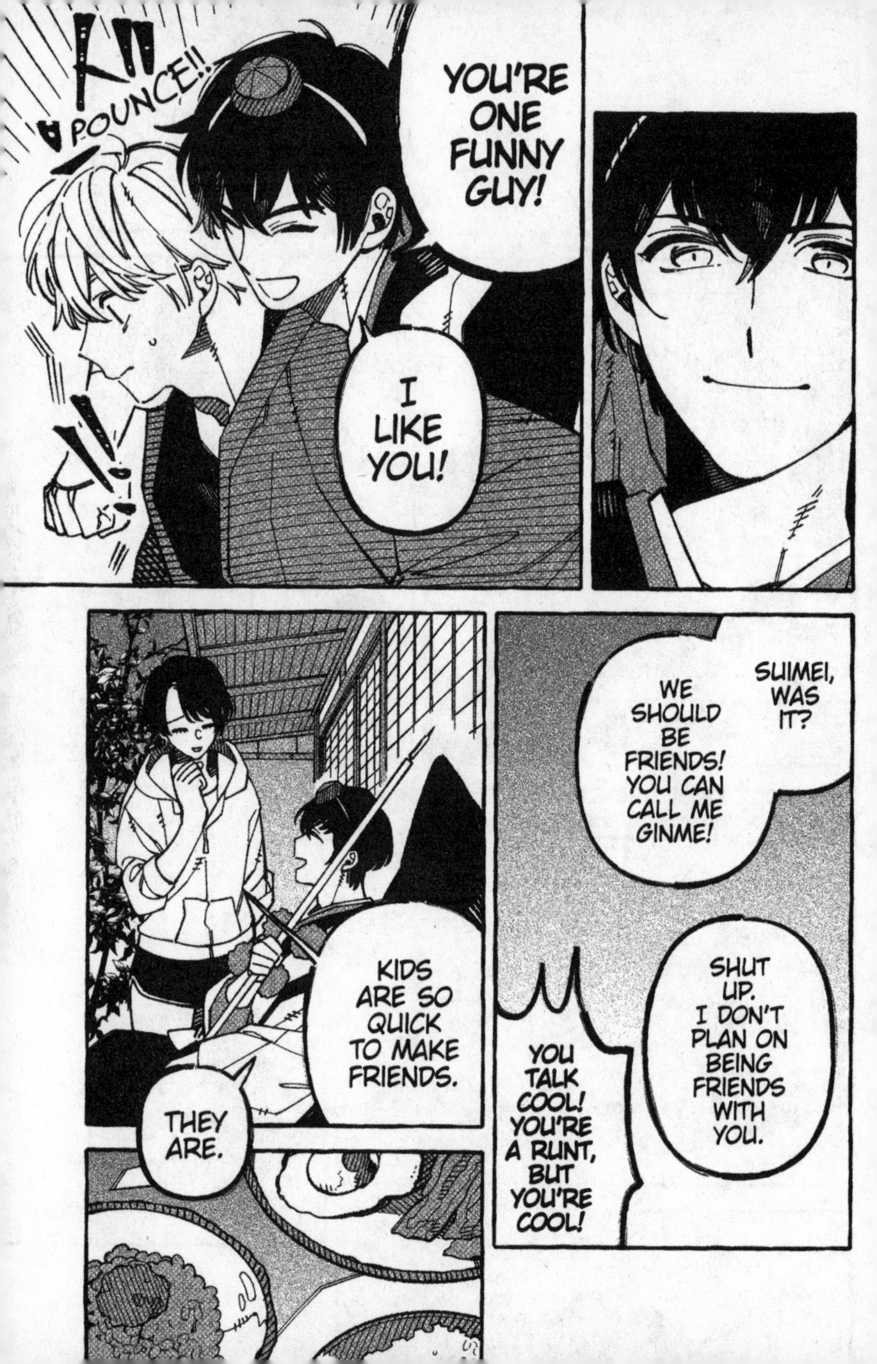
YOU'RE ONE FUNNY GUY!
POUNCE!!
I LIKE YOU!
SUIMEI, WAS IT?
WE SHOULD BE FRIENDS! YOU CAN CALL ME GINME!
SHUT UP. I DON'T PLAN ON BEING FRIENDS WITH YOU.
YOU TALK COOL! YOU'RE A RUNT, BUT YOU'RE COOL!
KIDS ARE SO QUICK TO MAKE FRIENDS.
THEY ARE.

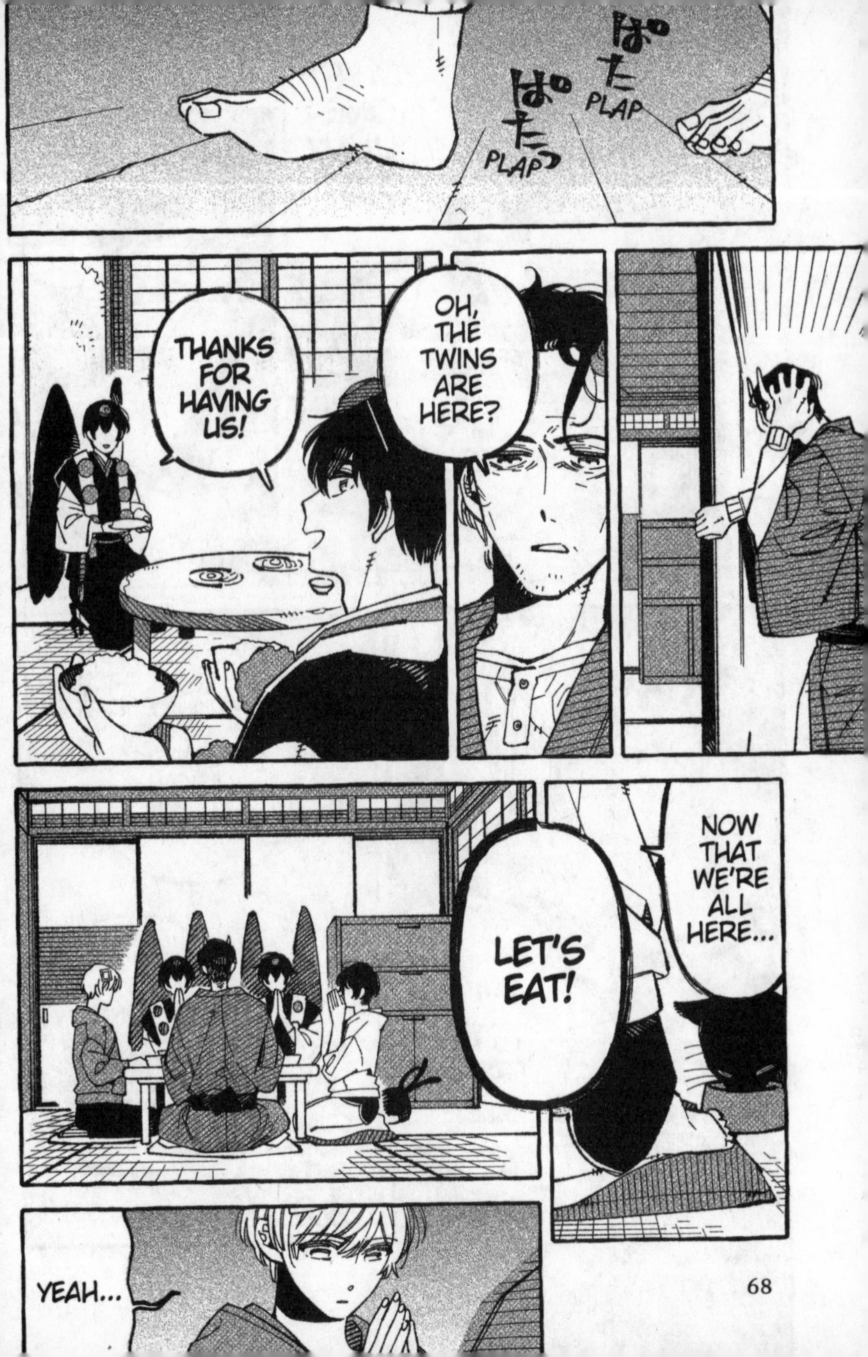
ぱた
PLAP
ぱた
PLAP
OH, THE TWINS ARE HERE?
THANKS FOR HAVING US!
NOW THAT WE'RE ALL HERE...
LET'S EAT!
YEAH...

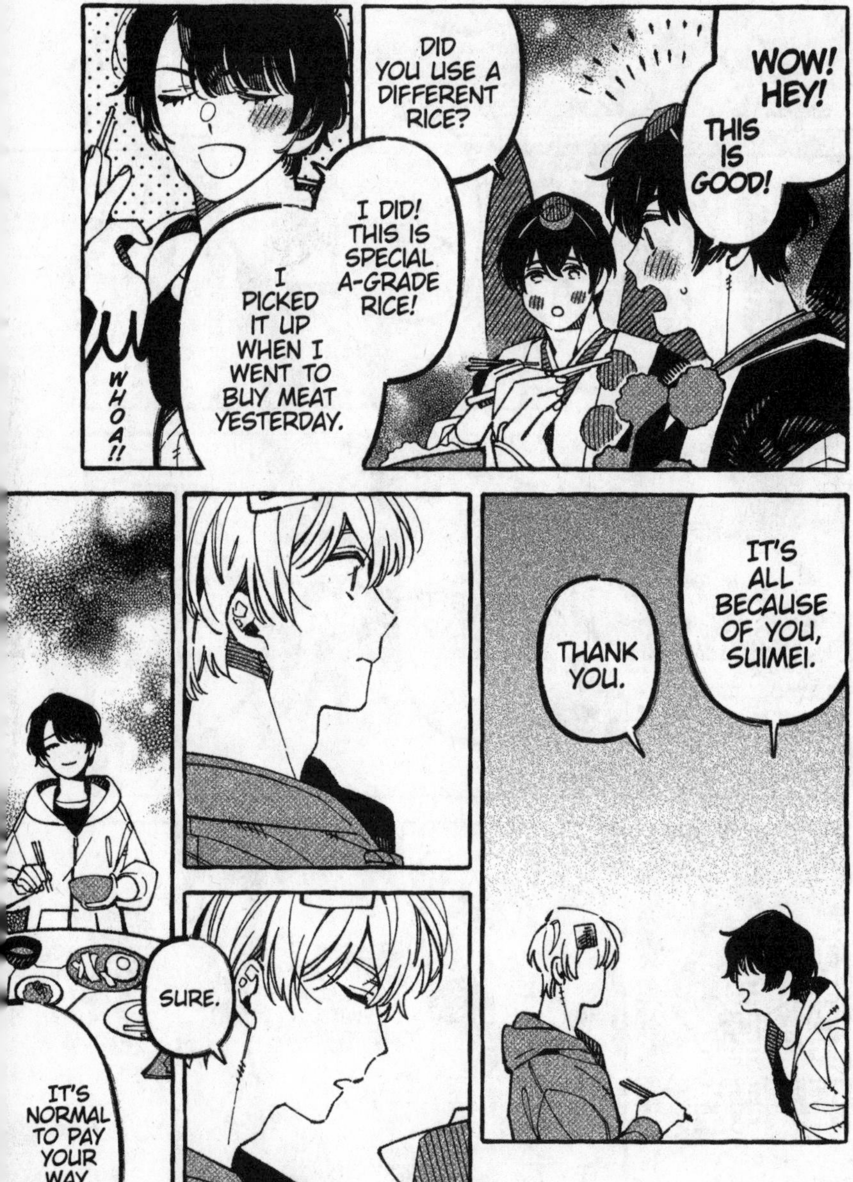
WOW! HEY!
THIS IS GOOD!
DID YOU USE A DIFFERENT RICE?
I DID! THIS IS SPECIAL A-GRADE RICE!
I PICKED IT UP WHEN I WENT TO BUY MEAT YESTERDAY.
WHOA!!
IT'S ALL BECAUSE OF YOU, SUIMEI.
THANK YOU.
SURE.
IT'S NORMAL TO PAY YOUR WAY. THAT'S ALL.

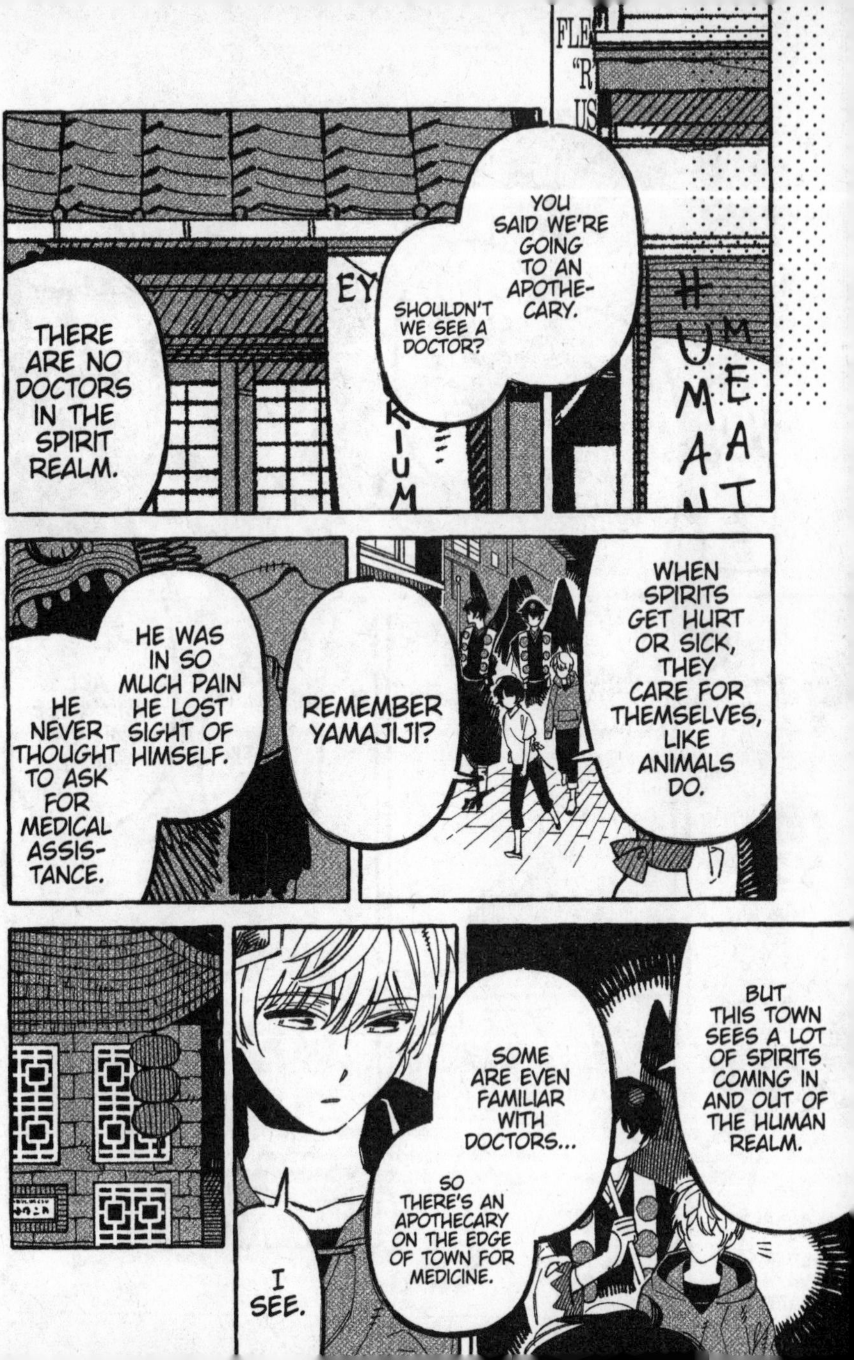
YOU SAID WE'RE GOING TO AN APOTHECARY.
SHOULDN'T WE SEE A DOCTOR?
THERE ARE NO DOCTORS IN THE SPIRIT REALM.
WHEN SPIRITS GET HURT OR SICK, THEY CARE FOR THEMSELVES, LIKE ANIMALS DO.
REMEMBER YAMAJIJI?
HE WAS IN SO MUCH PAIN HE LOST SIGHT OF HIMSELF.
HE NEVER THOUGHT TO ASK FOR MEDICAL ASSISTANCE.
BUT THIS TOWN SEES A LOT OF SPIRITS COMING IN AND OUT OF THE HUMAN REALM.
SOME ARE EVEN FAMILIAR WITH DOCTORS...
SO THERE'S AN APOTHECARY ON THE EDGE OF TOWN FOR MEDICINE.
I SEE.

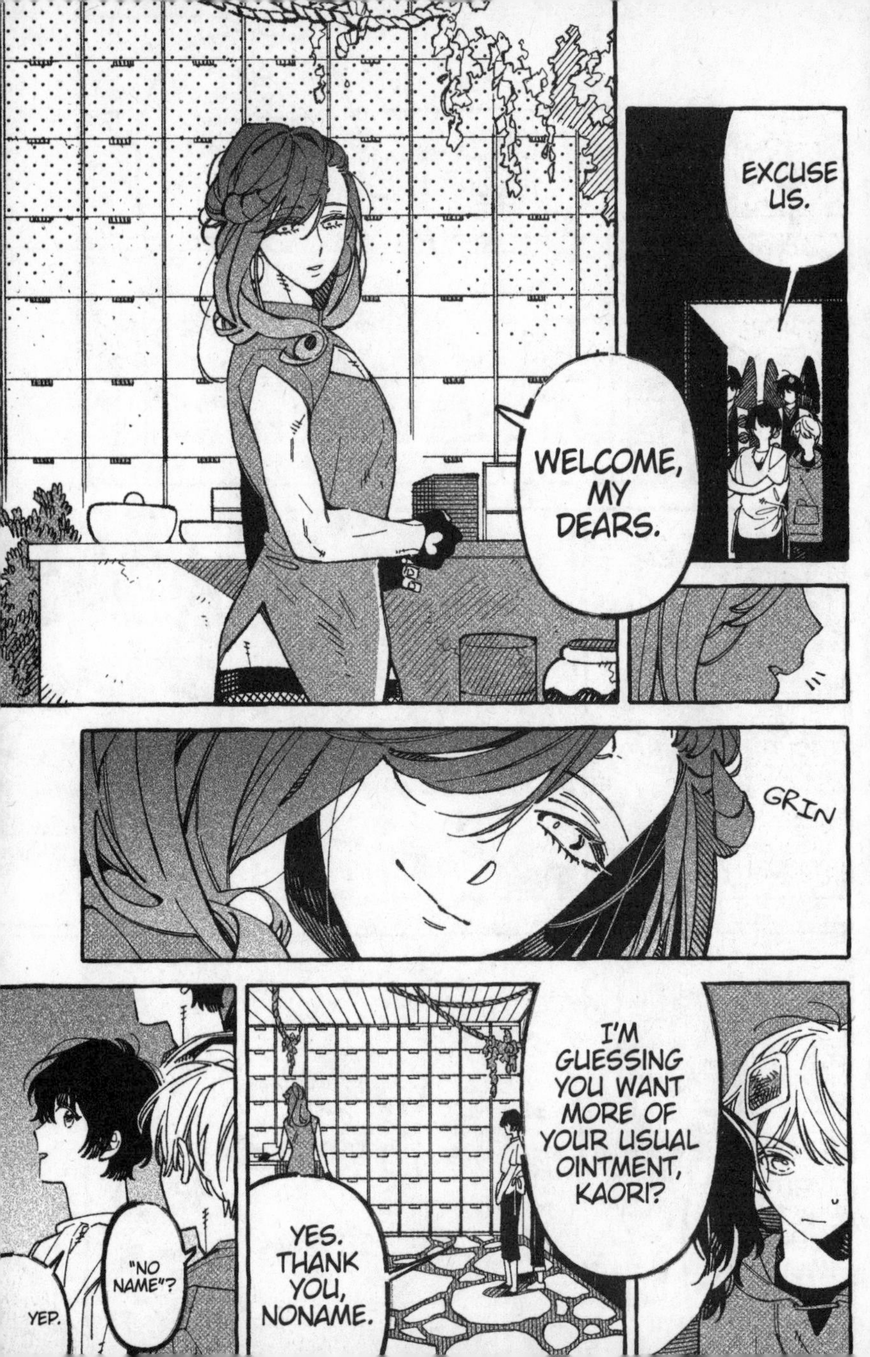
EXCUSE US.
WELCOME, MY DEARS.
GRIN
I'M GUESSING YOU WANT MORE OF YOUR USUAL OINTMENT, KAORI?
YES. THANK YOU, NONAME.
"NO NAME"?
YEP.

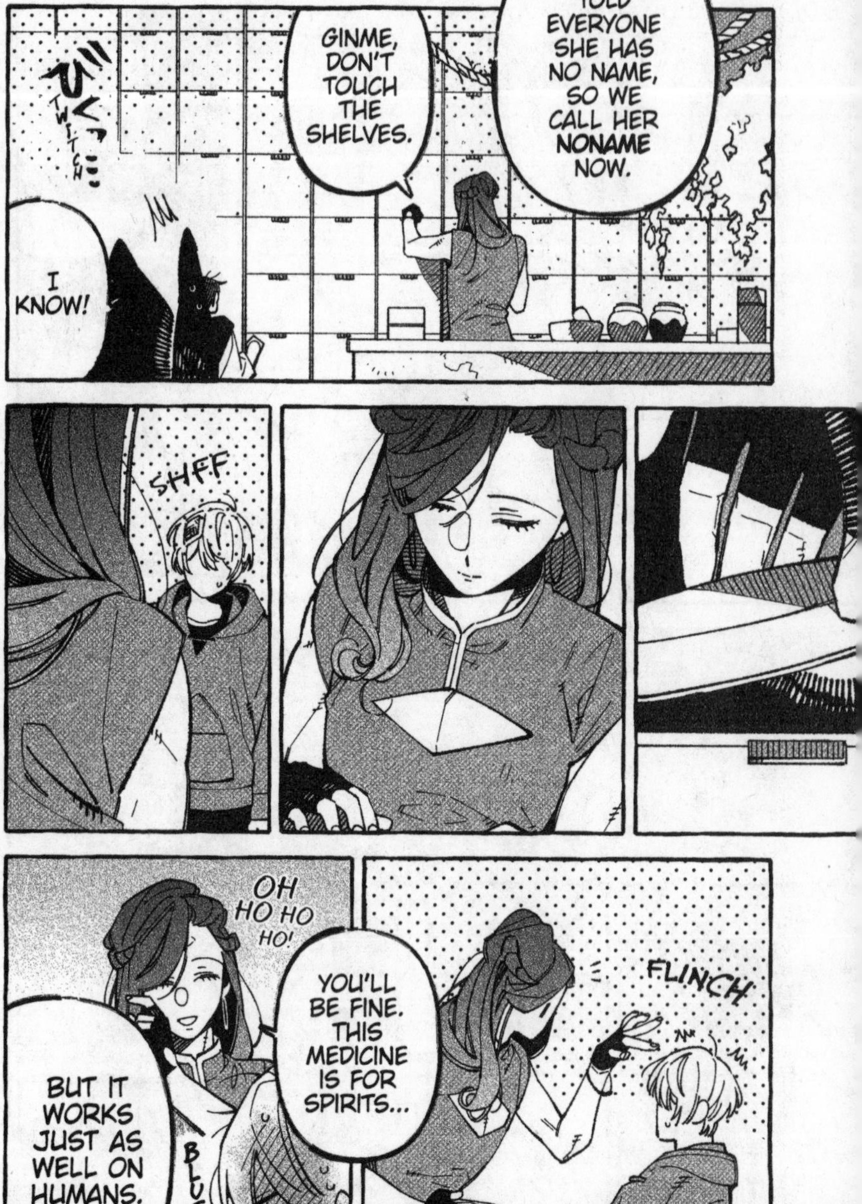
SHE TOLD EVERYONE SHE HAS NO NAME, SO WE CALL HER NONAME NOW.
GINME, DON'T TOUCH THE SHELVES.
TWITCH
I KNOW!
SHFF
FLINCH
YOU'LL BE FINE. THIS MEDICINE IS FOR SPIRITS...
OH HO HO HO!
BUT IT WORKS JUST AS WELL ON HUMANS.
BLUSH

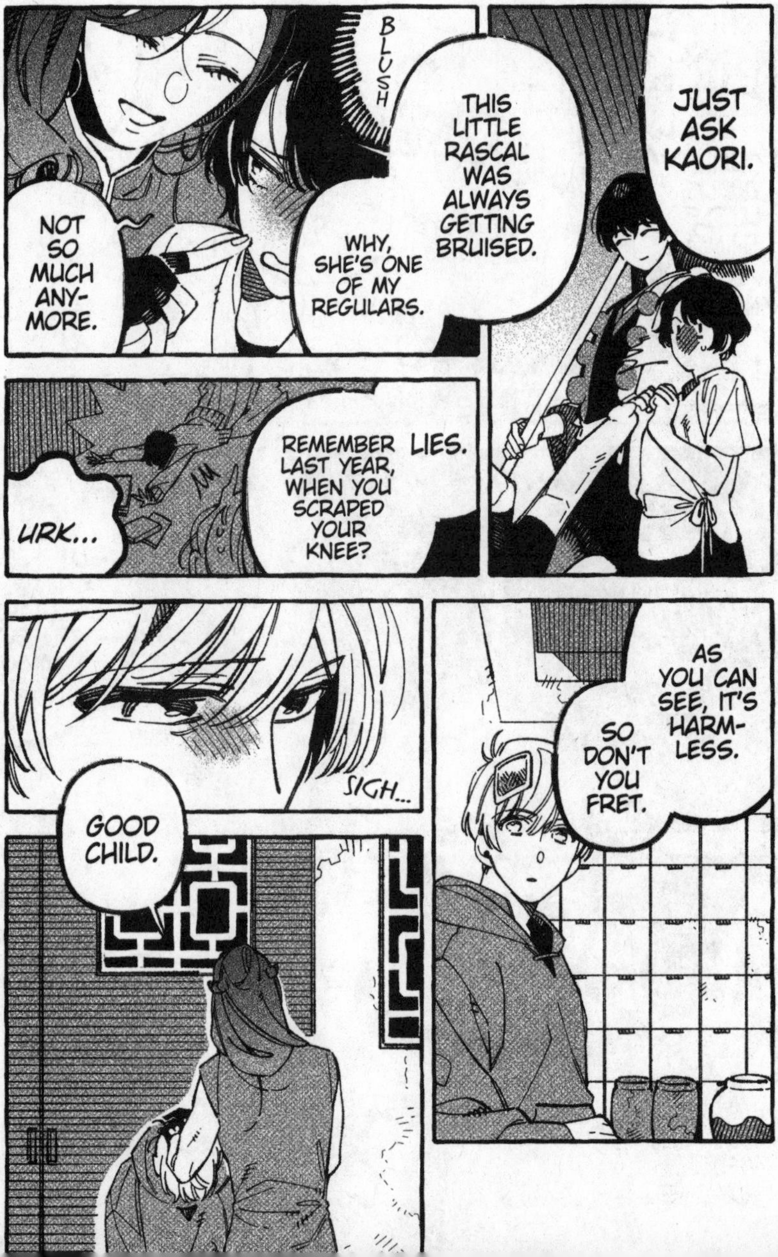
JUST ASK KAORI.
THIS LITTLE RASCAL WAS ALWAYS GETTING BRUISED.
BLUSH
WHY, SHE'S ONE OF MY REGULARS.
NOT SO MUCH ANY-MORE.
LIES.
REMEMBER LAST YEAR, WHEN YOU SCRAPED YOUR KNEE?
URK...
AS YOU CAN SEE, IT'S HARM-LESS.
SO DON'T YOU FRET.
SIGH...
GOOD CHILD.

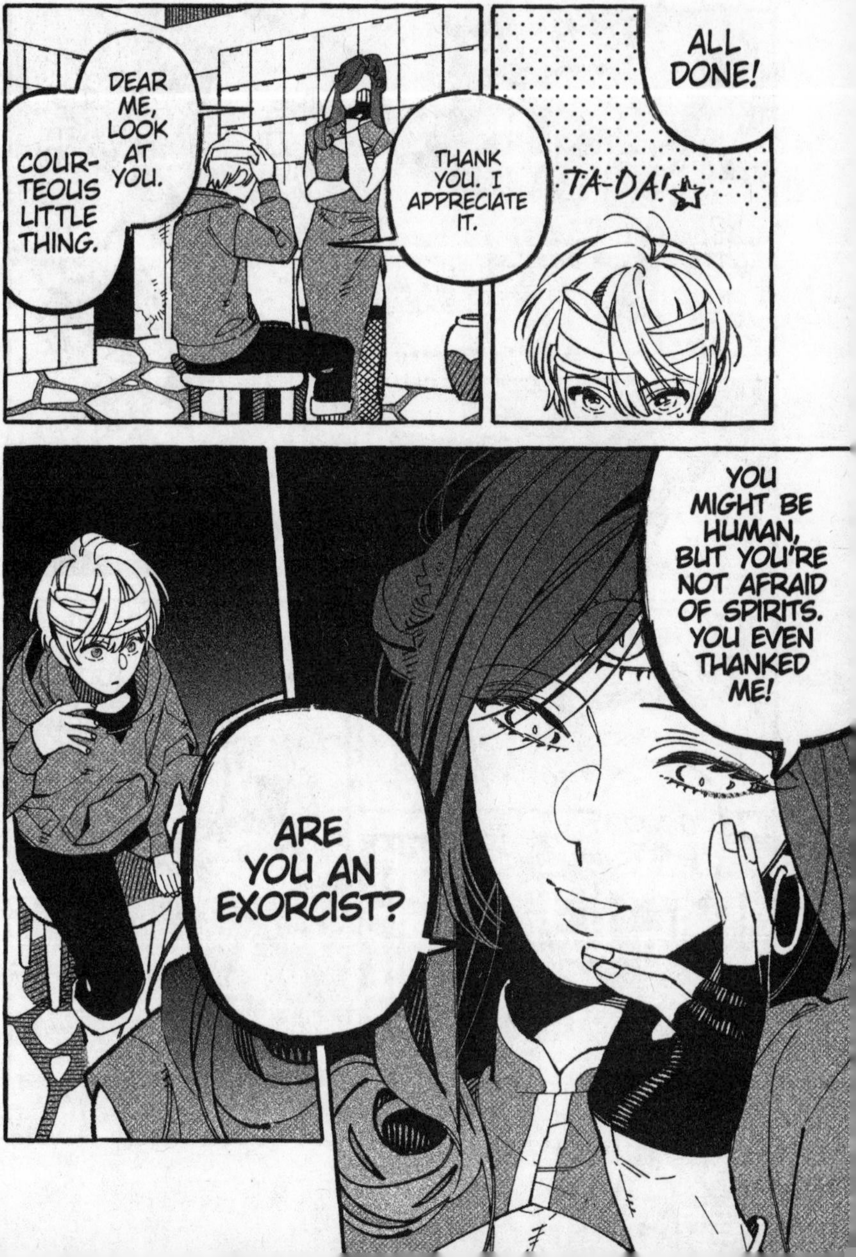
ALL DONE!
TA-DA!
THANK YOU. I APPRECIATE IT.
DEAR ME, LOOK AT YOU.
COURTEOUS LITTLE THING.
YOU MIGHT BE HUMAN, BUT YOU'RE NOT AFRAID OF SPIRITS. YOU EVEN THANKED ME!
ARE YOU AN EXORCIST?

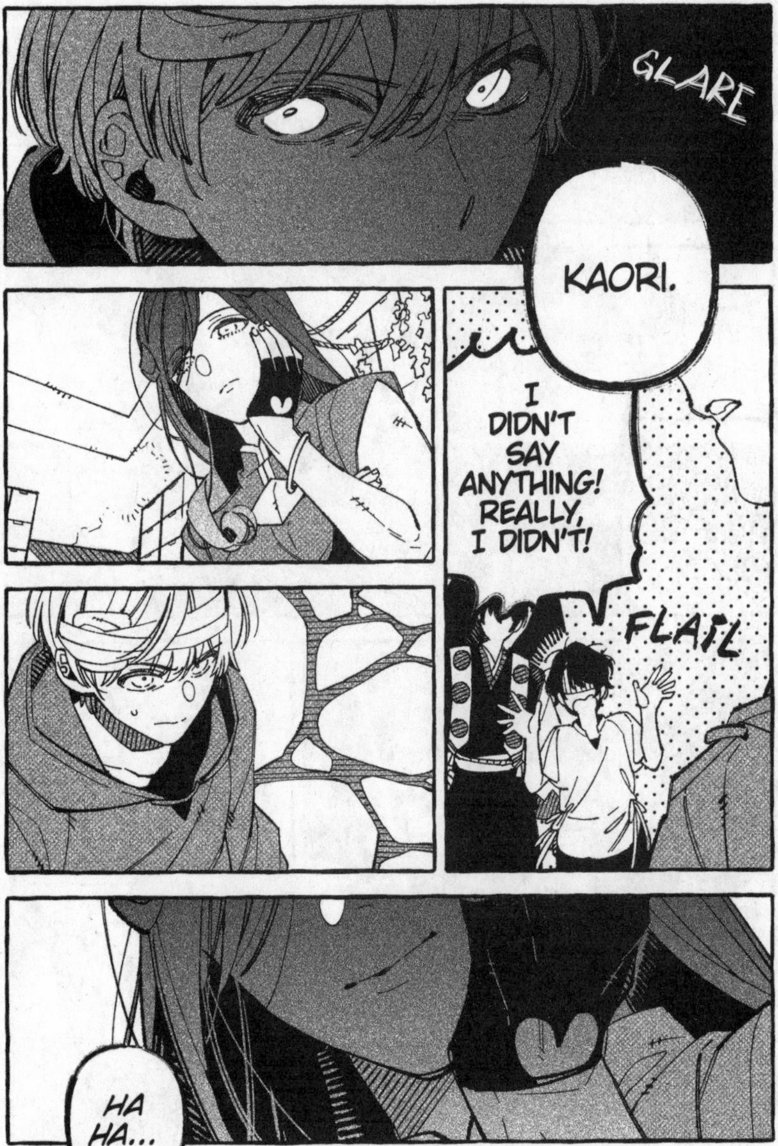
GLARE
KAORI.
I DIDN'T SAY ANYTHING! REALLY, I DIDN'T!
FLAIL
HA HA...

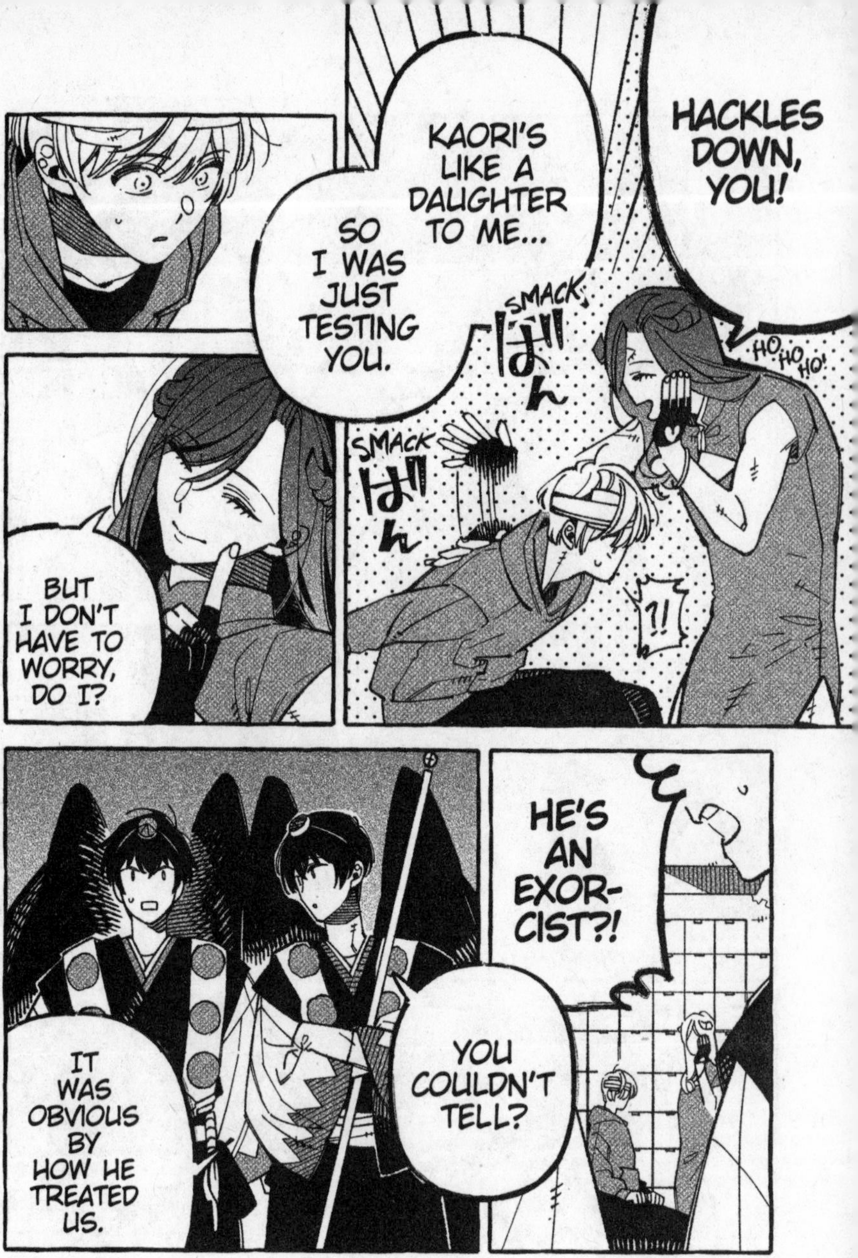
HACKLES DOWN, YOU!
HO HO HO!
KAORI'S LIKE A DAUGHTER TO ME...
SO I WAS JUST TESTING YOU.
SMACK ばん
SMACK ばん
?!
BUT I DON'T HAVE TO WORRY, DO I?
HE'S AN EXOR-CIST?!
YOU COULDN'T TELL?
IT WAS OBVIOUS BY HOW HE TREATED US.

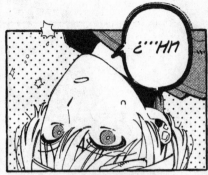

......
HATE ME FOR IT IF YOU WANT.
YOU HAVE THE RIGHT.
HUH?
WHY?
UH...?
ANY SPIRITS YOU KILLED WERE PROBABLY DOING BAD STUFF IN THE HUMAN REALM.
IT'S THEIR OWN FAULT.
AND WHAT'S THAT GOT TO DO WITH THIS?

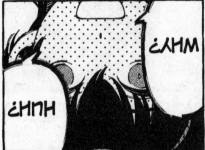

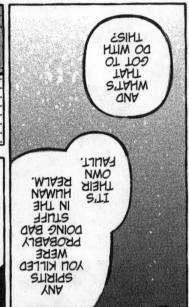

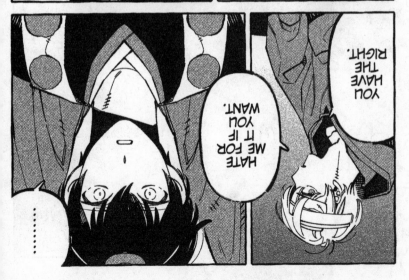

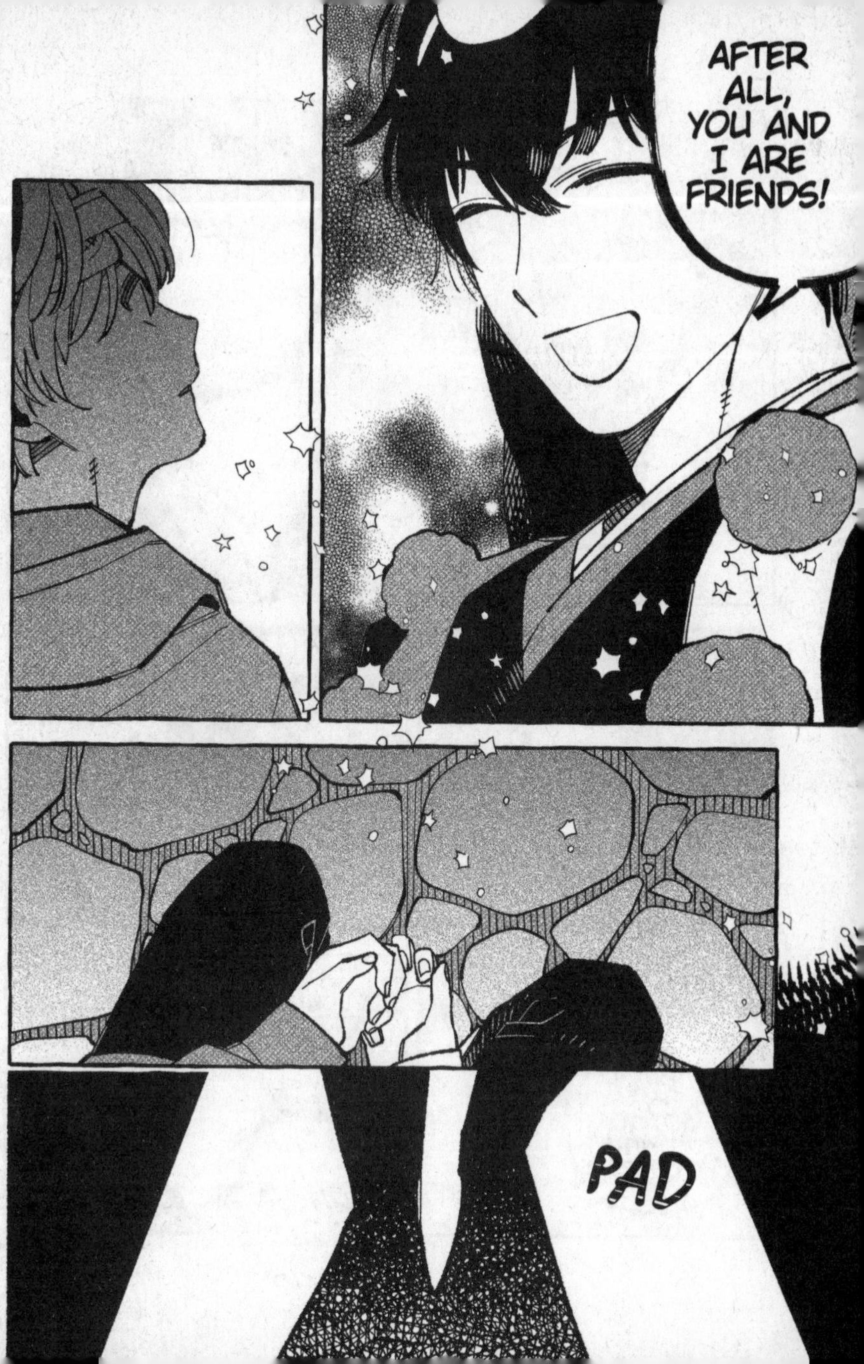
AFTER ALL, YOU AND I ARE FRIENDS!
PAD

THE HAUNTED BOOKSTORE

Gateway to a Parallel Universe

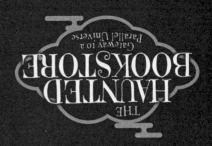

THE HAUNTED BOOKSTORE

Gateway to a Parallel Universe

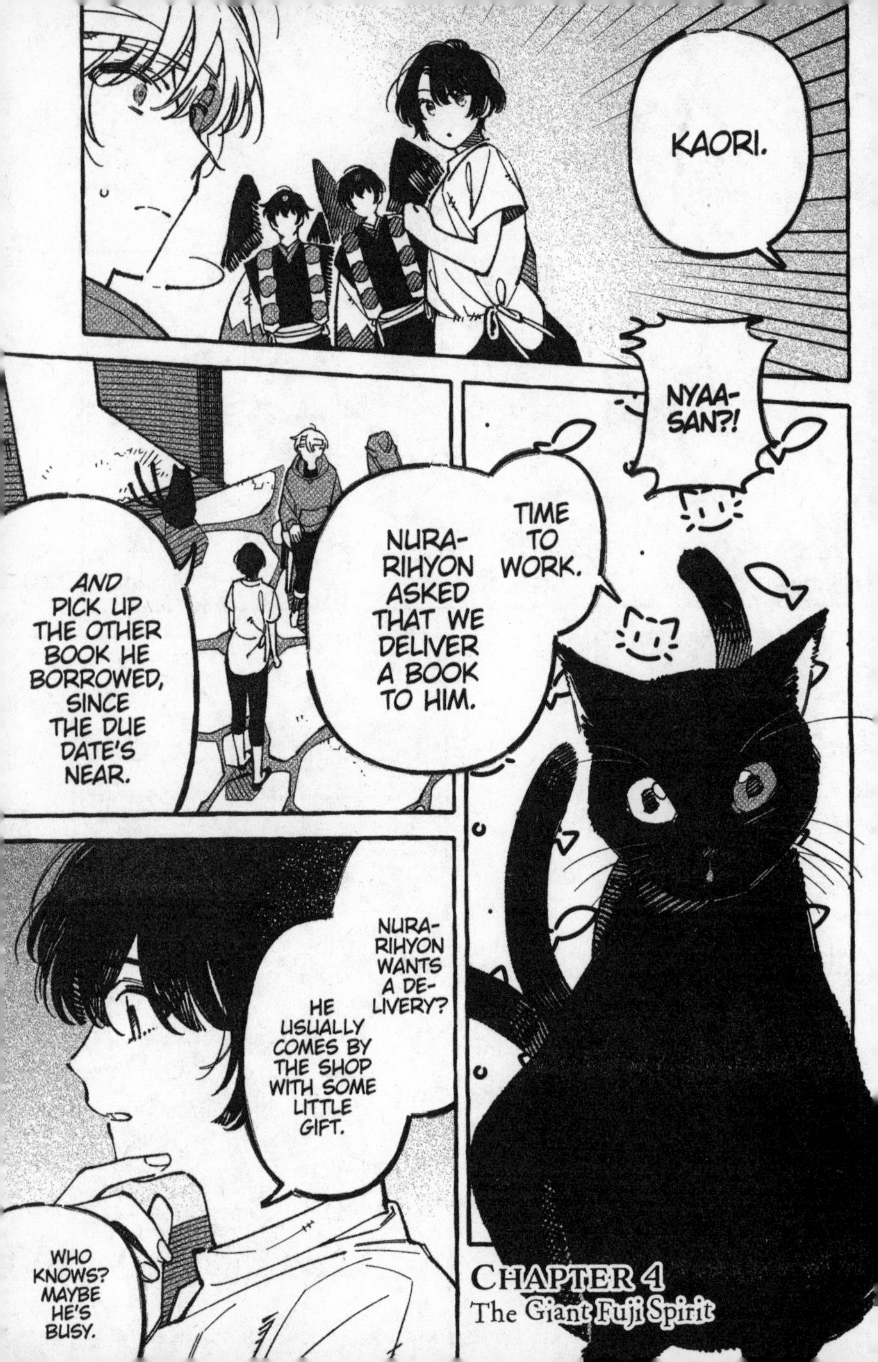
KAORI.
NYAA-SAN?!
TIME TO WORK. NURA-RIHYON ASKED THAT WE DELIVER A BOOK TO HIM.
AND PICK UP THE OTHER BOOK HE BORROWED, SINCE THE DUE DATE'S NEAR.
NURA-RIHYON WANTS A DELIVERY?
HE USUALLY COMES BY THE SHOP WITH SOME LITTLE GIFT.
WHO KNOWS? MAYBE HE'S BUSY.
CHAPTER 4
The Giant Fuji Spirit

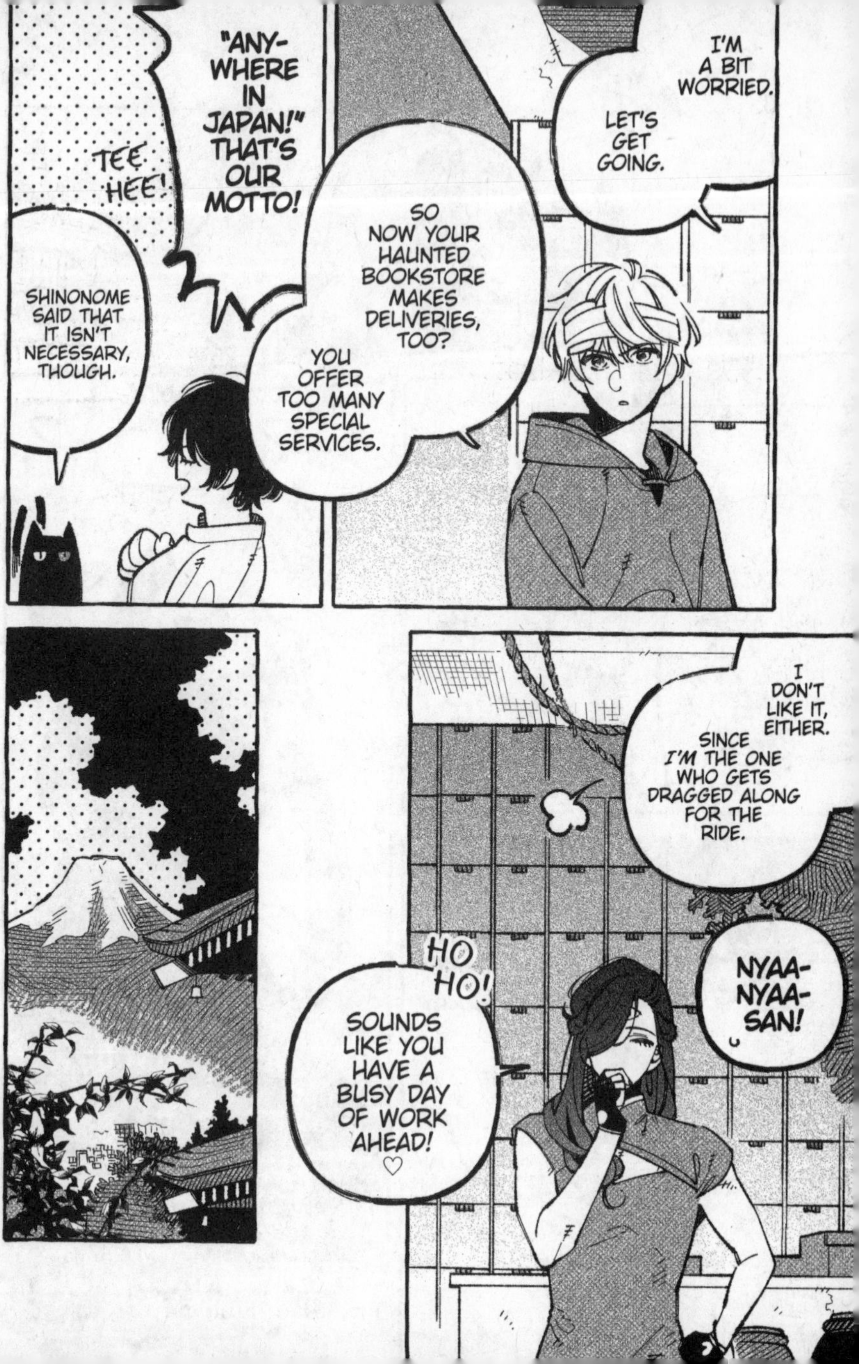
I'M A BIT WORRIED.
LET'S GET GOING.
SO NOW YOUR HAUNTED BOOKSTORE MAKES DELIVERIES, TOO?
YOU OFFER TOO MANY SPECIAL SERVICES.
"ANY-WHERE IN JAPAN!" THAT'S OUR MOTTO!
TEE HEE!
SHINONOME SAID THAT IT ISN'T NECESSARY, THOUGH.
I DON'T LIKE IT, EITHER.
SINCE I'M THE ONE WHO GETS DRAGGED ALONG FOR THE RIDE.
NYAA-NYAA-SAN!
HO HO!
SOUNDS LIKE YOU HAVE A BUSY DAY OF WORK AHEAD! ♡

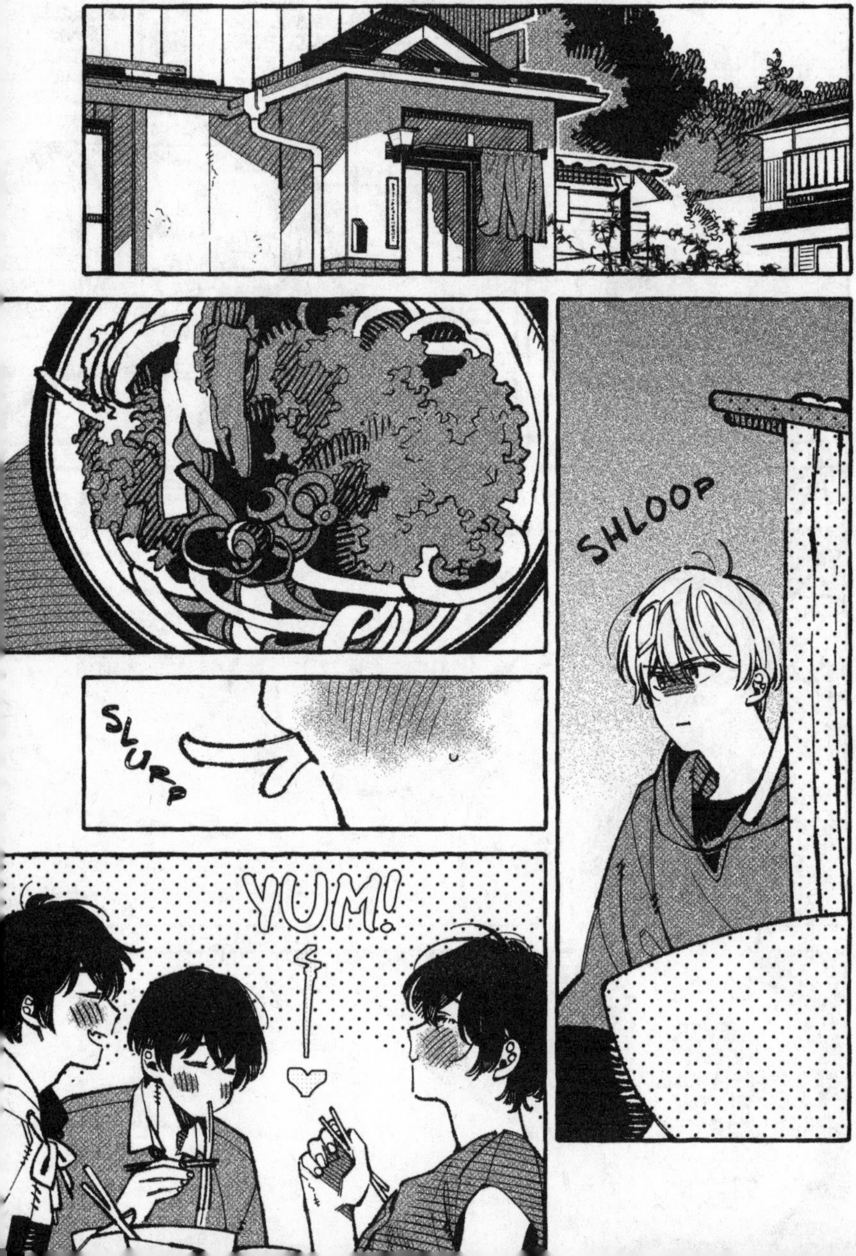
SHLOOP
SLURP
YUM!

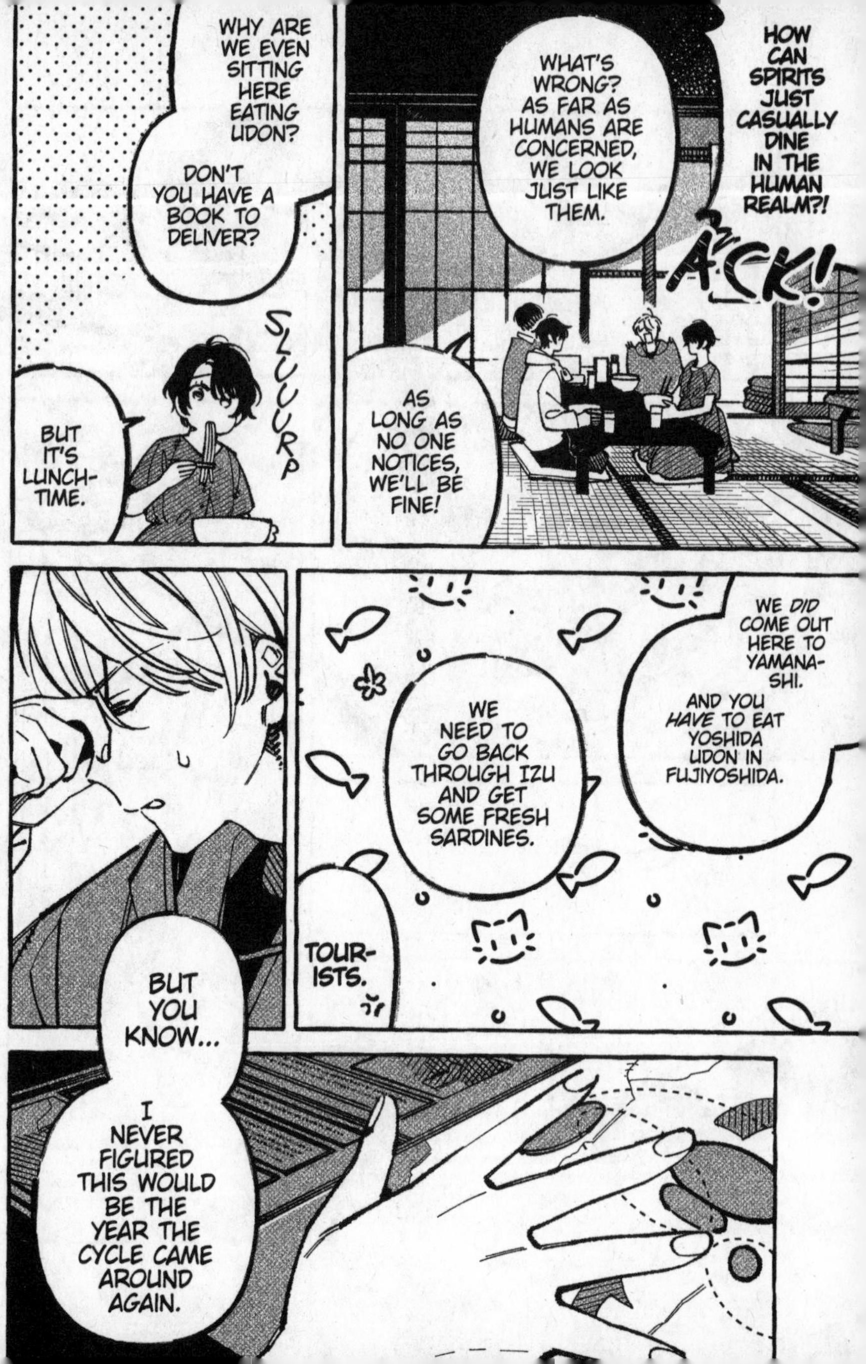
HOW CAN SPIRITS JUST CASUALLY DINE IN THE HUMAN REALM?!
A'CK!
WHAT'S WRONG? AS FAR AS HUMANS ARE CONCERNED, WE LOOK JUST LIKE THEM.
AS LONG AS NO ONE NOTICES, WE'LL BE FINE!
WHY ARE WE EVEN SITTING HERE EATING UDON?
DON'T YOU HAVE A BOOK TO DELIVER?
SLUUURP
BUT IT'S LUNCH-TIME.
WE *DID* COME OUT HERE TO YAMANA-SHI.
AND YOU *HAVE* TO EAT YOSHIDA UDON IN FUJIYOSHIDA.
WE NEED TO GO BACK THROUGH IZU AND GET SOME FRESH SARDINES.
TOUR-ISTS.
BUT YOU KNOW...
I NEVER FIGURED THIS WOULD BE THE YEAR THE CYCLE CAME AROUND AGAIN.

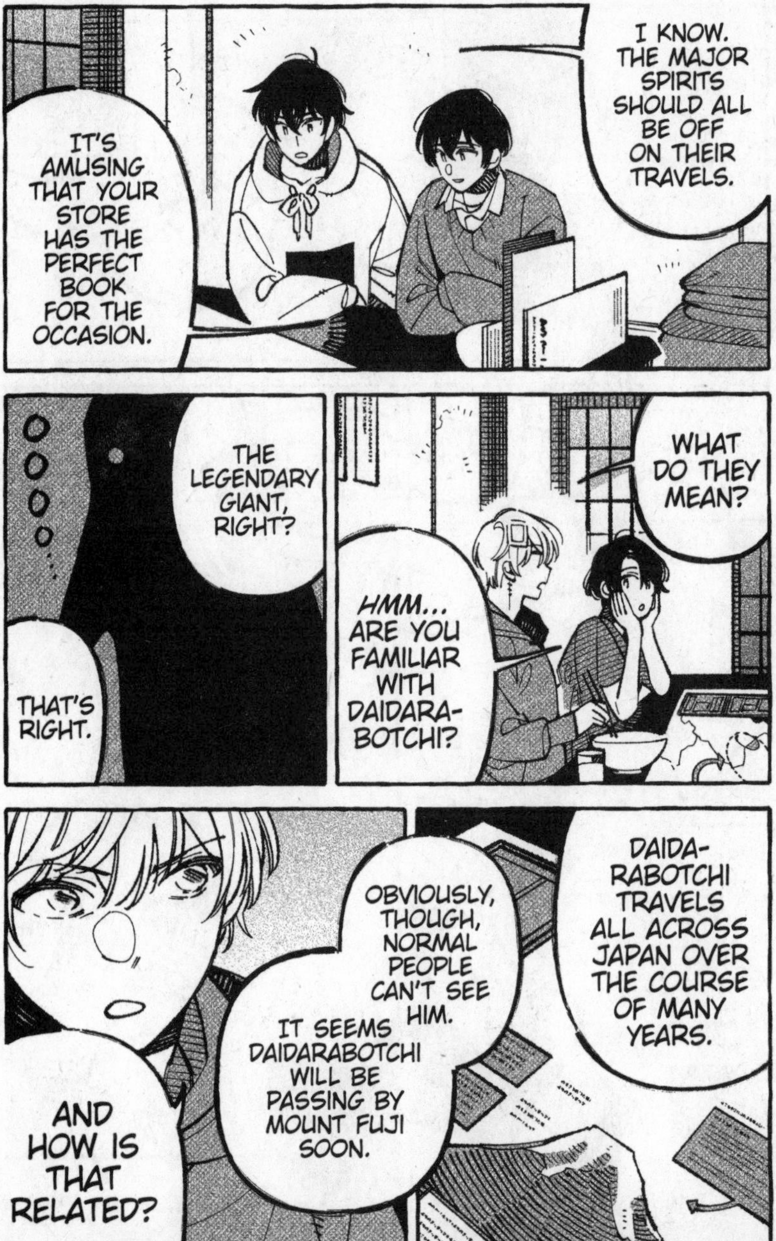
I KNOW. THE MAJOR SPIRITS SHOULD ALL BE OFF ON THEIR TRAVELS.
IT'S AMUSING THAT YOUR STORE HAS THE PERFECT BOOK FOR THE OCCASION.
WHAT DO THEY MEAN?
HMM... ARE YOU FAMILIAR WITH DAIDARA-BOTCHI?
THE LEGENDARY GIANT, RIGHT?
OOOO...
THAT'S RIGHT.
DAIDA-RABOTCHI TRAVELS ALL ACROSS JAPAN OVER THE COURSE OF MANY YEARS.
OBVIOUSLY, THOUGH, NORMAL PEOPLE CAN'T SEE HIM.
IT SEEMS DAIDARABOTCHI WILL BE PASSING BY MOUNT FUJI SOON.
AND HOW IS THAT RELATED?

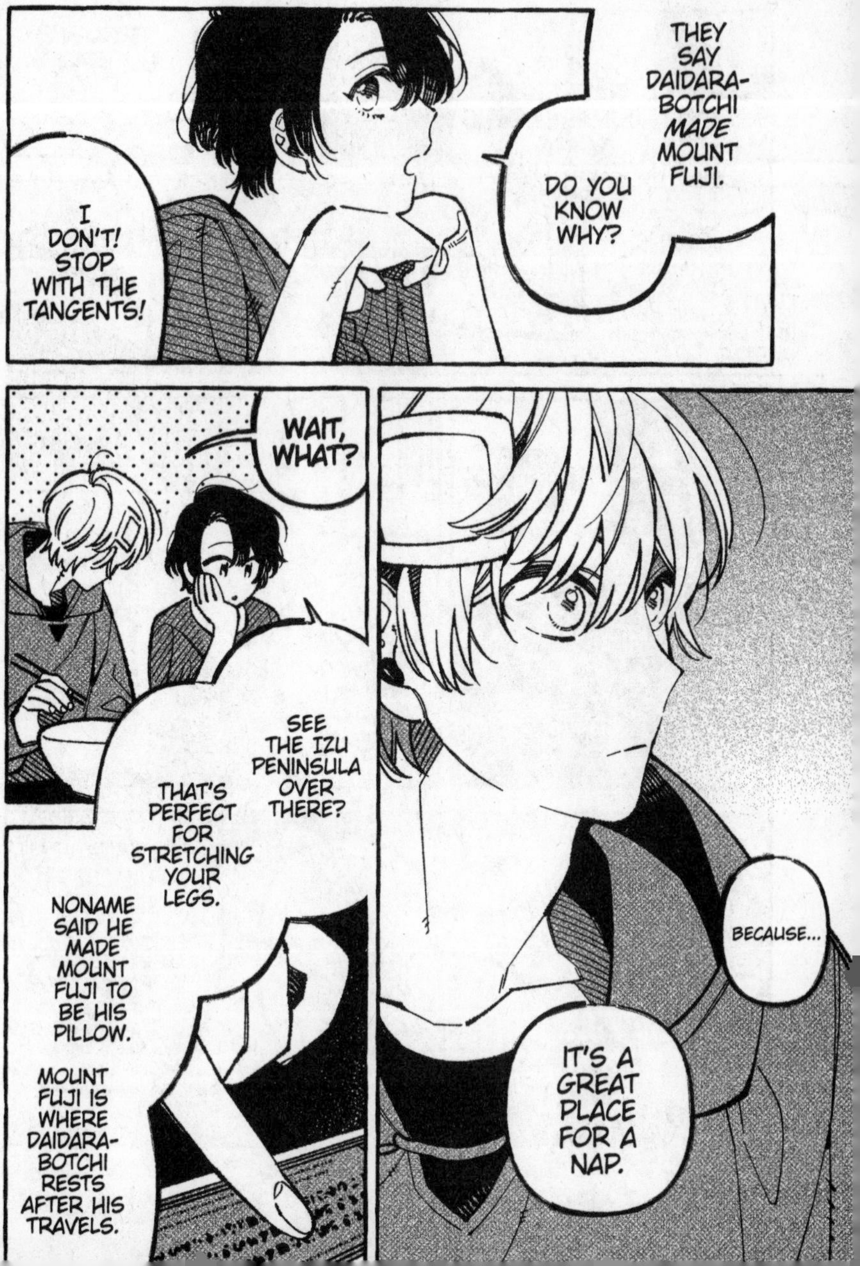
THEY SAY DAIDARA-BOTCHI MADE MOUNT FUJI.
DO YOU KNOW WHY?
I DON'T! STOP WITH THE TANGENTS!
BECAUSE...
IT'S A GREAT PLACE FOR A NAP.
WAIT, WHAT?
SEE THE IZU PENINSULA OVER THERE?
THAT'S PERFECT FOR STRETCHING YOUR LEGS.
NONAME SAID HE MADE MOUNT FUJI TO BE HIS PILLOW.
MOUNT FUJI IS WHERE DAIDARA-BOTCHI RESTS AFTER HIS TRAVELS.

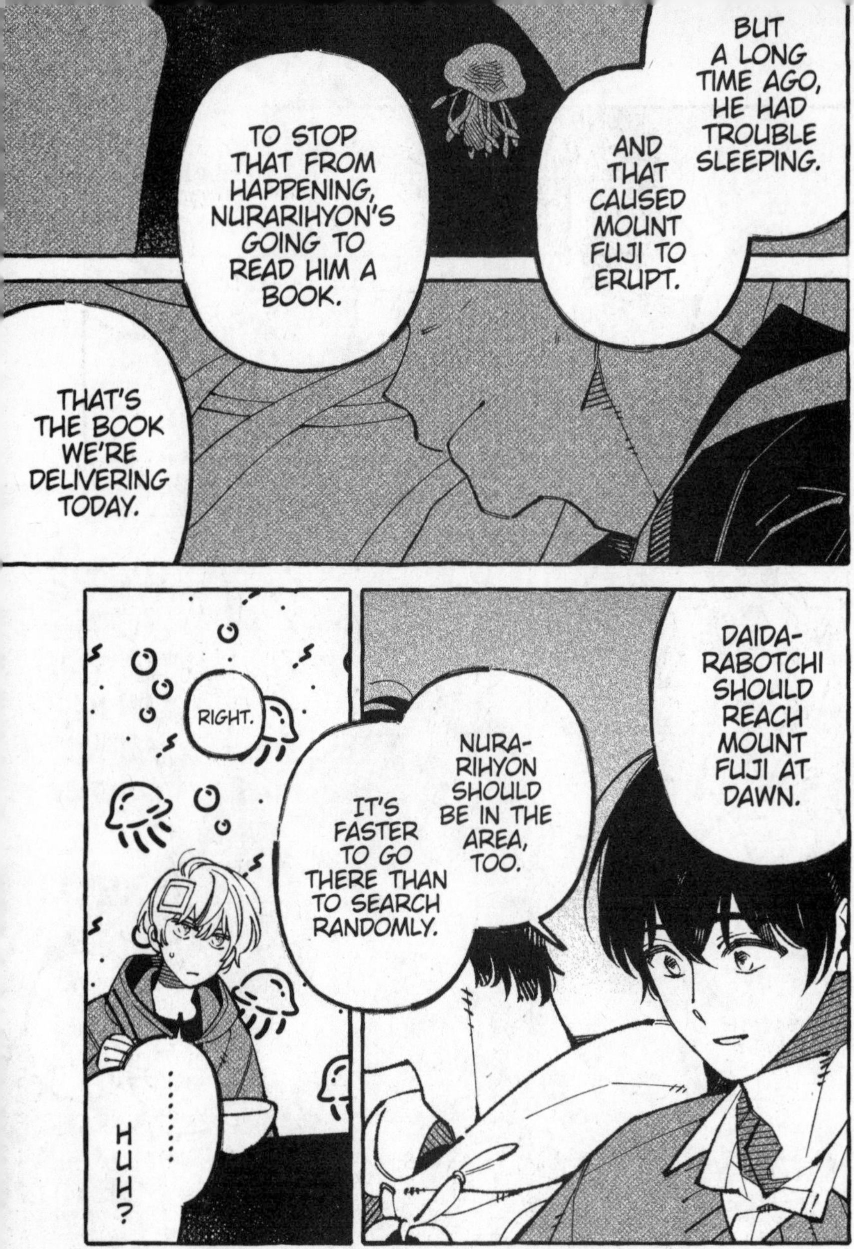
BUT A LONG TIME AGO, HE HAD TROUBLE SLEEPING.
AND THAT CAUSED MOUNT FUJI TO ERUPT.
TO STOP THAT FROM HAPPENING, NURARIHYON'S GOING TO READ HIM A BOOK.
THAT'S THE BOOK WE'RE DELIVERING TODAY.
DAIDA-RABOTCHI SHOULD REACH MOUNT FUJI AT DAWN.
NURA-RIHYON SHOULD BE IN THE AREA, TOO.
IT'S FASTER TO GO THERE THAN TO SEARCH RANDOMLY.
RIGHT.
......
HUH?

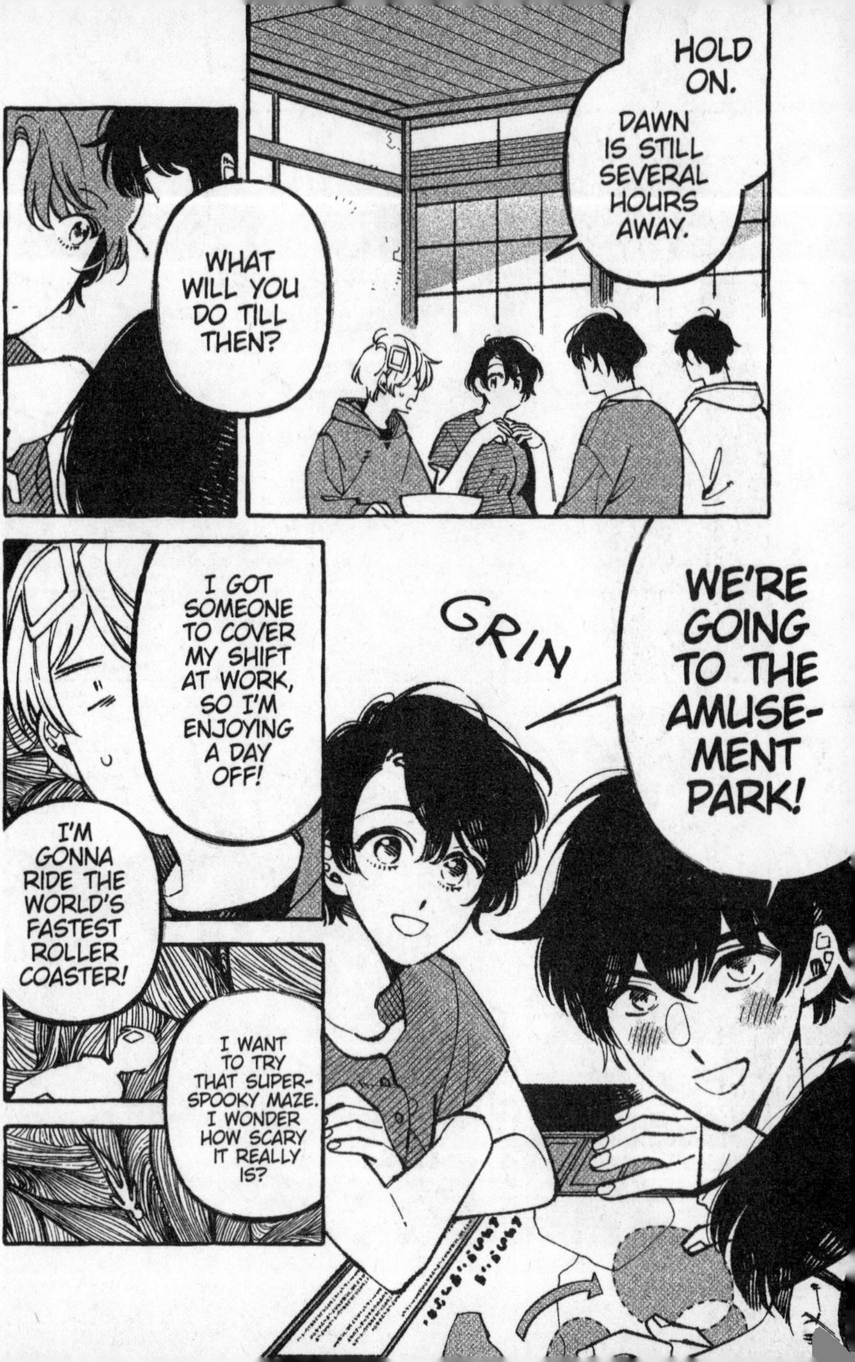
HOLD ON.
DAWN IS STILL SEVERAL HOURS AWAY.
WHAT WILL YOU DO TILL THEN?
WE'RE GOING TO THE AMUSEMENT PARK!
GRIN
I GOT SOMEONE TO COVER MY SHIFT AT WORK, SO I'M ENJOYING A DAY OFF!
I'M GONNA RIDE THE WORLD'S FASTEST ROLLER COASTER!
I WANT TO TRY THAT SUPER-SPOOKY MAZE. I WONDER HOW SCARY IT REALLY IS?

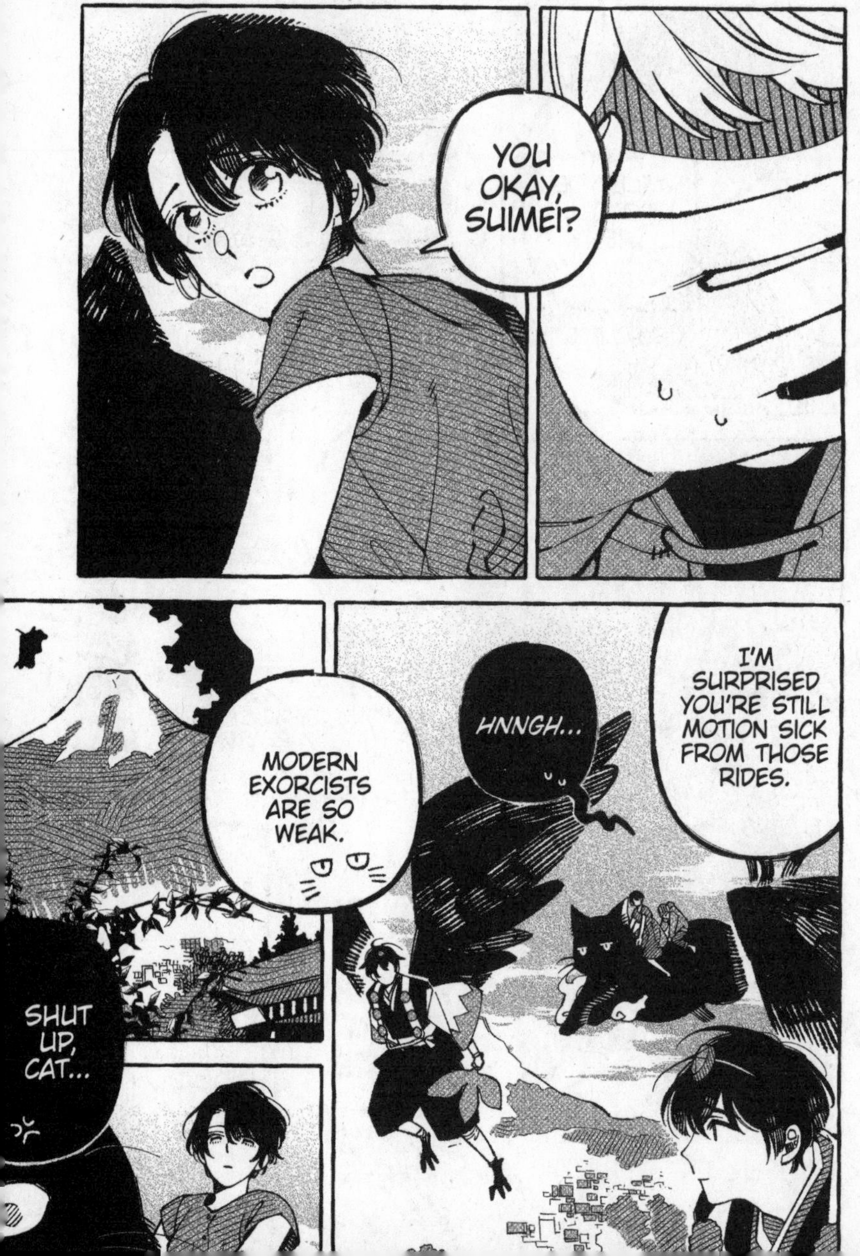
YOU OKAY, SUIMEI?
I'M SURPRISED YOU'RE STILL MOTION SICK FROM THOSE RIDES.
HNNGH...
MODERN EXORCISTS ARE SO WEAK.
SHUT UP, CAT...

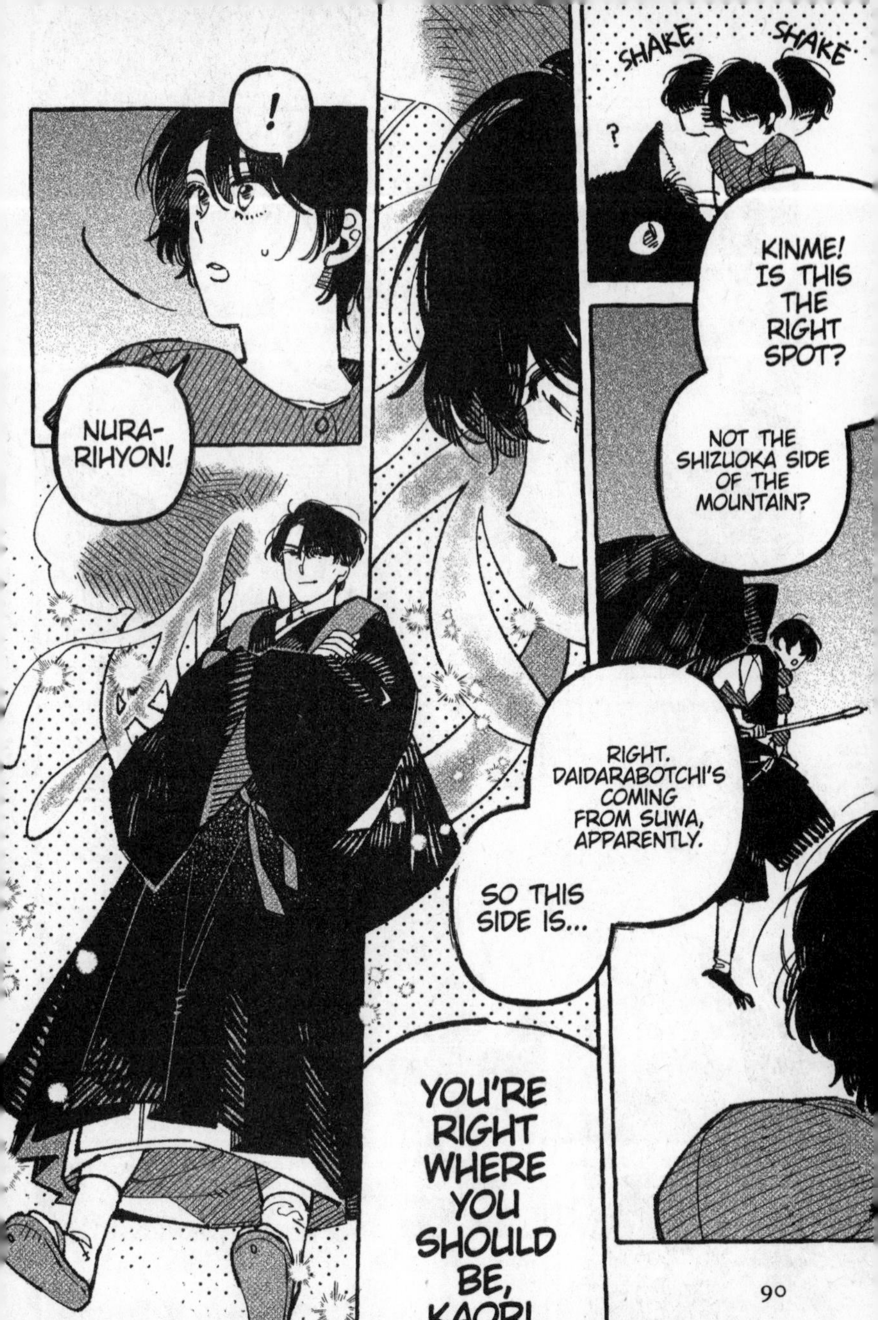
SHAKE SHAKE
?
KINME! IS THIS THE RIGHT SPOT?
NOT THE SHIZUOKA SIDE OF THE MOUNTAIN?
RIGHT. DAIDARABOTCHI'S COMING FROM SUWA, APPARENTLY.
SO THIS SIDE IS...
!
NURA-RIHYON!
YOU'RE RIGHT WHERE YOU SHOULD BE, KAORI.

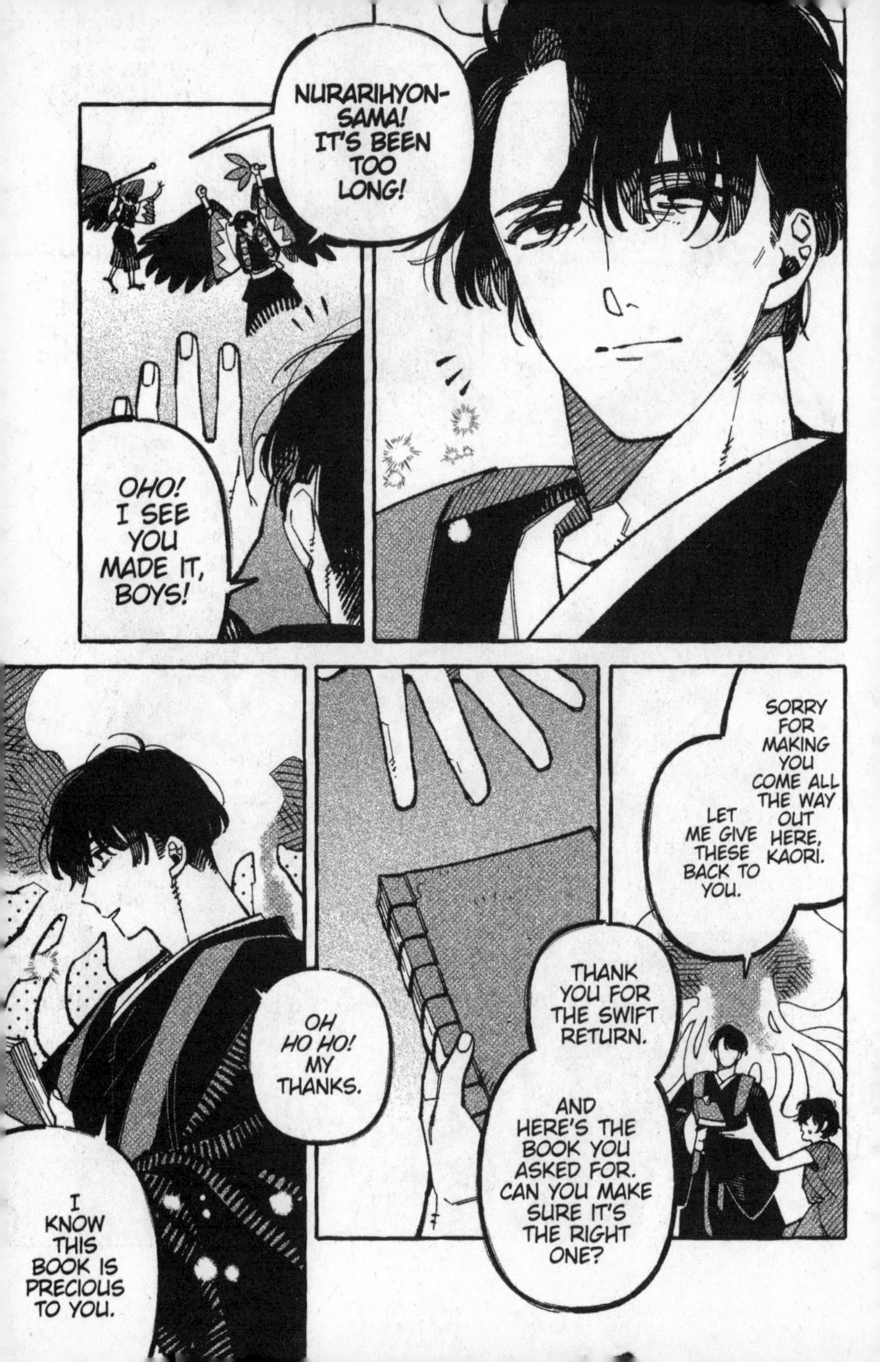
NURARIHYON-SAMA! IT'S BEEN TOO LONG!
OHO! I SEE YOU MADE IT, BOYS!
SORRY FOR MAKING YOU COME ALL THE WAY OUT HERE, KAORI.
LET ME GIVE THESE BACK TO YOU.
THANK YOU FOR THE SWIFT RETURN.
AND HERE'S THE BOOK YOU ASKED FOR. CAN YOU MAKE SURE IT'S THE RIGHT ONE?
OH HO HO! MY THANKS.
I KNOW THIS BOOK IS PRECIOUS TO YOU.

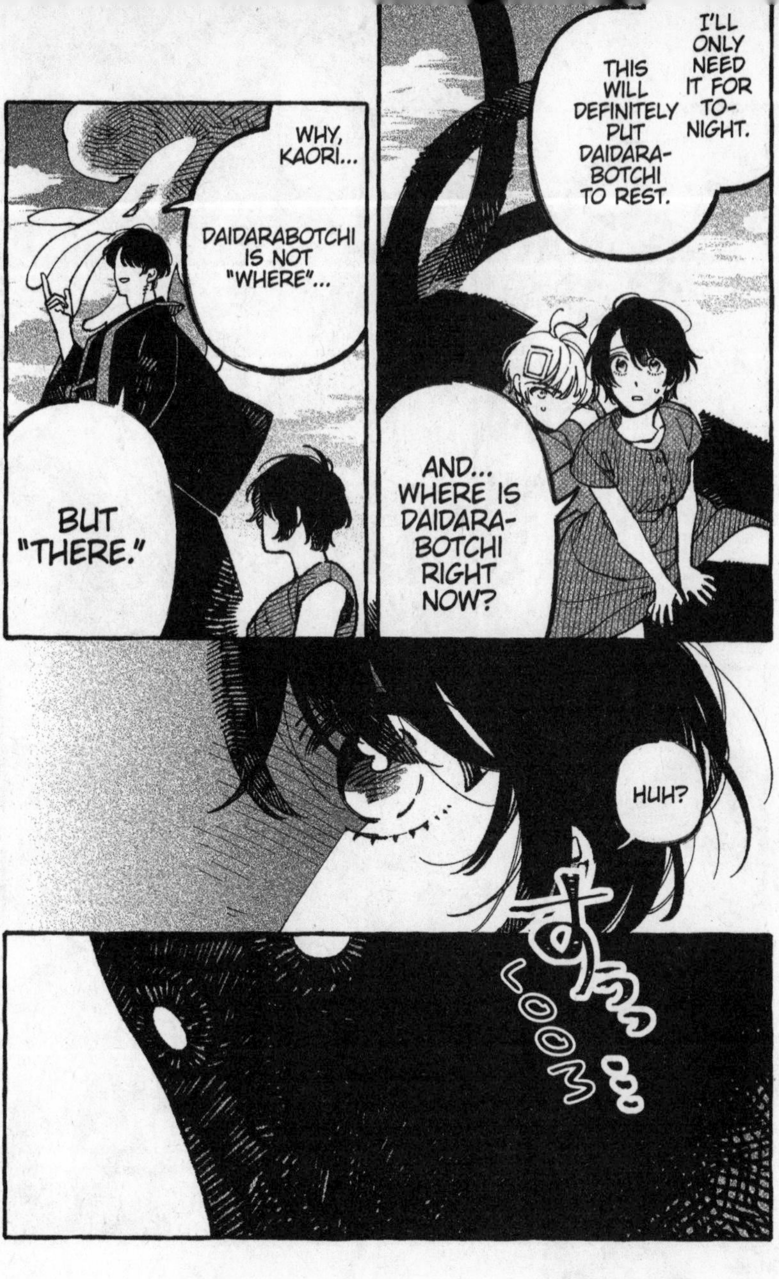
I'LL ONLY NEED IT FOR TO-NIGHT.
THIS WILL DEFINITELY PUT DAIDARA-BOTCHI TO REST.
AND... WHERE IS DAIDARA-BOTCHI RIGHT NOW?
WHY, KAORI...
DAIDARABOTCHI IS NOT "WHERE"...
BUT "THERE."
HUH?
LOOOM...

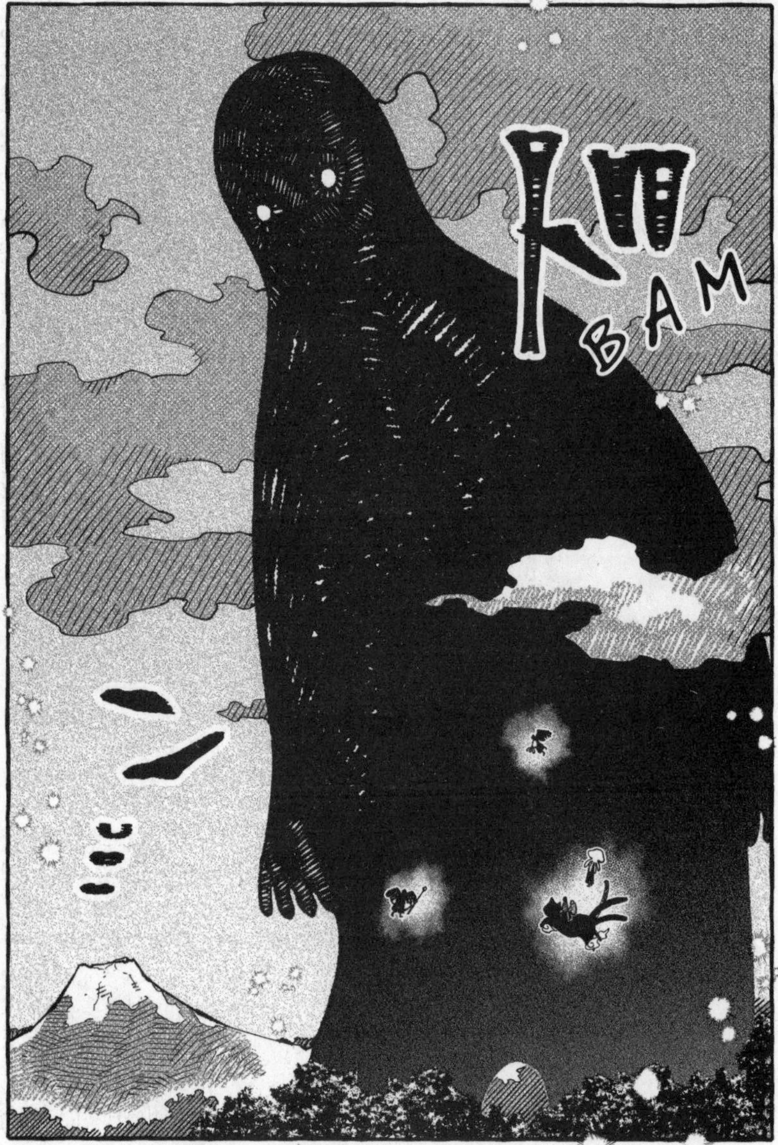
BAM

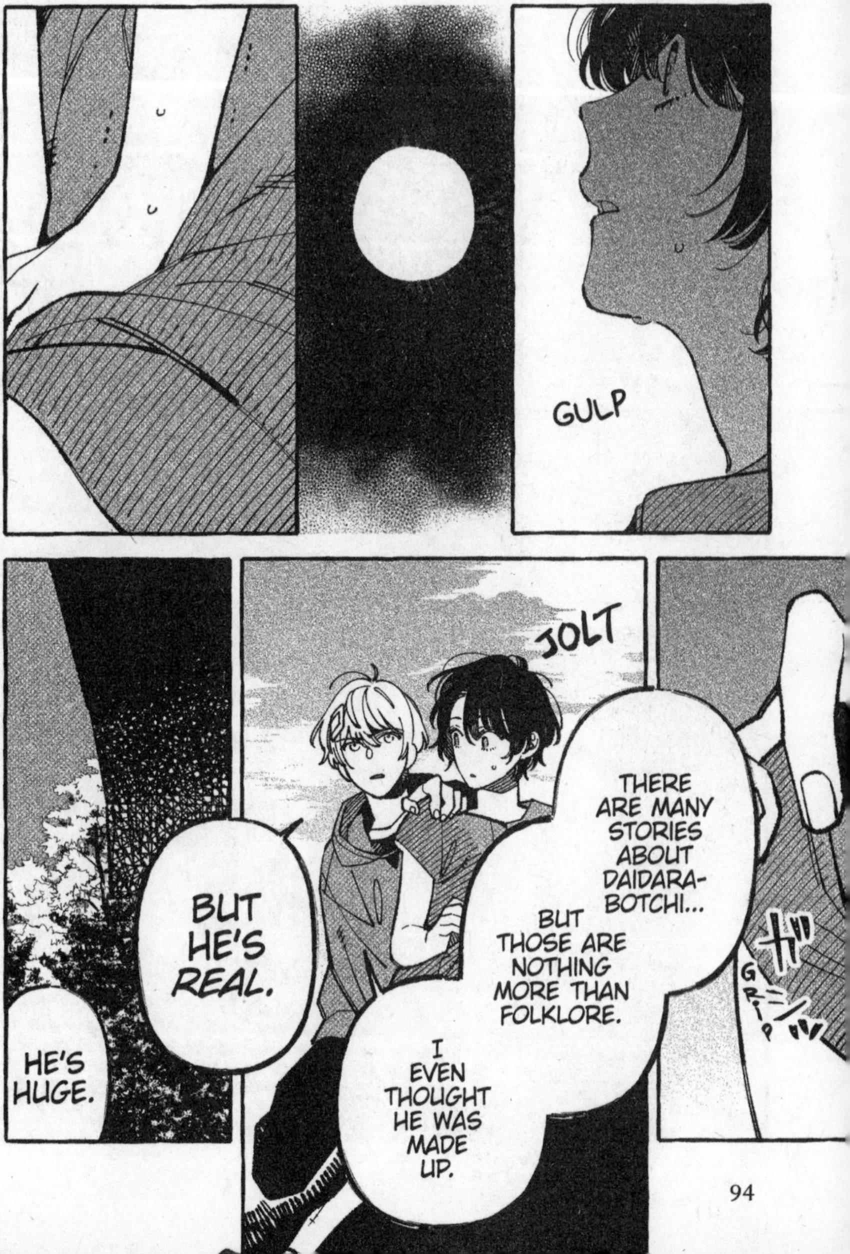
GULP
GRIP
JOLT
THERE ARE MANY STORIES ABOUT DAIDARA-BOTCHI...
BUT THOSE ARE NOTHING MORE THAN FOLKLORE.
I EVEN THOUGHT HE WAS MADE UP.
BUT HE'S REAL.
HE'S HUGE.

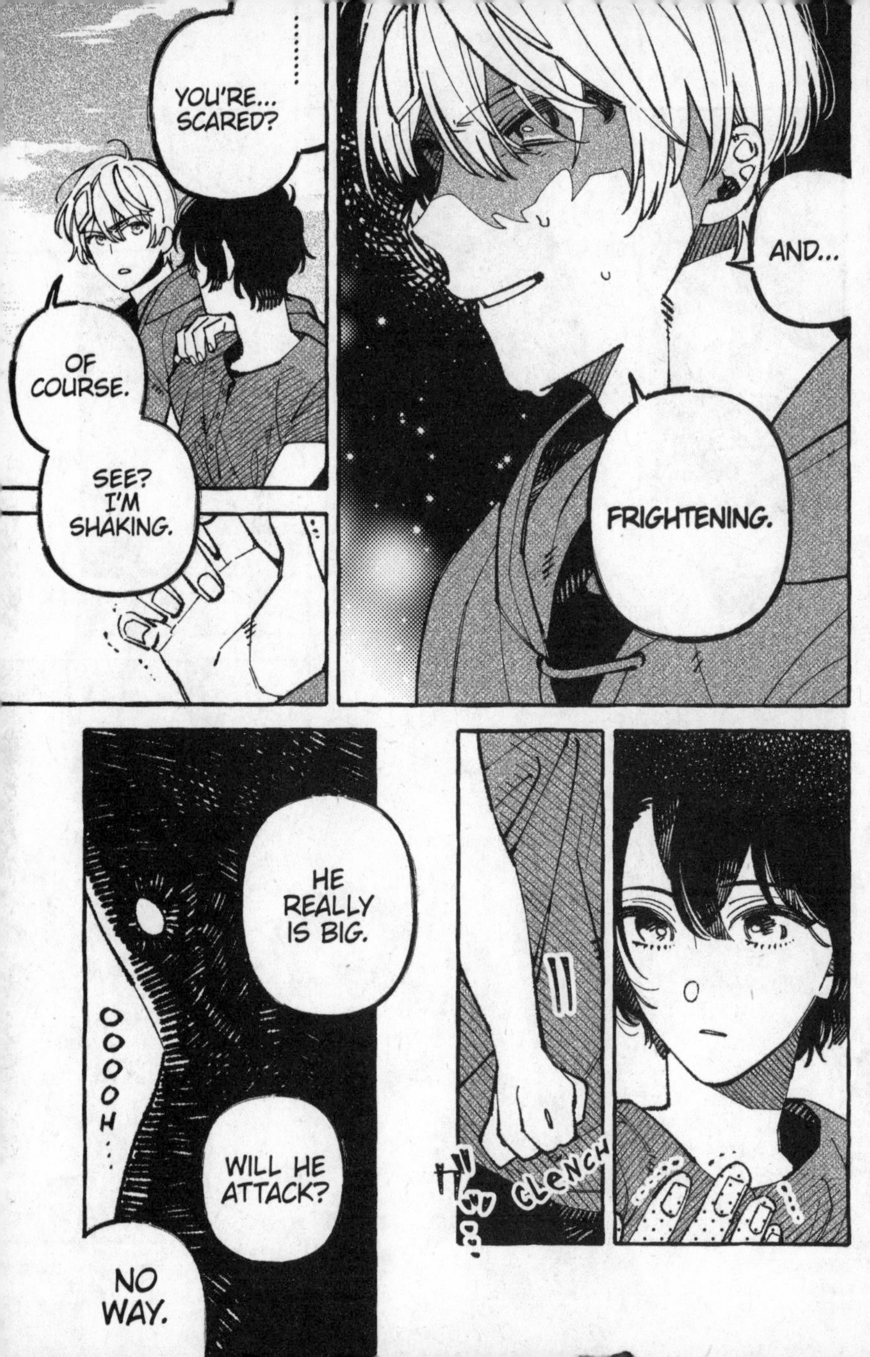
AND...
FRIGHTENING.
......
YOU'RE... SCARED?
OF COURSE.
SEE? I'M SHAKING.
!!
CLENCH
HE REALLY IS BIG.
OOOOOH...
WILL HE ATTACK?
NO WAY.

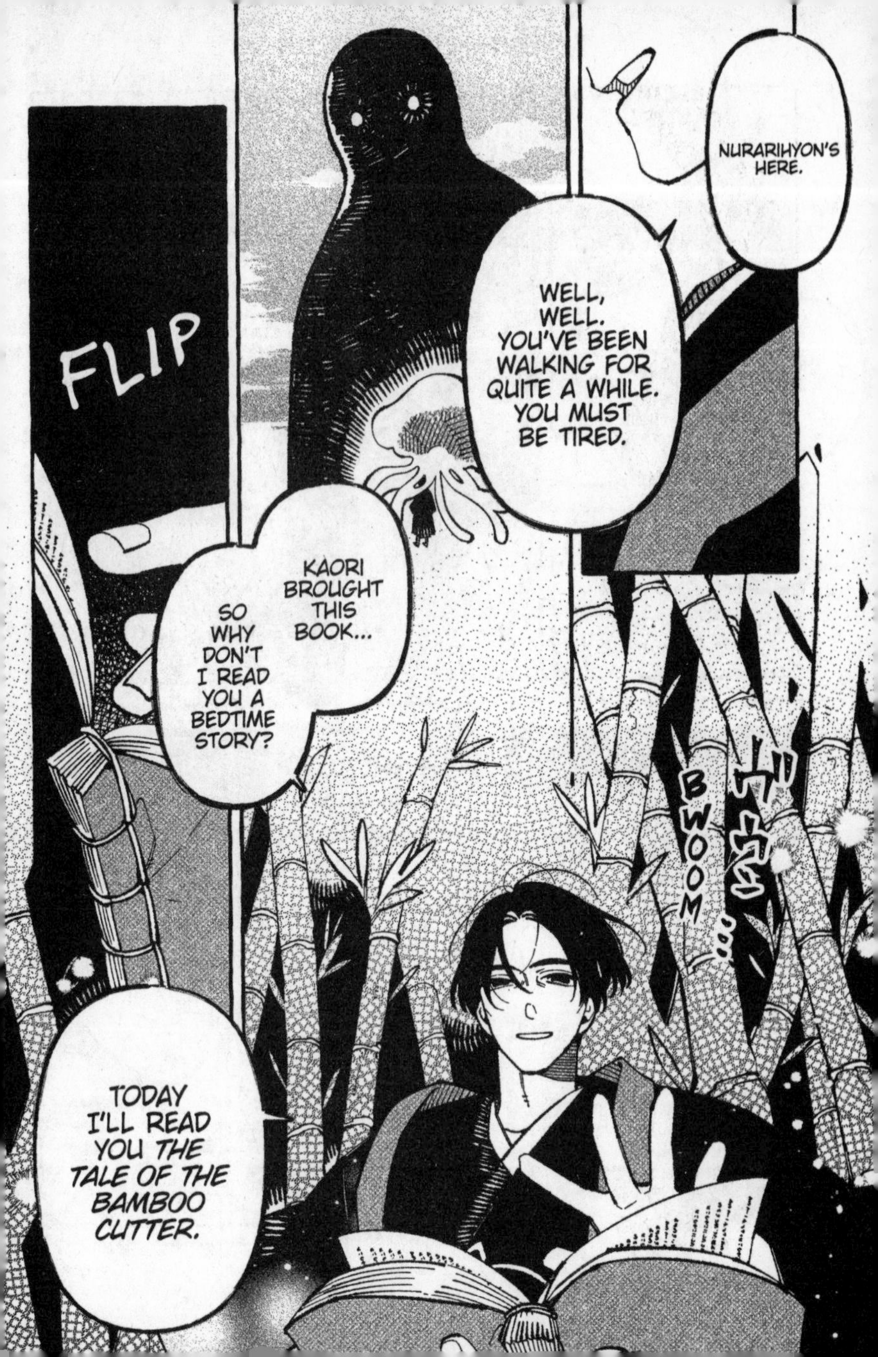
NURARIHYON'S HERE.
WELL, WELL. YOU'VE BEEN WALKING FOR QUITE A WHILE. YOU MUST BE TIRED.
FLIP
KAORI BROUGHT THIS BOOK...
SO WHY DON'T I READ YOU A BEDTIME STORY?
BWOOM...
TODAY I'LL READ YOU THE TALE OF THE BAMBOO CUTTER.

"I KNOW THIS BOOK IS PRECIOUS TO YOU."
MY TREASURE.
A VERY SPECIAL BOOK...
MADE BY SHINONOME-SAN.
IT'S THE ONLY PICTURE BOOK OF ITS KIND.
I WAS A REAL CRYBABY WHEN I WAS YOUNG.

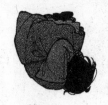

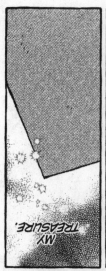

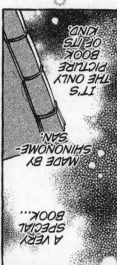

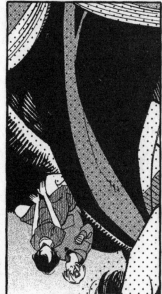

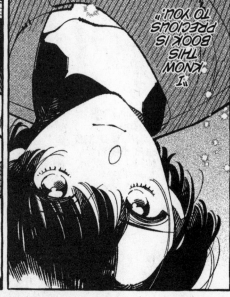

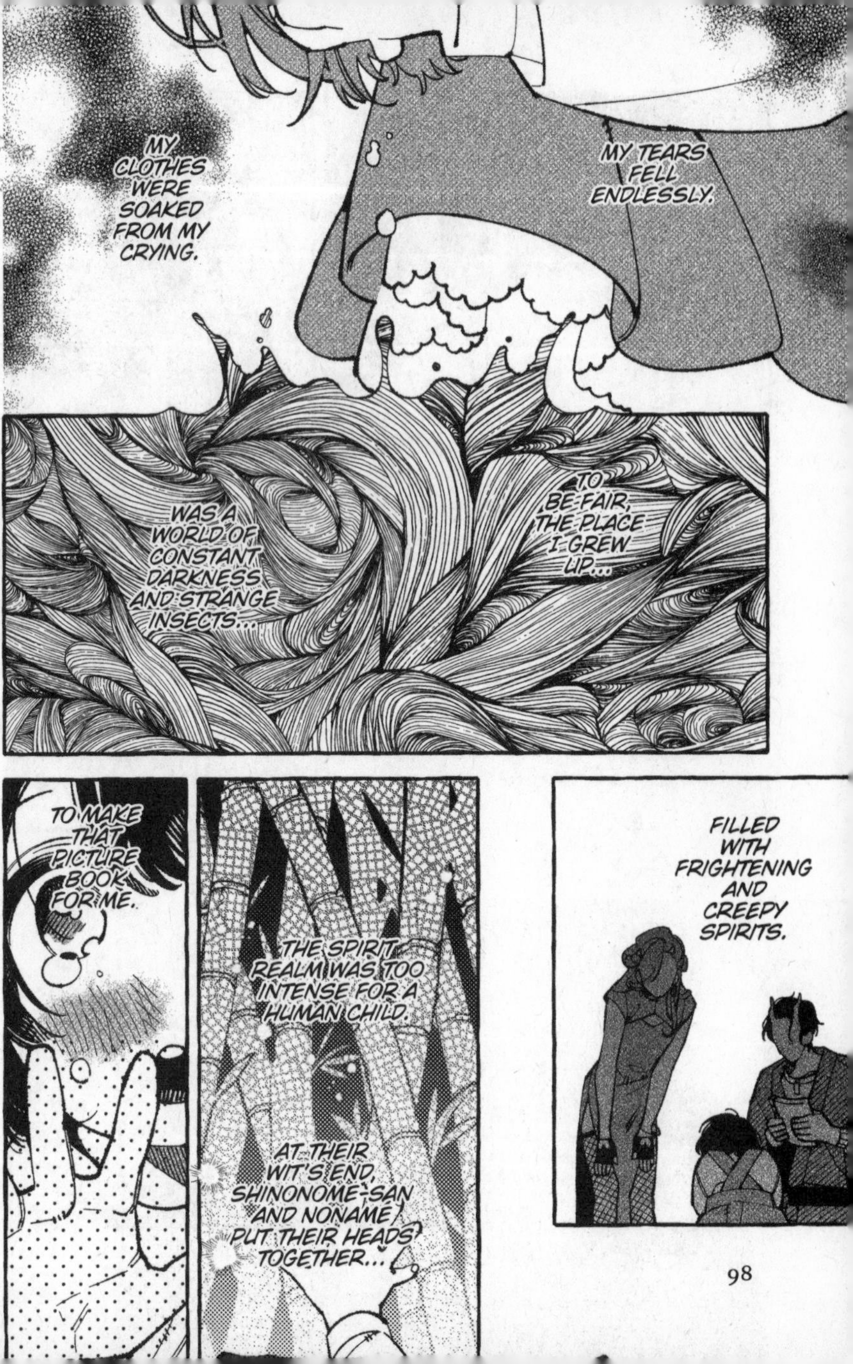
MY TEARS FELL ENDLESSLY.
MY CLOTHES WERE SOAKED FROM MY CRYING.
TO BE FAIR, THE PLACE I GREW UP...
WAS A WORLD OF CONSTANT DARKNESS AND STRANGE INSECTS...
FILLED WITH FRIGHTENING AND CREEPY SPIRITS.
THE SPIRIT REALM WAS TOO INTENSE FOR A HUMAN CHILD.
AT THEIR WIT'S END, SHINONOME-SAN AND NONAME PUT THEIR HEADS TOGETHER...
TO MAKE THAT PICTURE BOOK FOR ME.

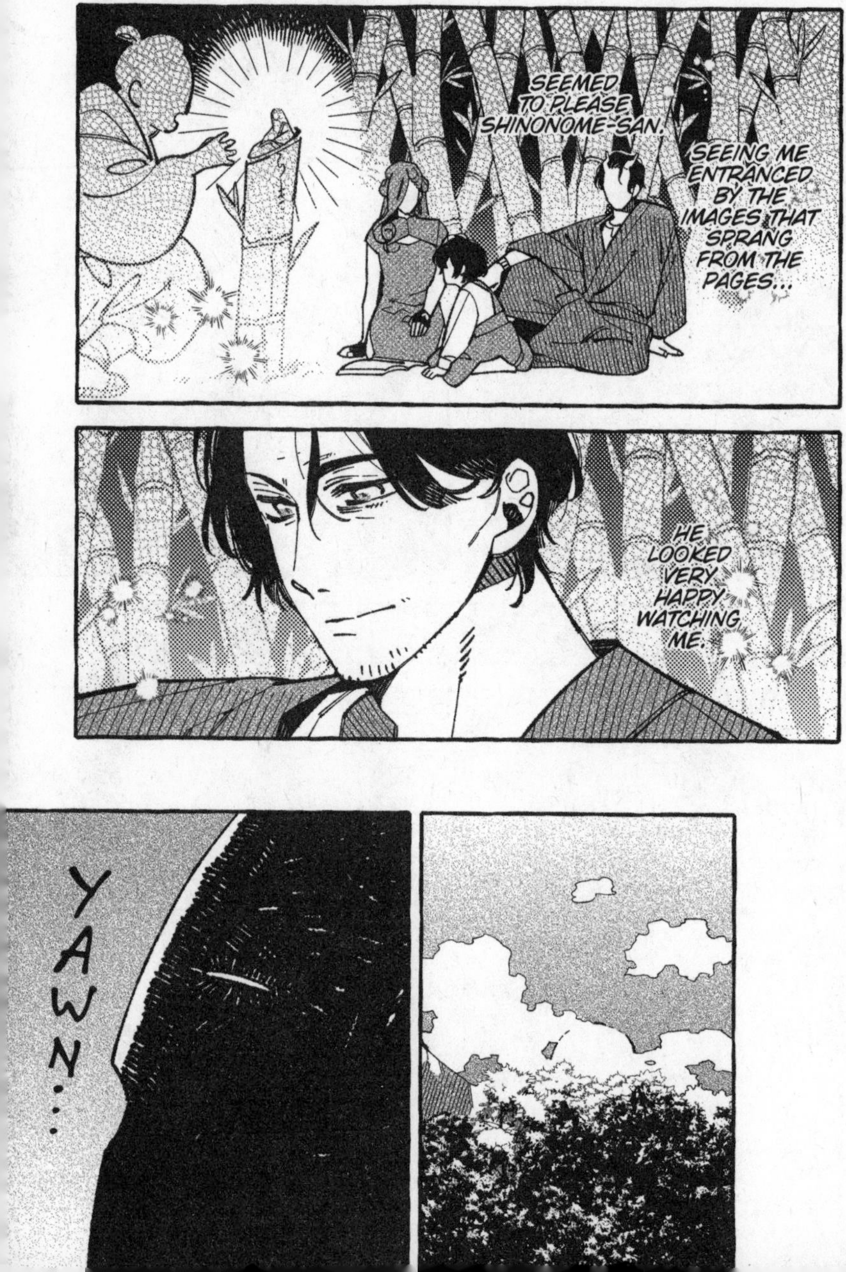
SEEING ME ENTRANCED BY THE IMAGES THAT SPRANG FROM THE PAGES...
SEEMED TO PLEASE SHINONOME-SAN.
HE LOOKED VERY HAPPY WATCHING ME.
YAWN...

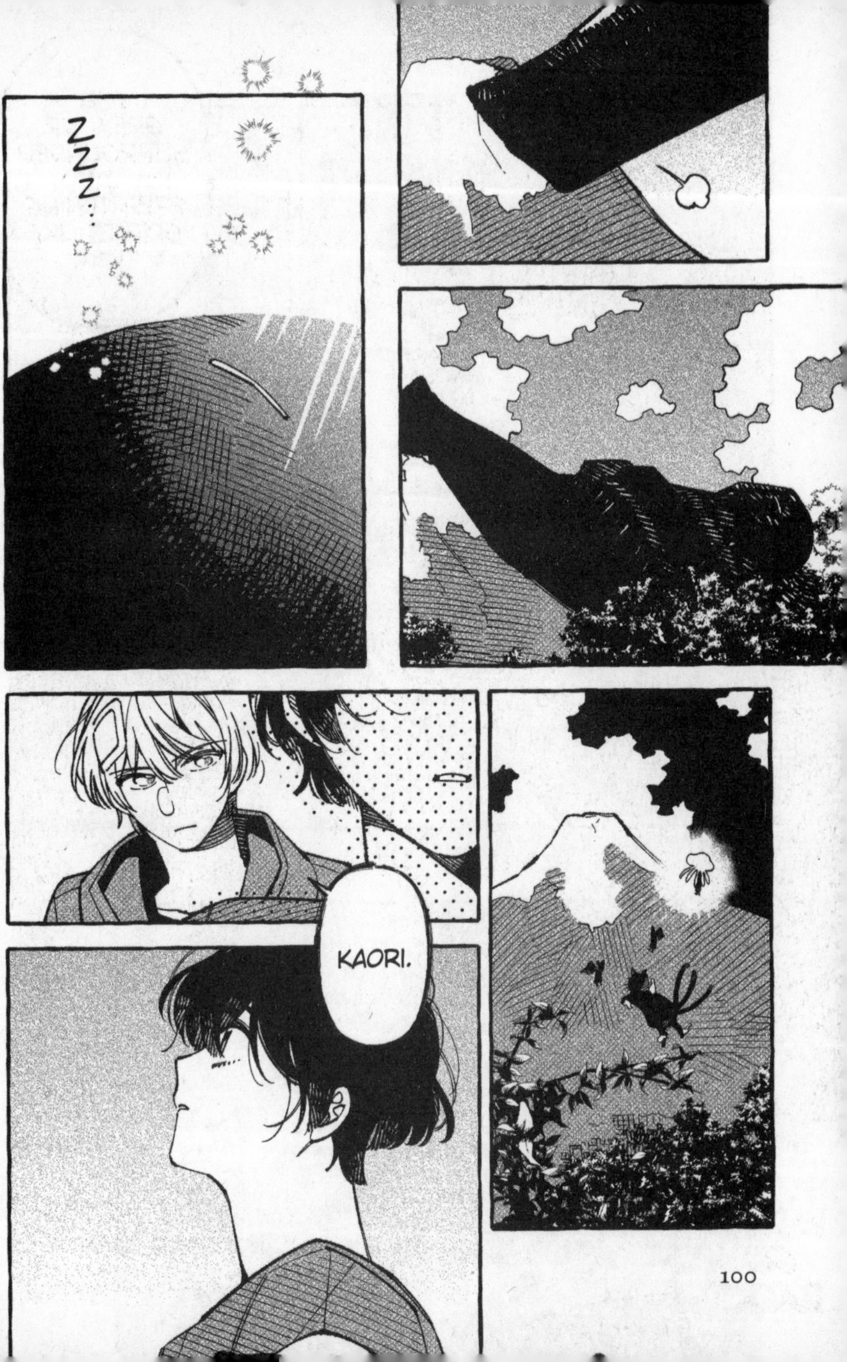
ZZZ...
KAORI.

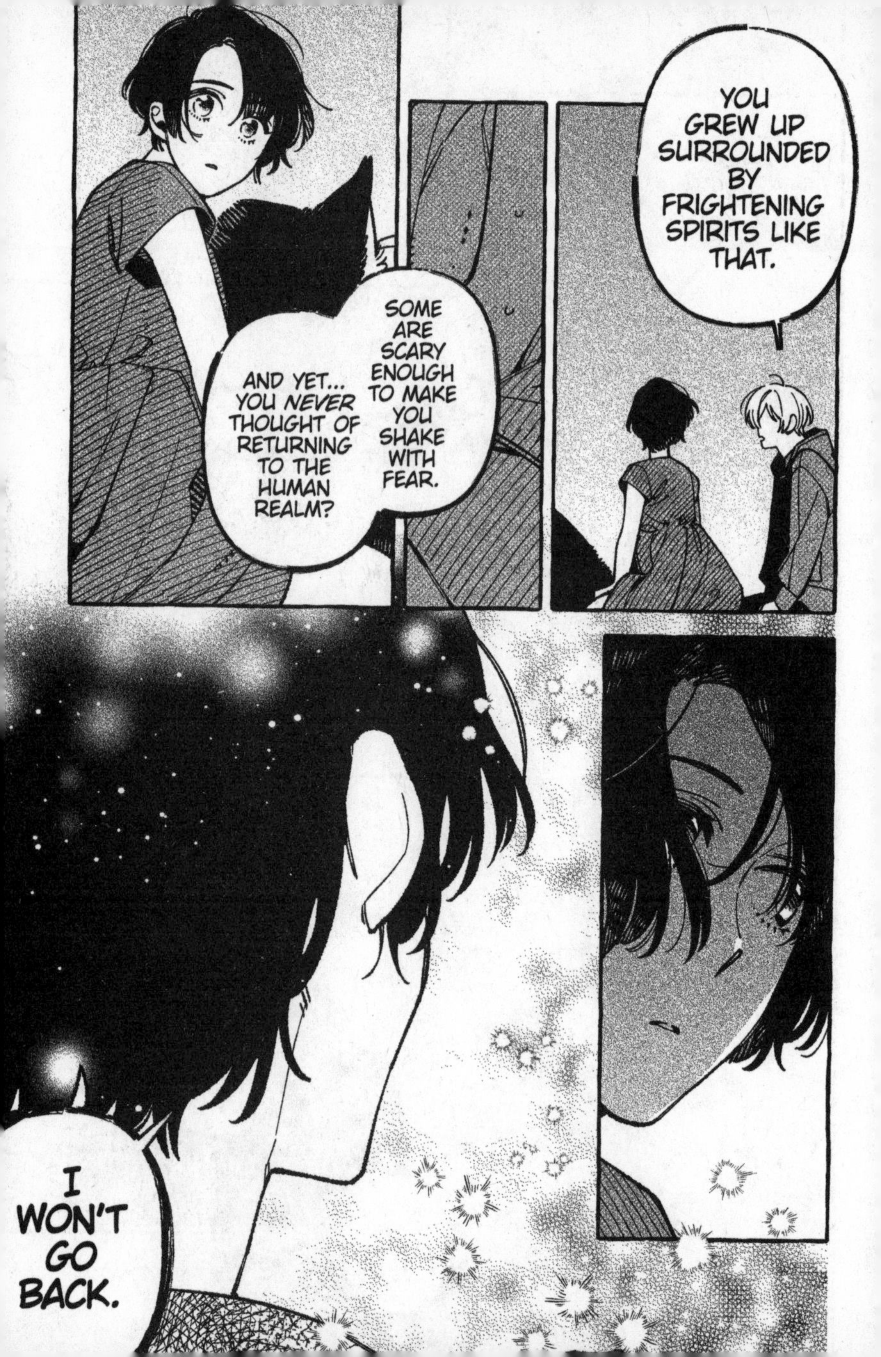
YOU GREW UP SURROUNDED BY FRIGHTENING SPIRITS LIKE THAT.
SOME ARE SCARY ENOUGH TO MAKE YOU SHAKE WITH FEAR.
AND YET... YOU NEVER THOUGHT OF RETURNING TO THE HUMAN REALM?
I WON'T GO BACK.

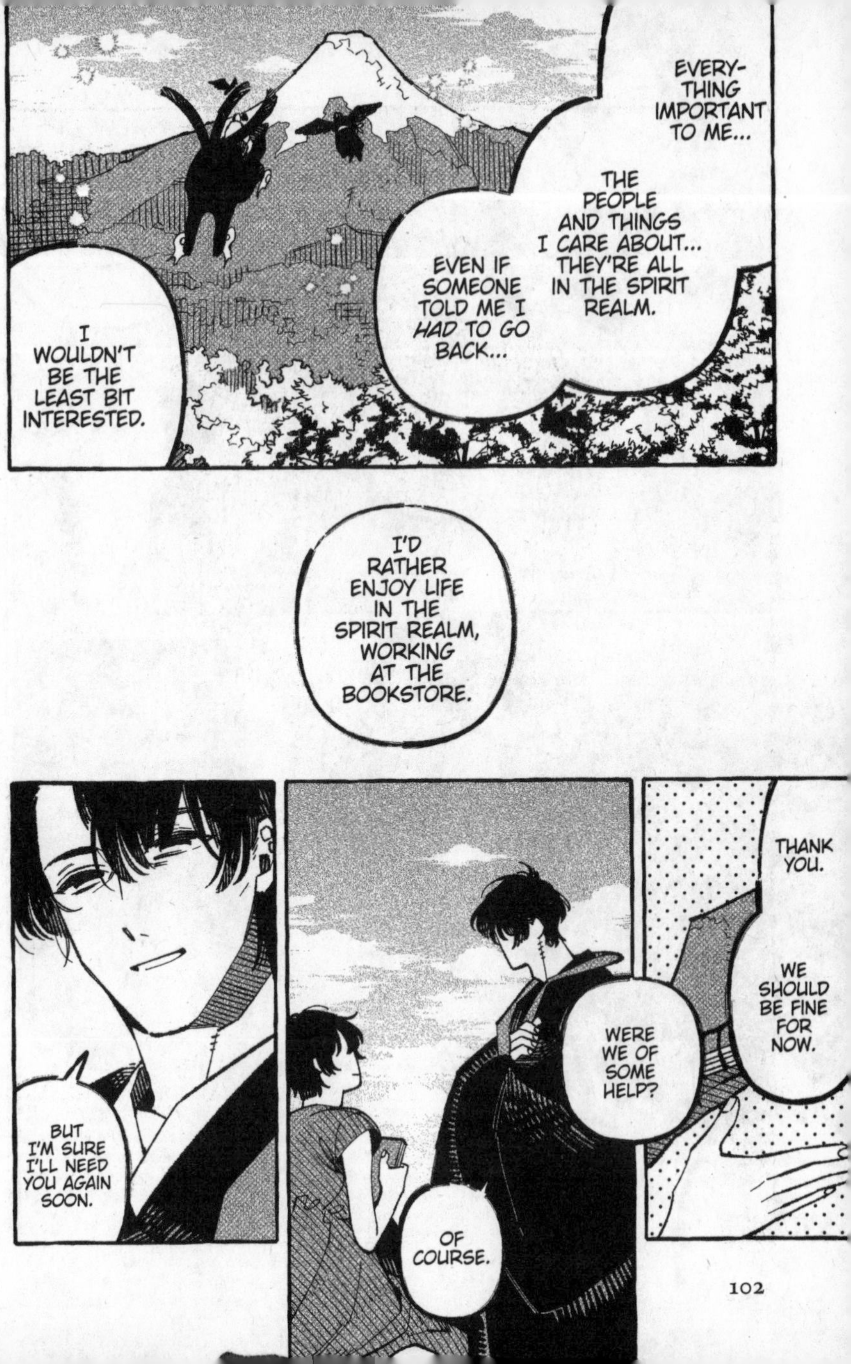
EVERY-THING IMPORTANT TO ME...
THE PEOPLE AND THINGS I CARE ABOUT... THEY'RE ALL IN THE SPIRIT REALM.
EVEN IF SOMEONE TOLD ME I *HAD* TO GO BACK...
I WOULDN'T BE THE LEAST BIT INTERESTED.
I'D RATHER ENJOY LIFE IN THE SPIRIT REALM, WORKING AT THE BOOKSTORE.
THANK YOU.
WE SHOULD BE FINE FOR NOW.
WERE WE OF SOME HELP?
OF COURSE.
BUT I'M SURE I'LL NEED YOU AGAIN SOON.

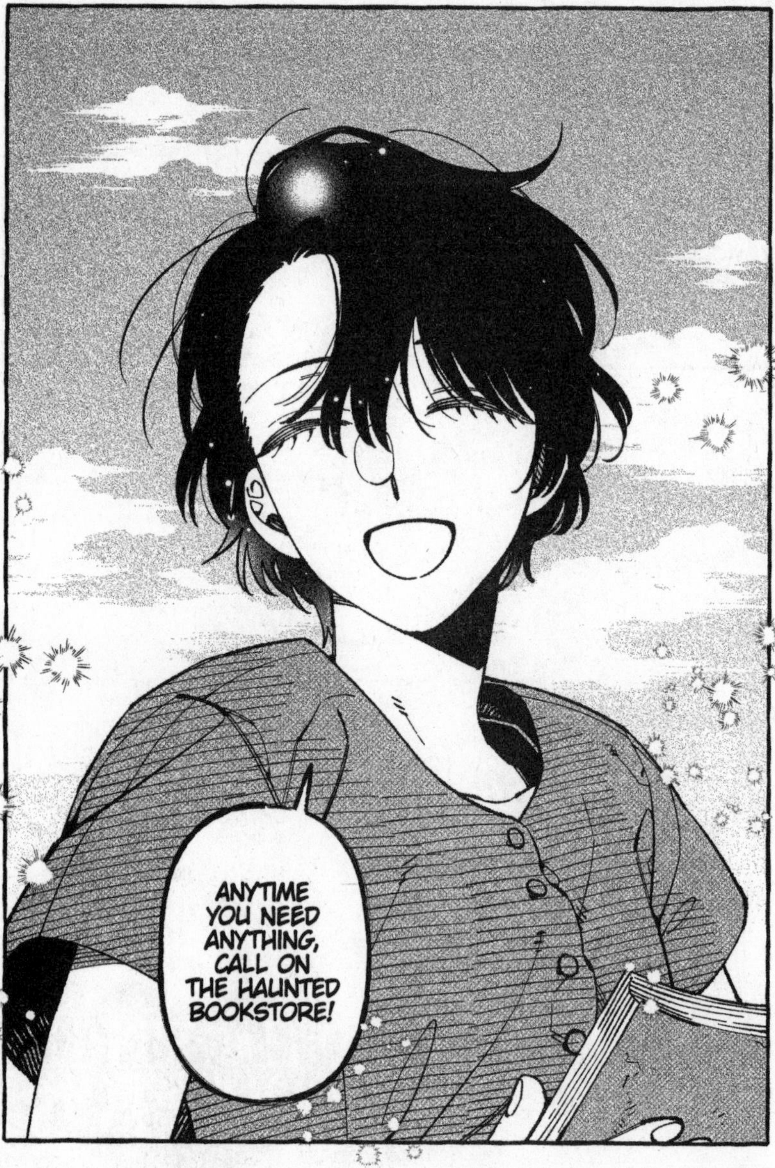
ANYTIME YOU NEED ANYTHING, CALL ON THE HAUNTED BOOKSTORE!

THE
HAUNTED BOOKSTORE
Gateway to a
Parallel Universe

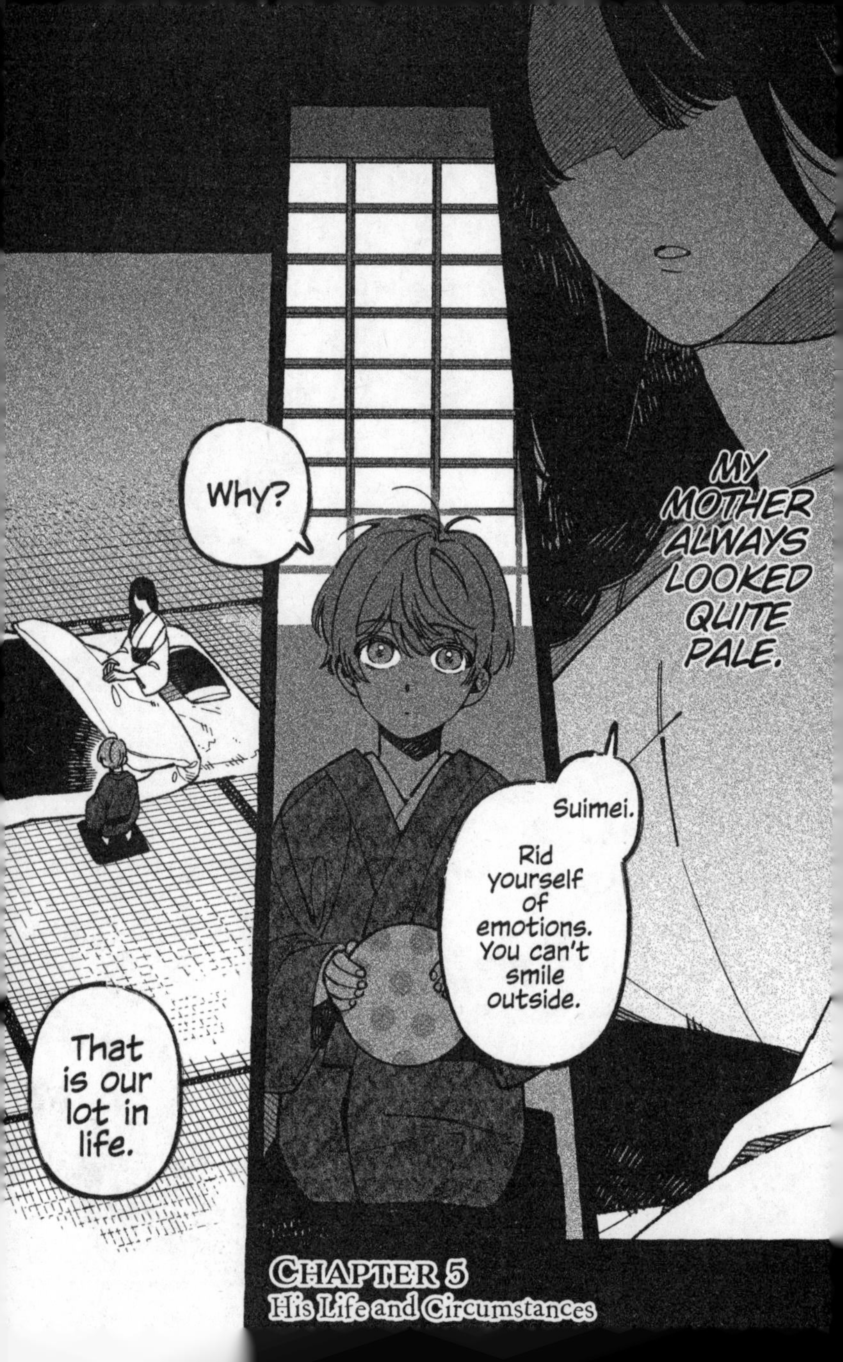
MY MOTHER ALWAYS LOOKED QUITE PALE.
Suimei.
Rid yourself of emotions. You can't smile outside.
Why?
That is our lot in life.
CHAPTER 5
His Life and Circumstances

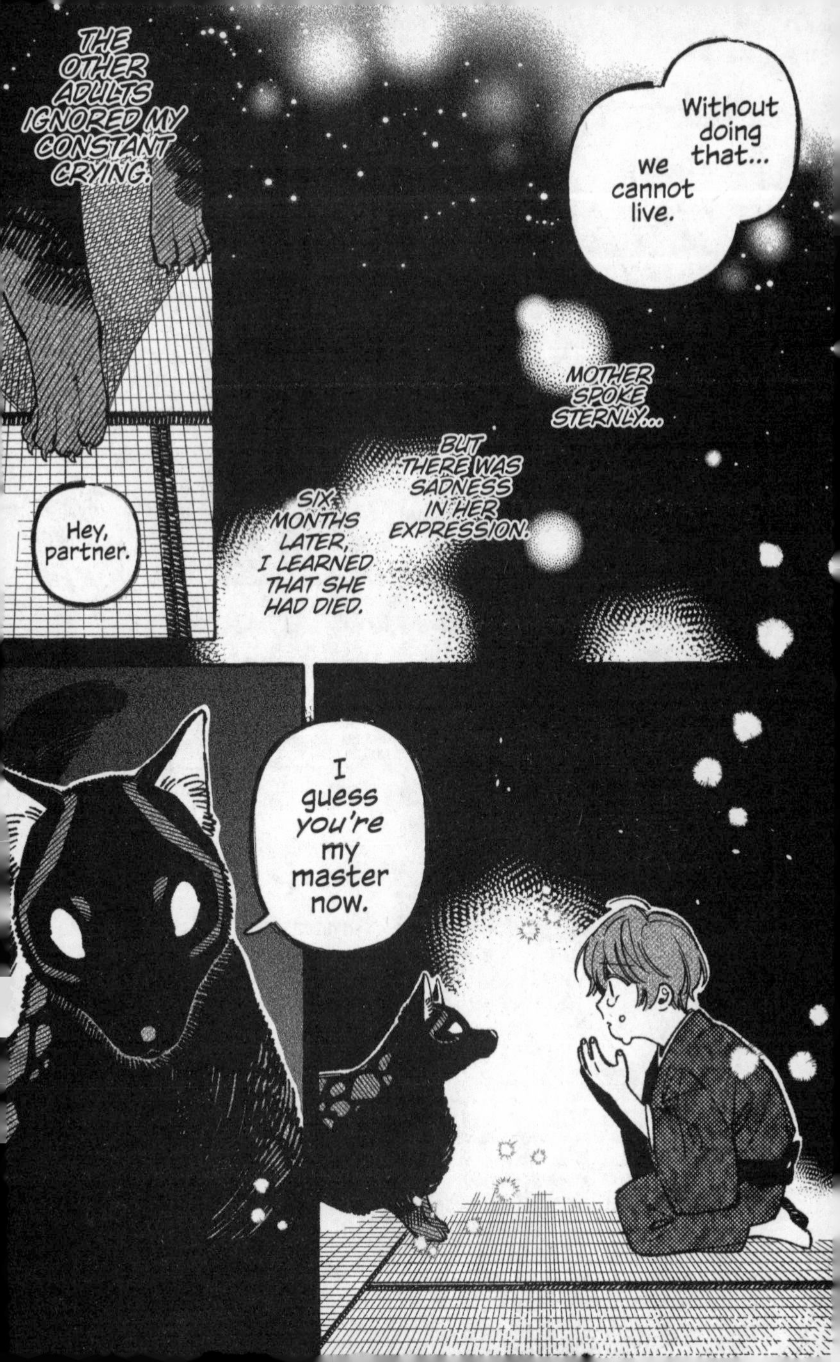
Without doing that... we cannot live.
MOTHER SPOKE STERNLY...
BUT THERE WAS SADNESS IN HER EXPRESSION.
SIX MONTHS LATER, I LEARNED THAT SHE HAD DIED.
THE OTHER ADULTS IGNORED MY CONSTANT CRYING.
Hey, partner.
I guess you're my master now.

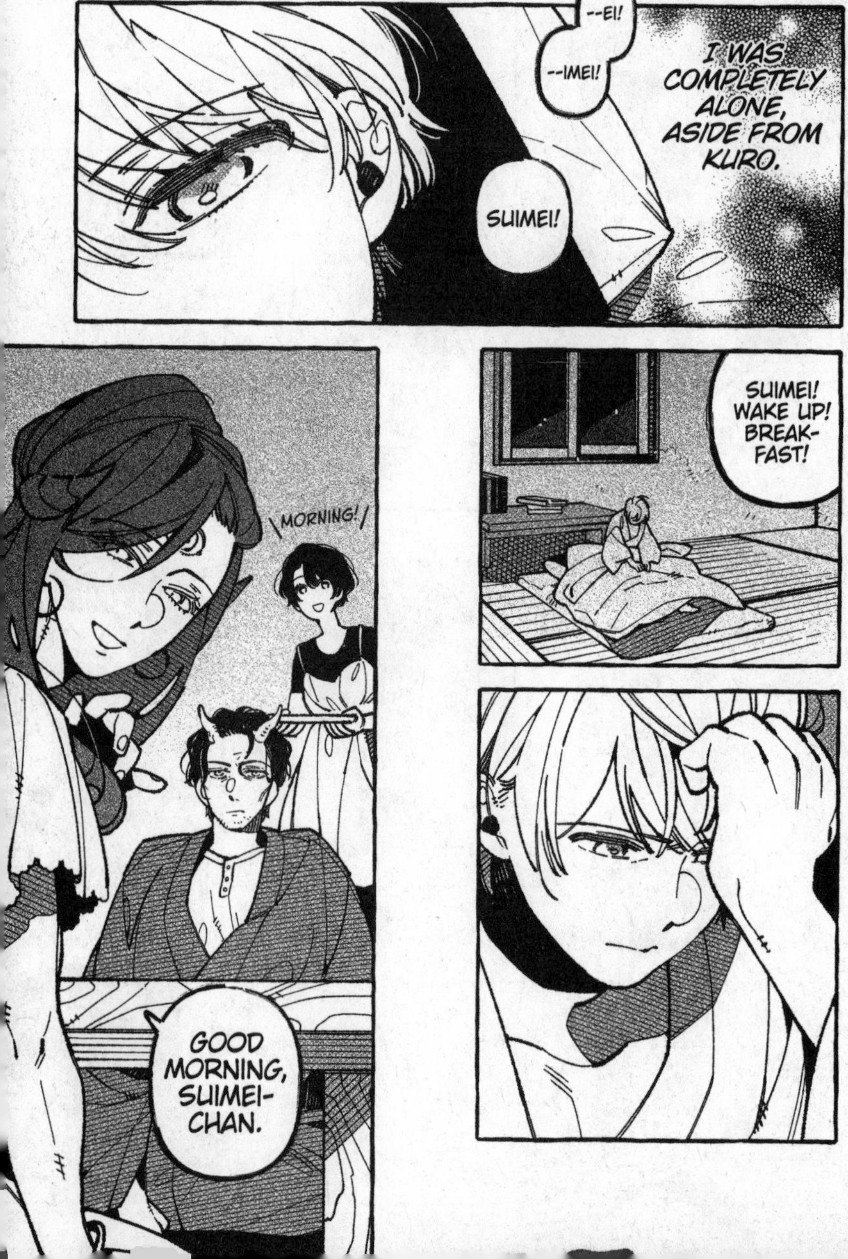
I WAS COMPLETELY ALONE, ASIDE FROM KURO.
--EI!
--IMEI!
SUIMEI!
SUIMEI! WAKE UP! BREAK-FAST!
GOOD MORNING, SUIMEI-CHAN.
MORNING!

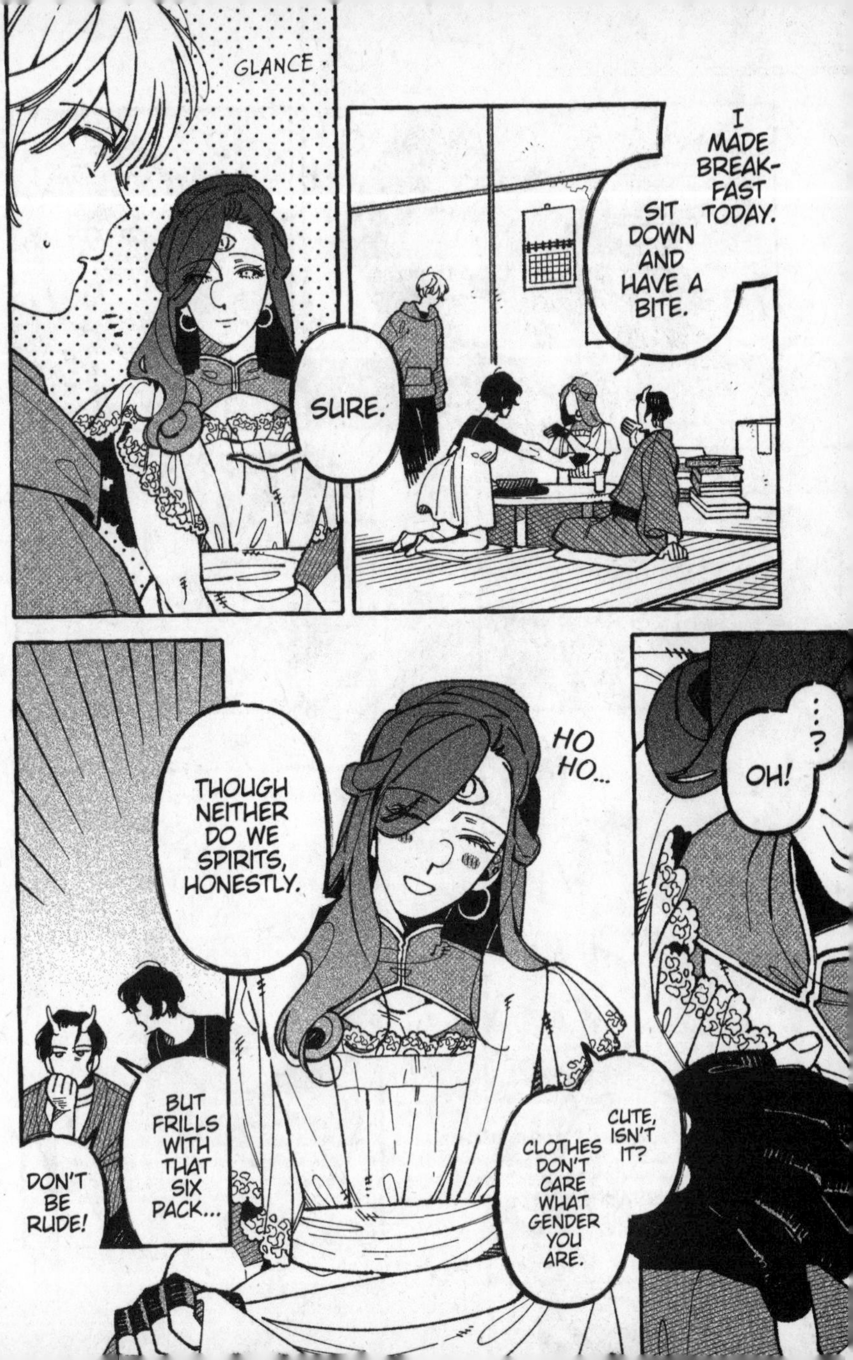
I MADE BREAKFAST TODAY.
SIT DOWN AND HAVE A BITE.
SURE.
GLANCE
...?
OH!
CUTE, ISN'T IT?
CLOTHES DON'T CARE WHAT GENDER YOU ARE.
HO HO...
THOUGH NEITHER DO WE SPIRITS, HONESTLY.
BUT FRILLS WITH THAT SIX PACK...
DON'T BE RUDE!

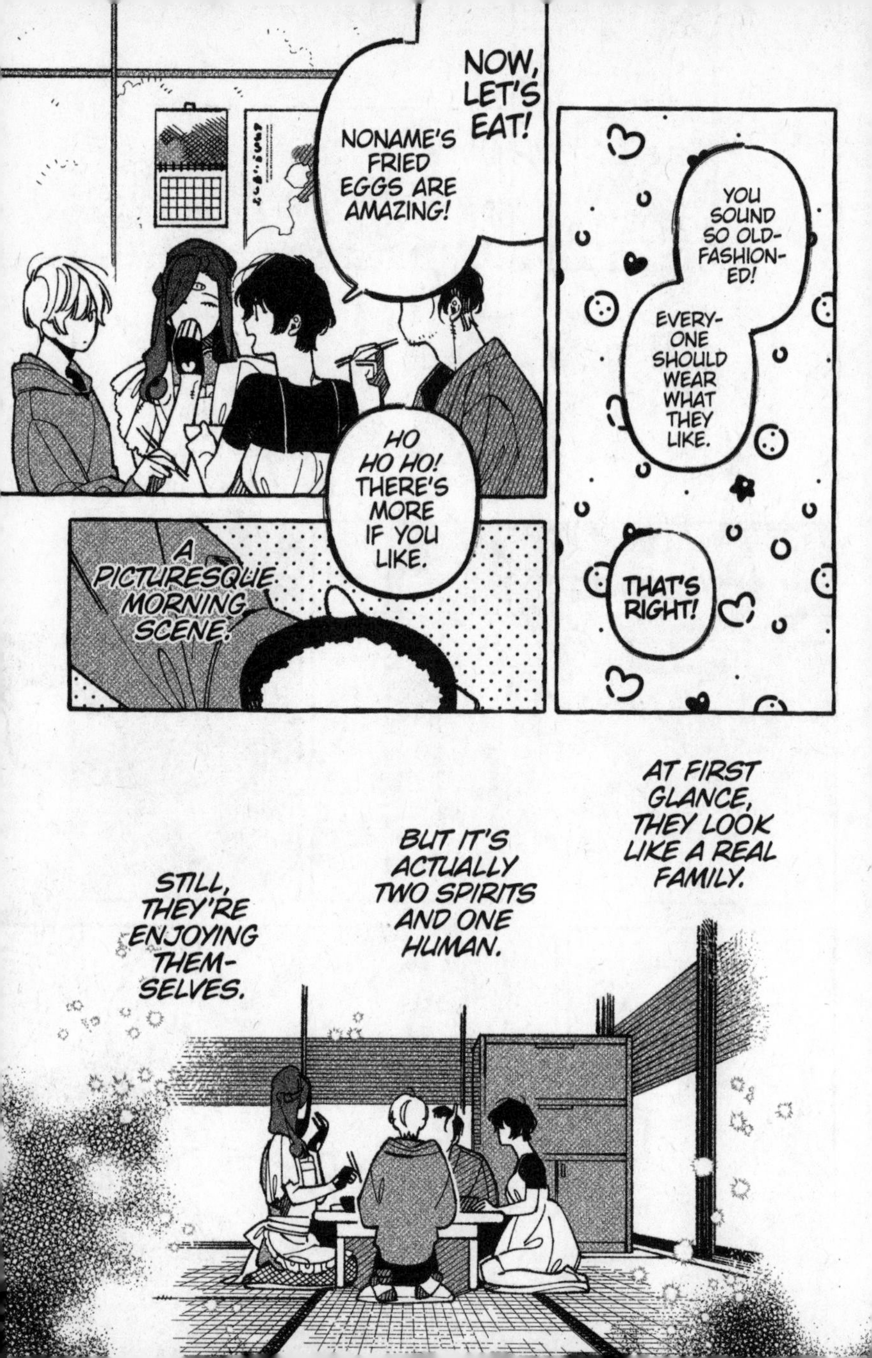
YOU SOUND SO OLD-FASHIONED!
EVERYONE SHOULD WEAR WHAT THEY LIKE.
THAT'S RIGHT!
NOW, LET'S EAT!
NONAME'S FRIED EGGS ARE AMAZING!
HO HO HO! THERE'S MORE IF YOU LIKE.
A PICTURESQUE MORNING SCENE.
AT FIRST GLANCE, THEY LOOK LIKE A REAL FAMILY.
BUT IT'S ACTUALLY TWO SPIRITS AND ONE HUMAN.
STILL, THEY'RE ENJOYING THEMSELVES.

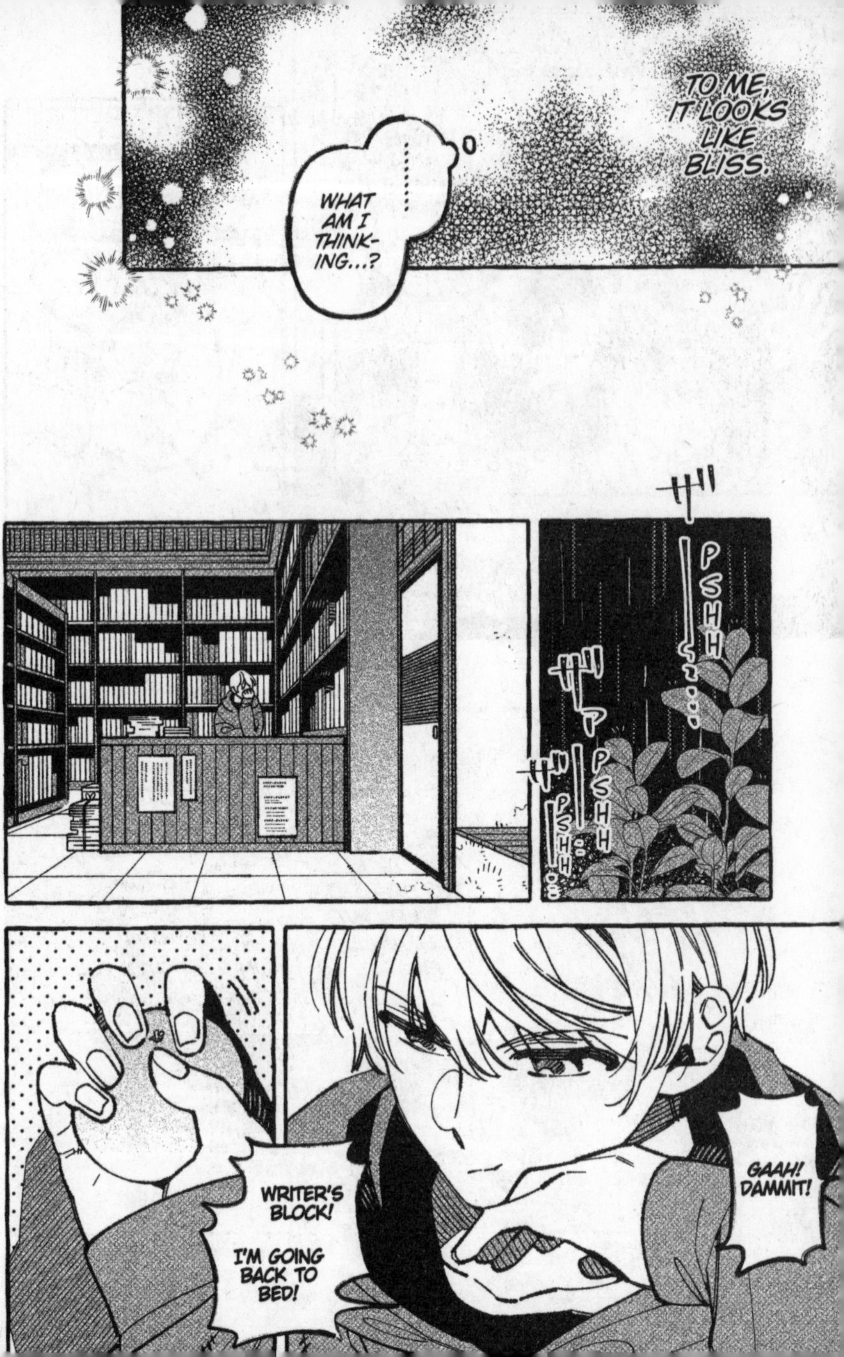
TO ME, IT LOOKS LIKE BLISS.
......
WHAT AM I THINKING...?
PSHH...
PSHH...
PSHH...
GAAH! DAMMIT!
WRITER'S BLOCK!
I'M GOING BACK TO BED!

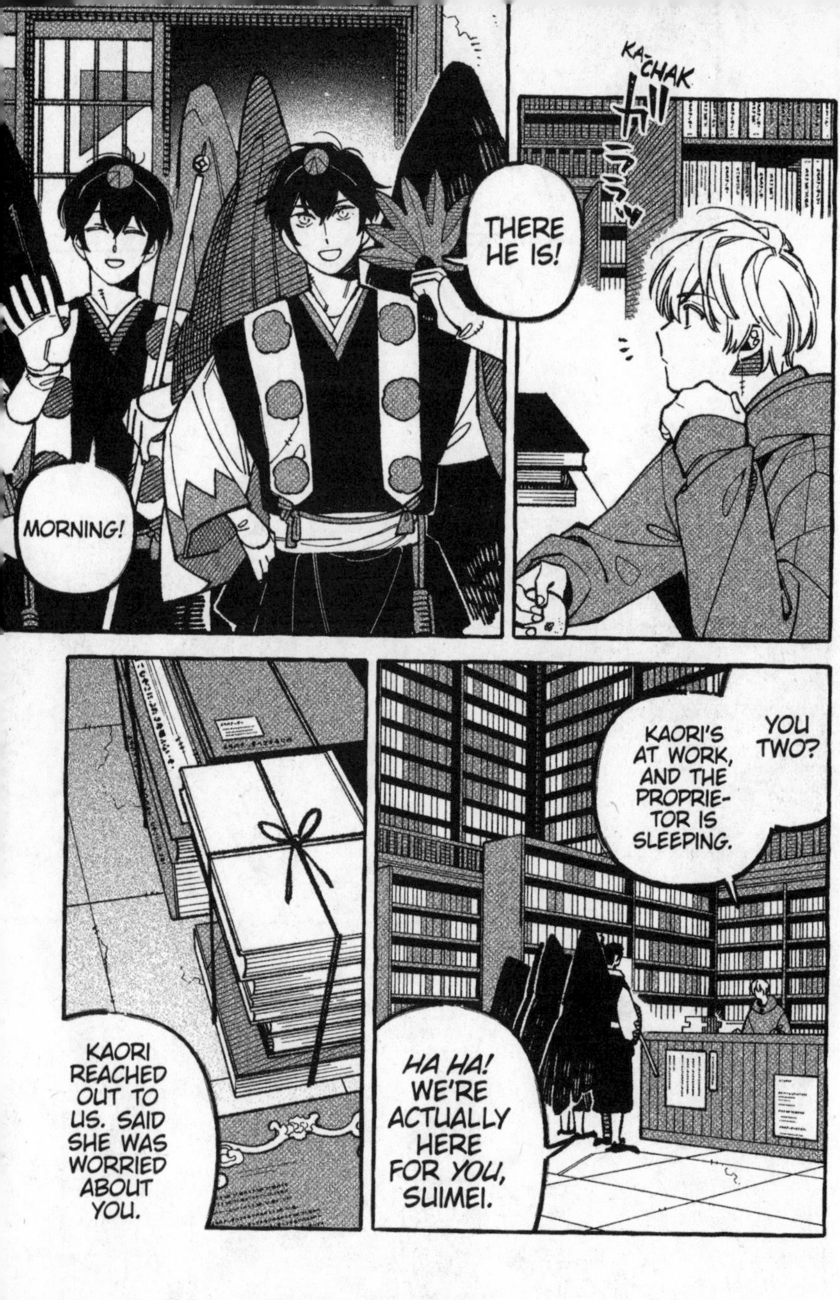
KA-CHAK
THERE HE IS!
MORNING!
YOU TWO?
KAORI'S AT WORK, AND THE PROPRIETOR IS SLEEPING.
HA HA! WE'RE ACTUALLY HERE FOR YOU, SUIMEI.
KAORI REACHED OUT TO US. SAID SHE WAS WORRIED ABOUT YOU.

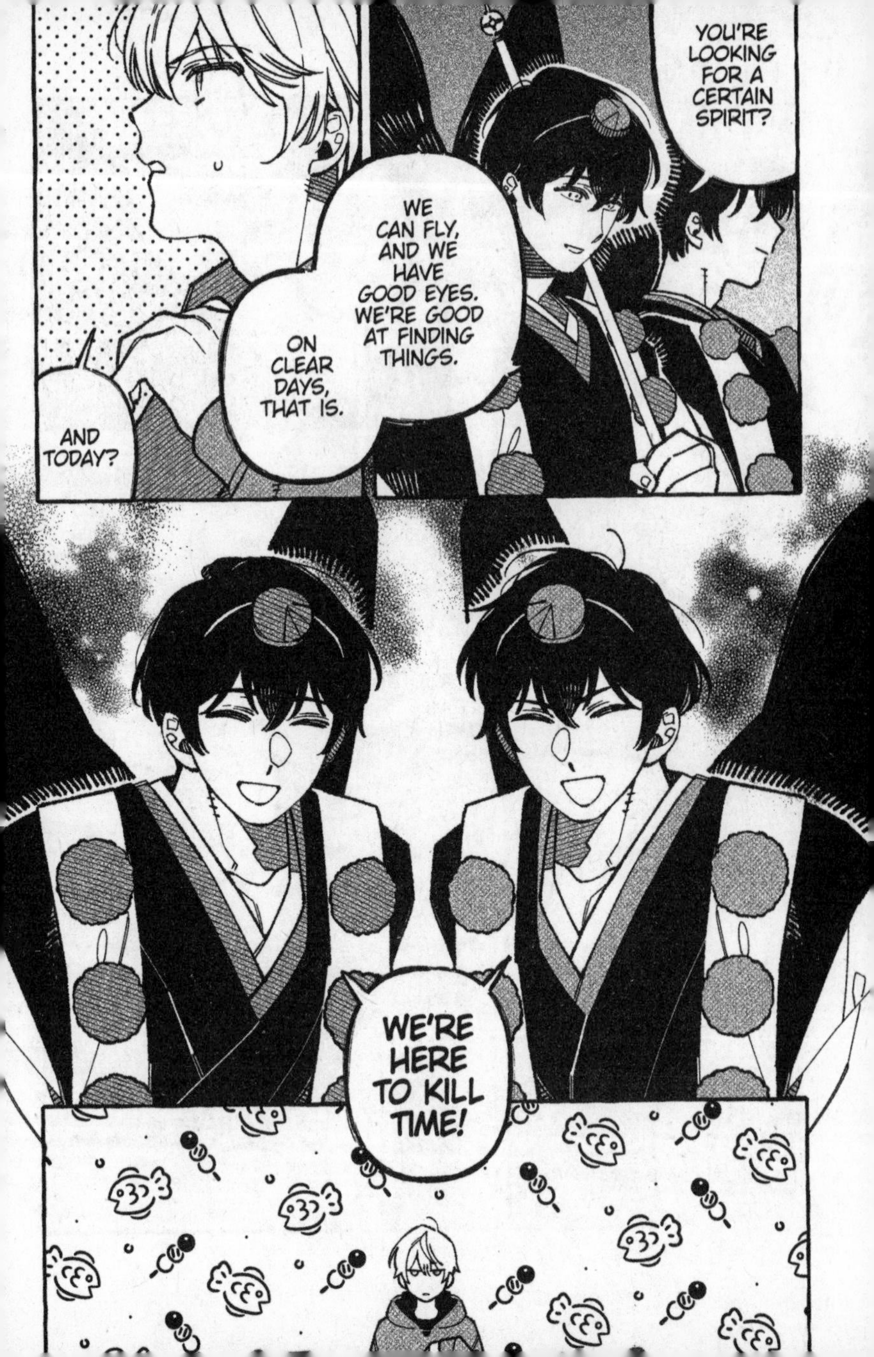
YOU'RE LOOKING FOR A CERTAIN SPIRIT?
WE CAN FLY, AND WE HAVE GOOD EYES. WE'RE GOOD AT FINDING THINGS.
ON CLEAR DAYS, THAT IS.
AND TODAY?
WE'RE HERE TO KILL TIME!

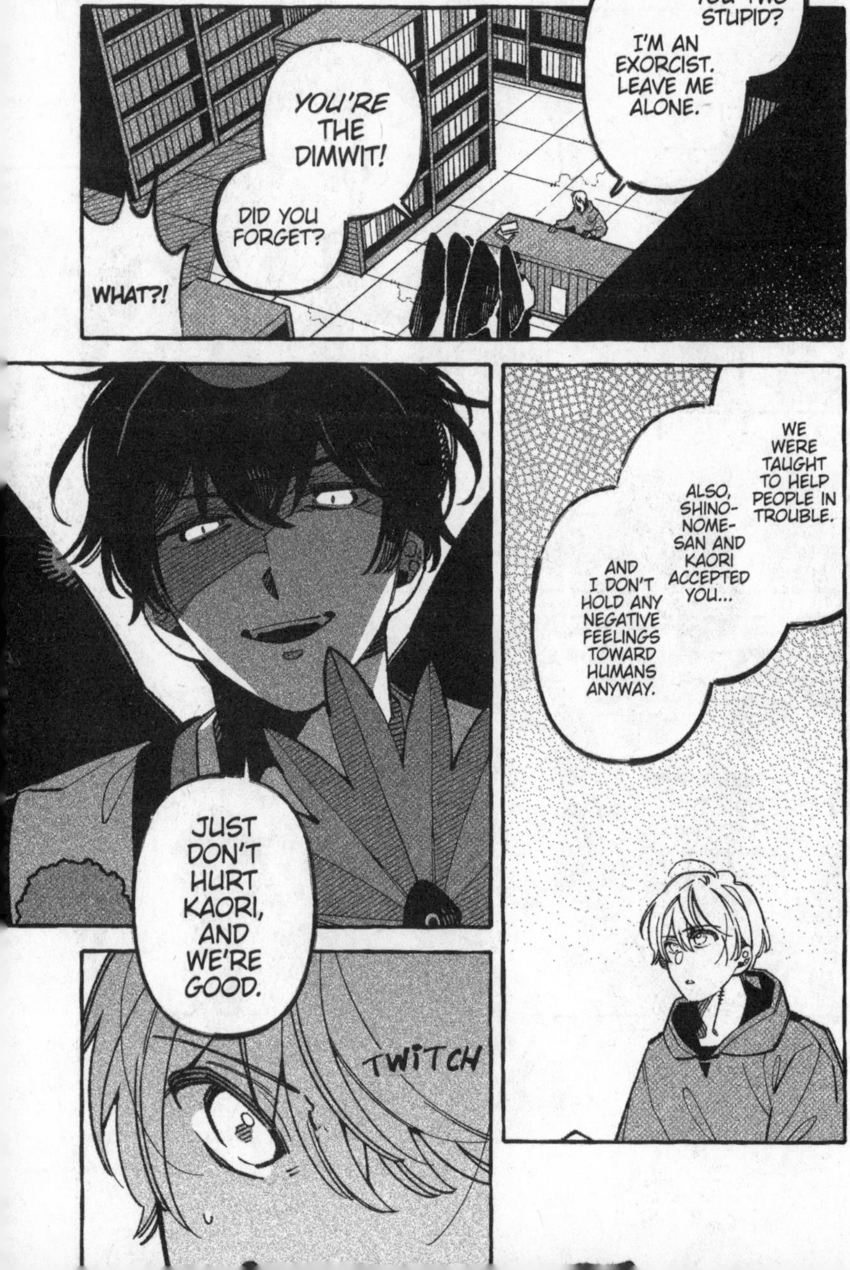
ARE YOU TWO STUPID?
I'M AN EXORCIST. LEAVE ME ALONE.
YOU'RE THE DIMWIT!
DID YOU FORGET?
WHAT?!
WE WERE TAUGHT TO HELP PEOPLE IN TROUBLE.
ALSO, SHINO-NOME-SAN AND KAORI ACCEPTED YOU...
AND I DON'T HOLD ANY NEGATIVE FEELINGS TOWARD HUMANS ANYWAY.
JUST DON'T HURT KAORI, AND WE'RE GOOD.
TWITCH

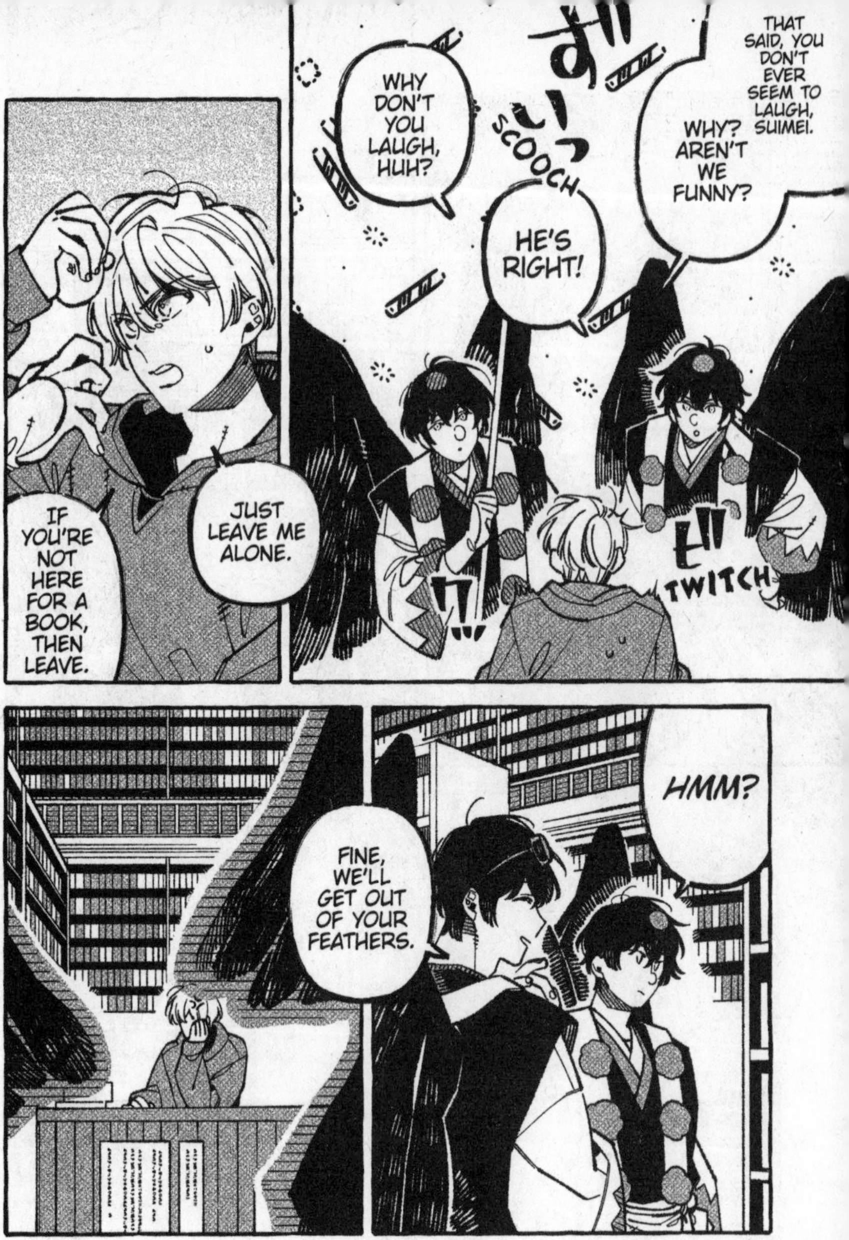
THAT SAID, YOU DON'T EVER SEEM TO LAUGH, SUIMEI.
WHY? AREN'T WE FUNNY?
SCOOCH
WHY DON'T YOU LAUGH, HUH?
HE'S RIGHT!
TWITCH
JUST LEAVE ME ALONE.
IF YOU'RE NOT HERE FOR A BOOK, THEN LEAVE.
HMM?
FINE, WE'LL GET OUT OF YOUR FEATHERS.

SHINONOME'S THE SAME WAY.

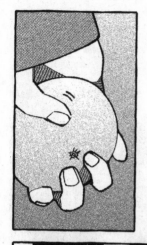

GLANCE

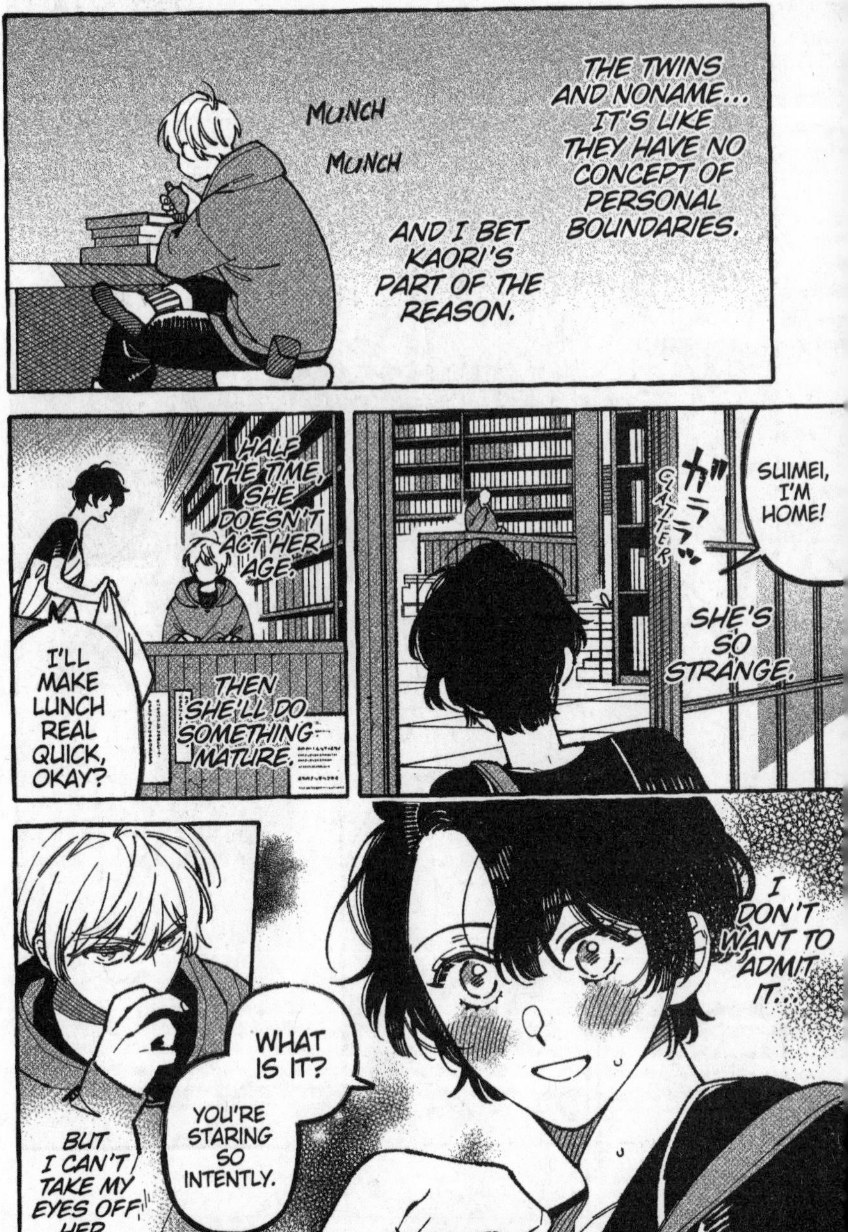
THE TWINS AND NONAME... IT'S LIKE THEY HAVE NO CONCEPT OF PERSONAL BOUNDARIES.
MUNCH
MUNCH
AND I BET KAORI'S PART OF THE REASON.
SUIMEI, I'M HOME!
CLATTER
SHE'S SO STRANGE.
HALF THE TIME, SHE DOESN'T ACT HER AGE.
THEN SHE'LL DO SOMETHING MATURE.
I'LL MAKE LUNCH REAL QUICK, OKAY?
I DON'T WANT TO ADMIT IT...
WHAT IS IT?
YOU'RE STARING SO INTENTLY.
BUT I CAN'T TAKE MY EYES OFF HER.

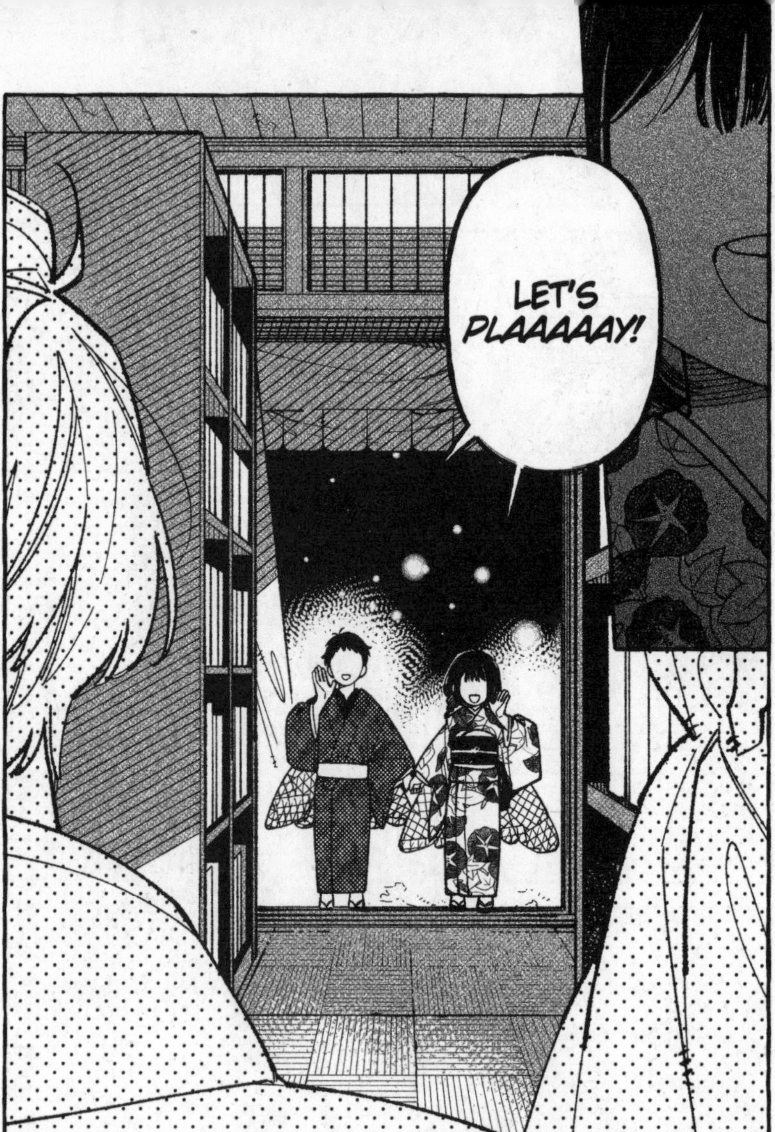
LET'S PLAAAAAY!

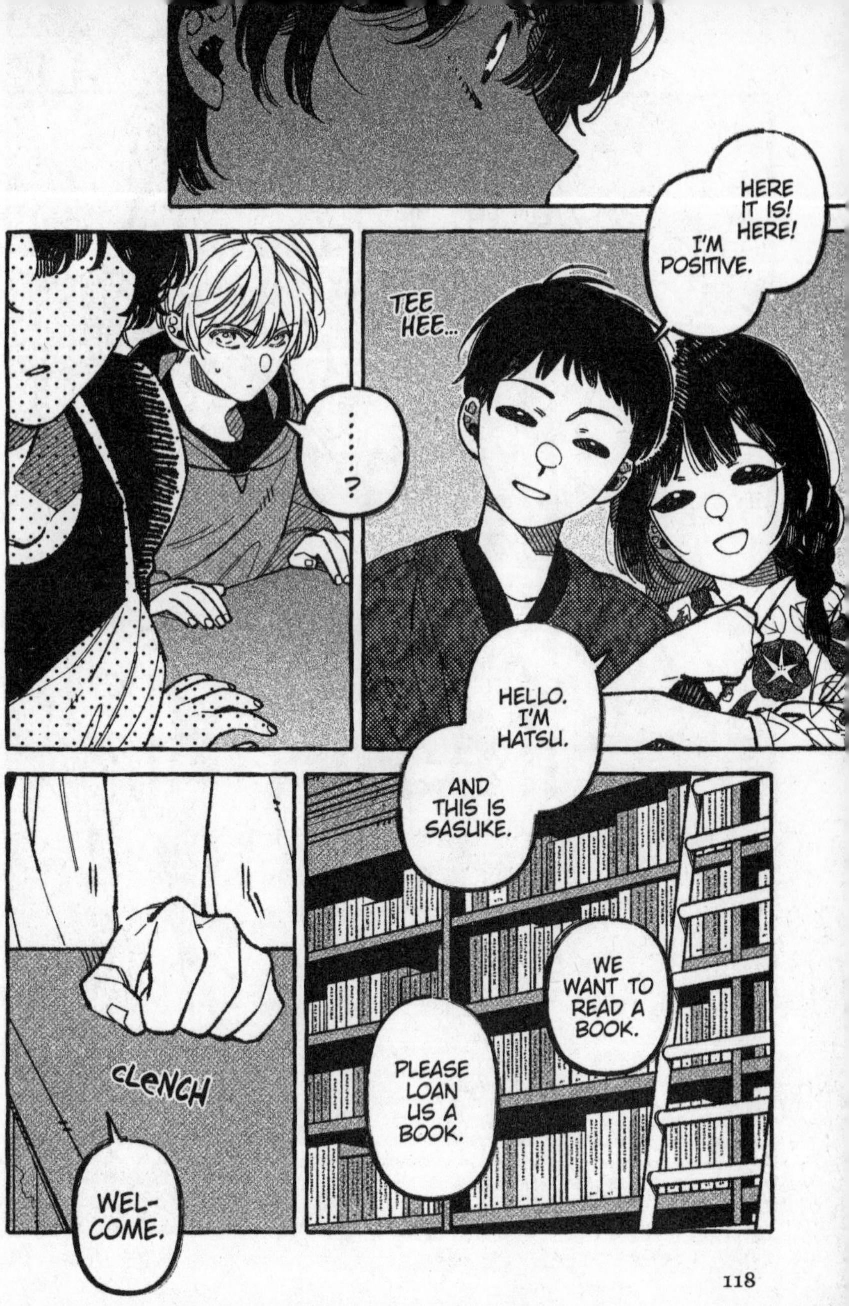
HERE IT IS! HERE!
I'M POSITIVE.
TEE HEE...
HELLO. I'M HATSU.
AND THIS IS SASUKE.
......?
WE WANT TO READ A BOOK.
PLEASE LOAN US A BOOK.
CLENCH
WEL-COME.

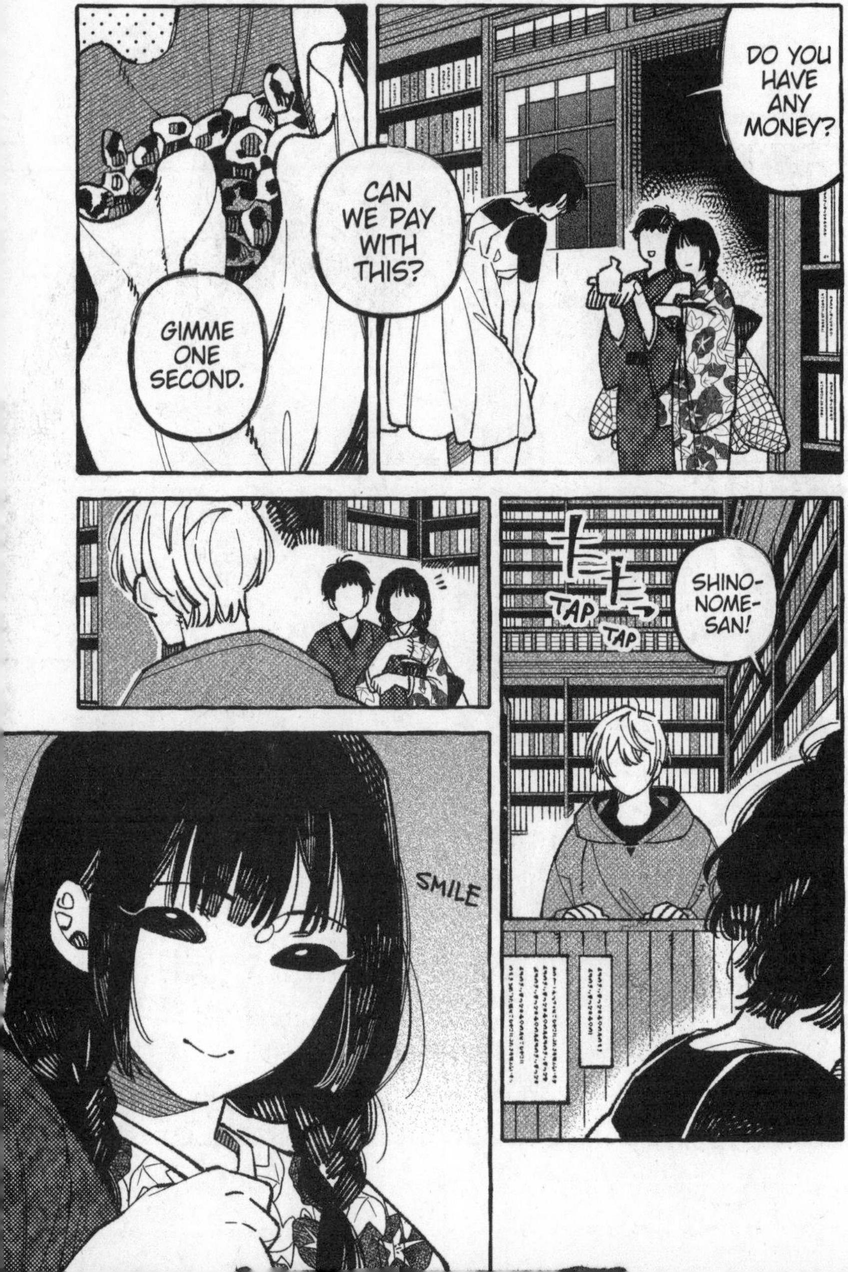
DO YOU HAVE ANY MONEY?
CAN WE PAY WITH THIS?
GIMME ONE SECOND.
SHINO-NOME-SAN!
TAP TAP
SMILE

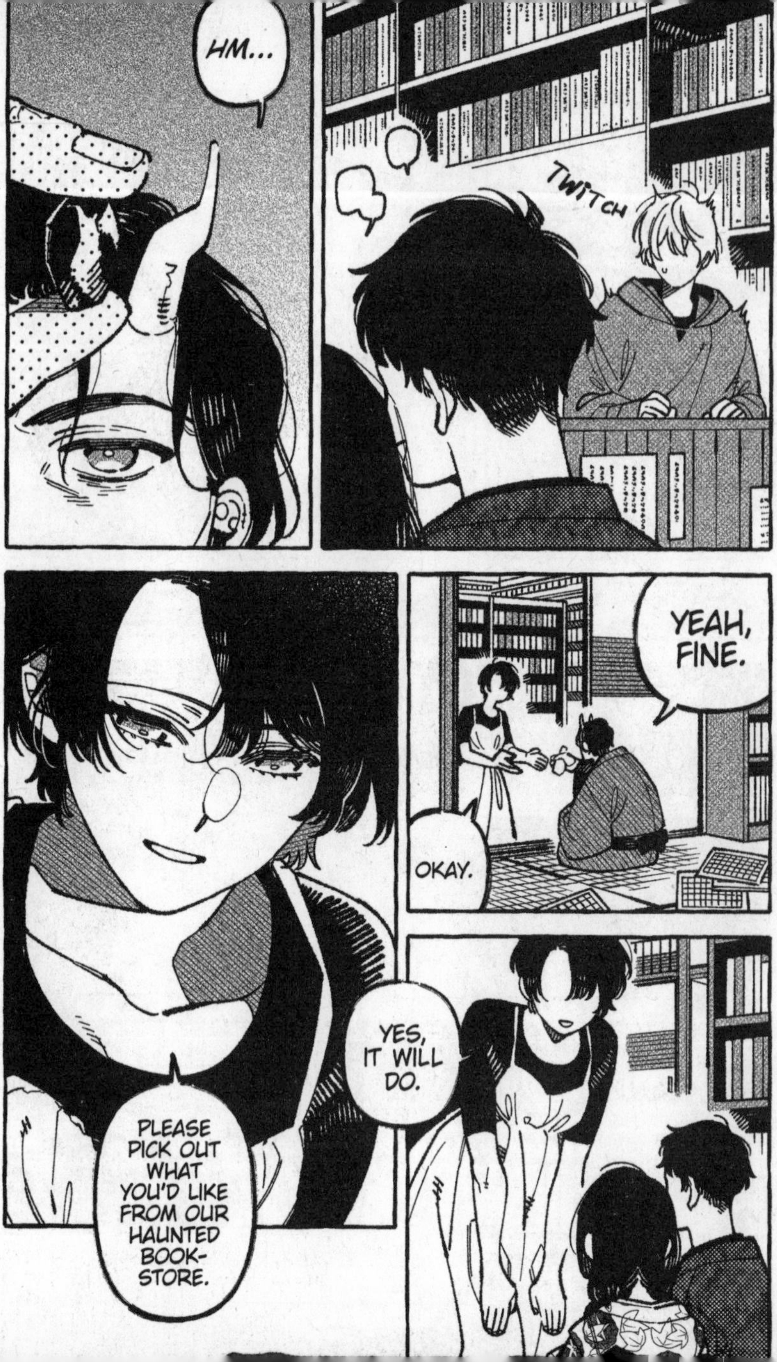
TWITCH
HM...
YEAH, FINE.
OKAY.
YES, IT WILL DO.
PLEASE PICK OUT WHAT YOU'D LIKE FROM OUR HAUNTED BOOK-STORE.

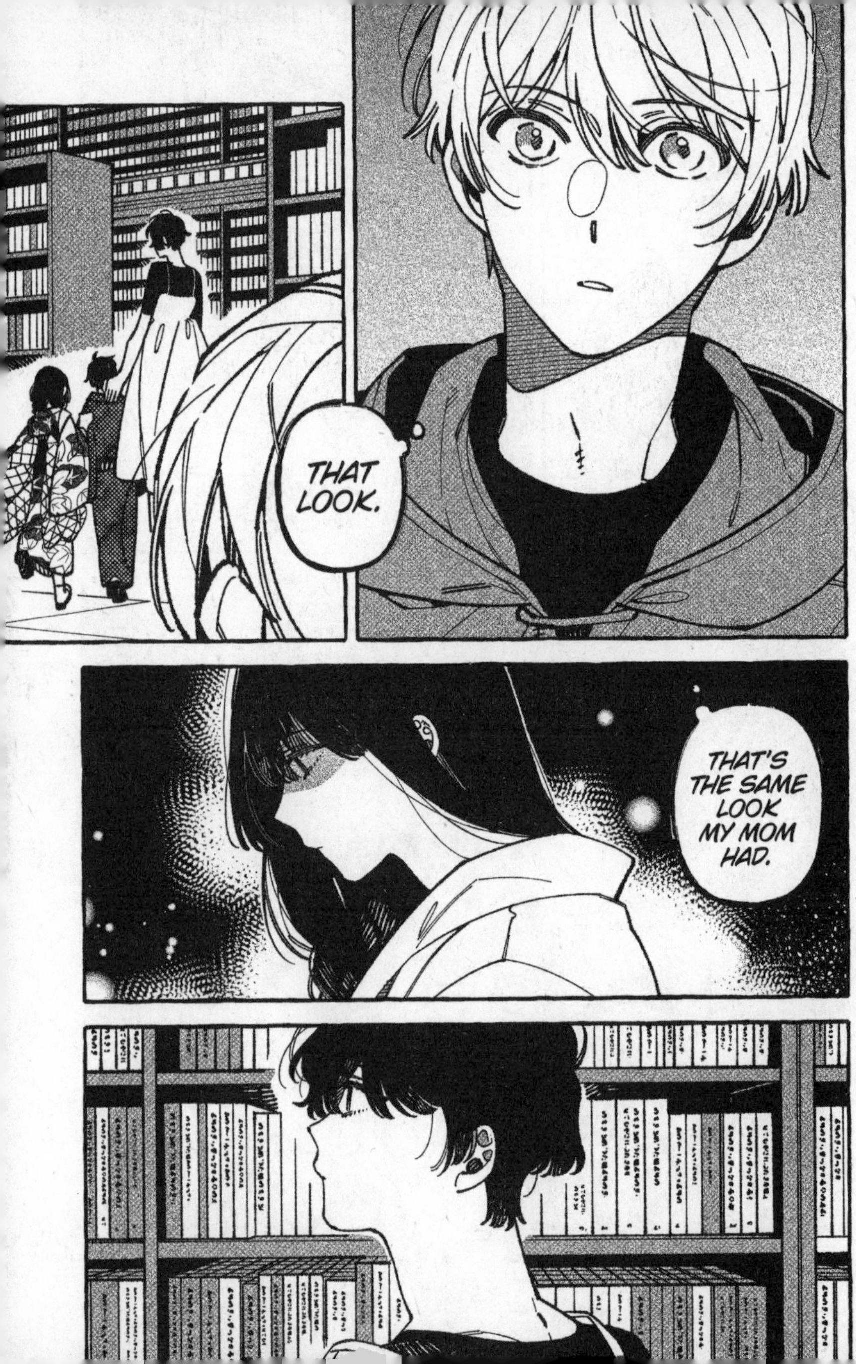
THAT LOOK.
THAT'S THE SAME LOOK MY MOM HAD.

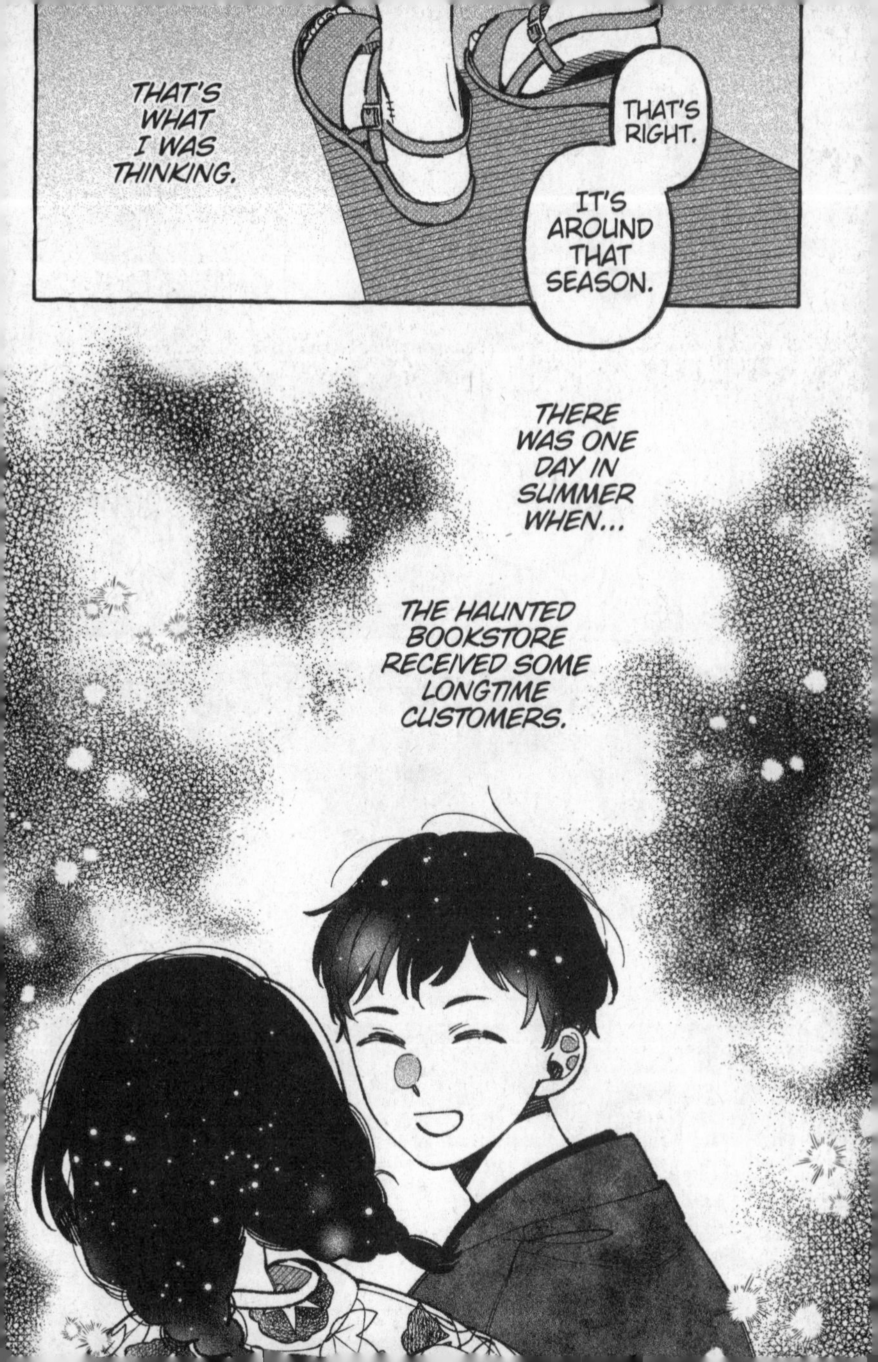
THAT'S RIGHT.
IT'S AROUND THAT SEASON.
THAT'S WHAT I WAS THINKING.
THERE WAS ONE DAY IN SUMMER WHEN...
THE HAUNTED BOOKSTORE RECEIVED SOME LONGTIME CUSTOMERS.

THE HAUNTED BOOKSTORE

Gateway to a Parallel Universe

THE
HAUNTED
BOOKSTORE
Gateway to a
Parallel Universe

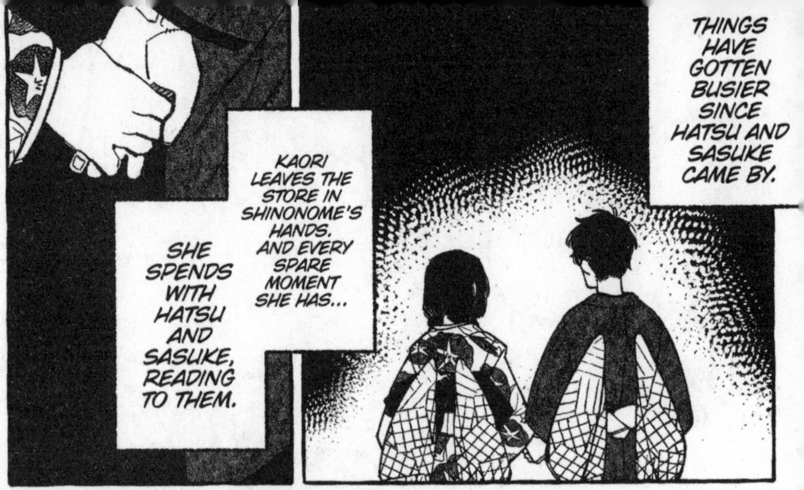
THINGS HAVE GOTTEN BUSIER SINCE HATSU AND SASUKE CAME BY.
KAORI LEAVES THE STORE IN SHINONOME'S HANDS. AND EVERY SPARE MOMENT SHE HAS...
SHE SPENDS WITH HATSU AND SASUKE, READING TO THEM.
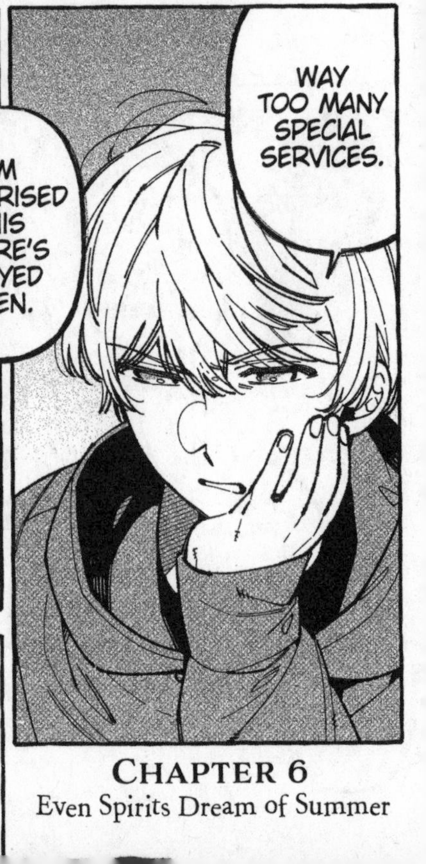
WAY TOO MANY SPECIAL SERVICES.
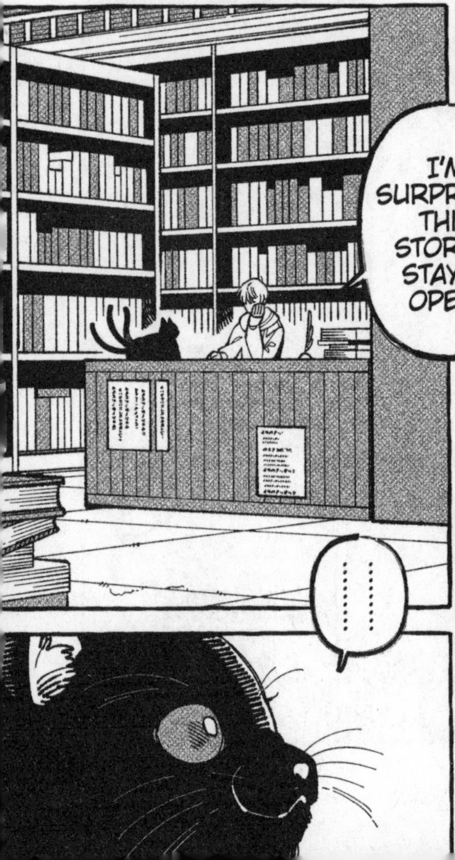
I'M SURPRISED THIS STORE'S STAYED OPEN.
......

CHAPTER 6
Even Spirits Dream of Summer

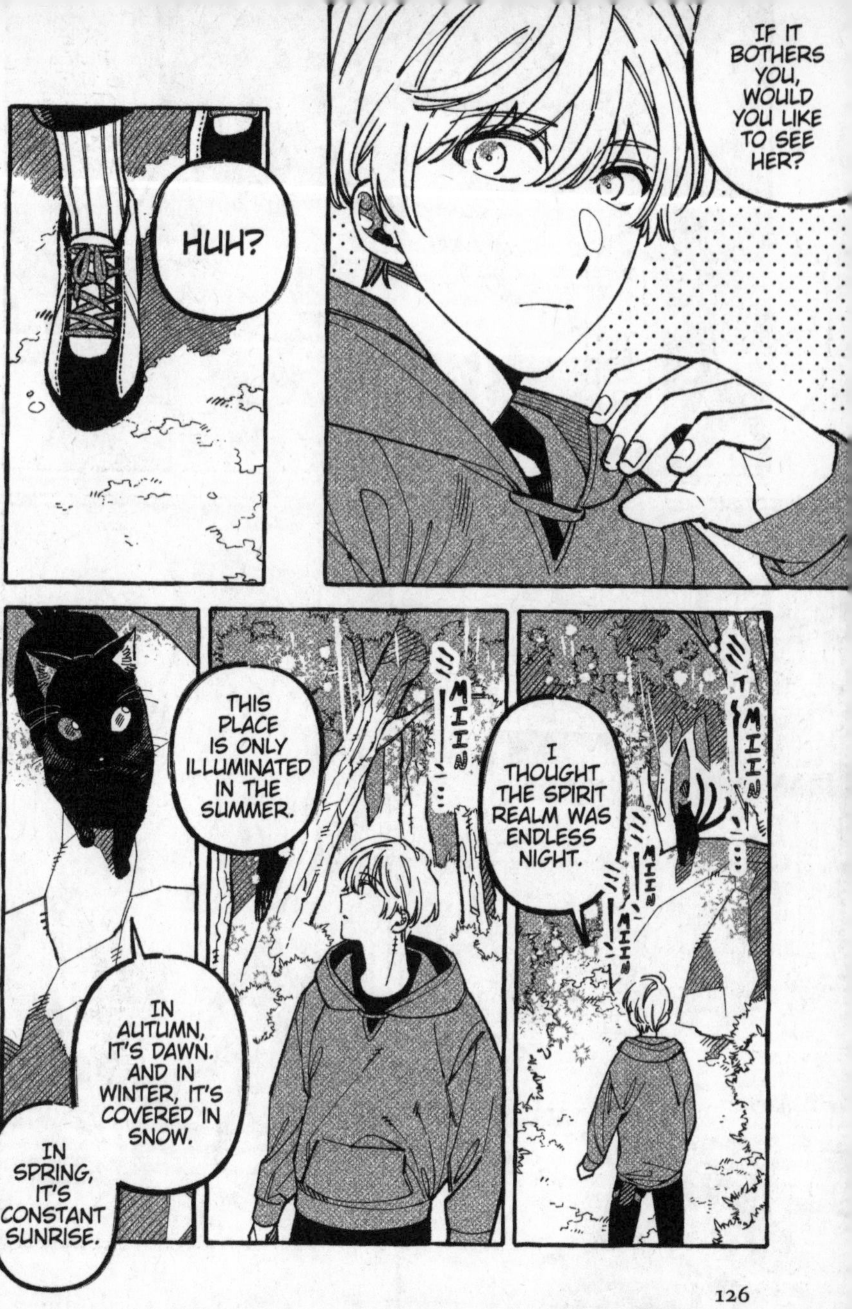
IF IT BOTHERS YOU, WOULD YOU LIKE TO SEE HER?
HUH?
MIIN
MIIN
MIIN
I THOUGHT THE SPIRIT REALM WAS ENDLESS NIGHT.
MIIN
THIS PLACE IS ONLY ILLUMINATED IN THE SUMMER.
IN AUTUMN, IT'S DAWN. AND IN WINTER, IT'S COVERED IN SNOW.
IN SPRING, IT'S CONSTANT SUNRISE.

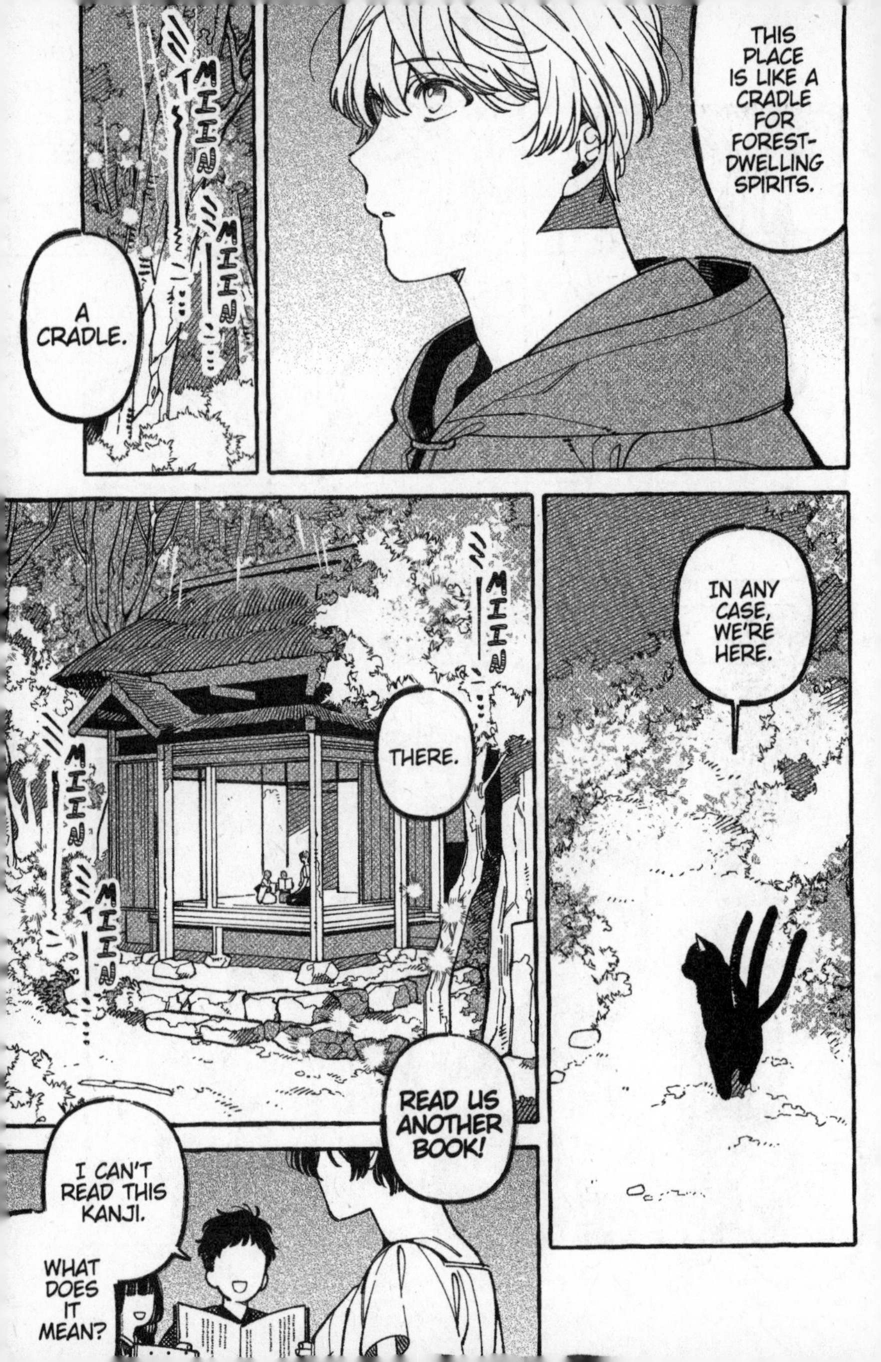
THIS PLACE IS LIKE A CRADLE FOR FOREST-DWELLING SPIRITS.
MIIN MIIN...
A CRADLE.
IN ANY CASE, WE'RE HERE.
MIIN...
THERE.
MIIN MIIN...
READ US ANOTHER BOOK!
I CAN'T READ THIS KANJI.
WHAT DOES IT MEAN?

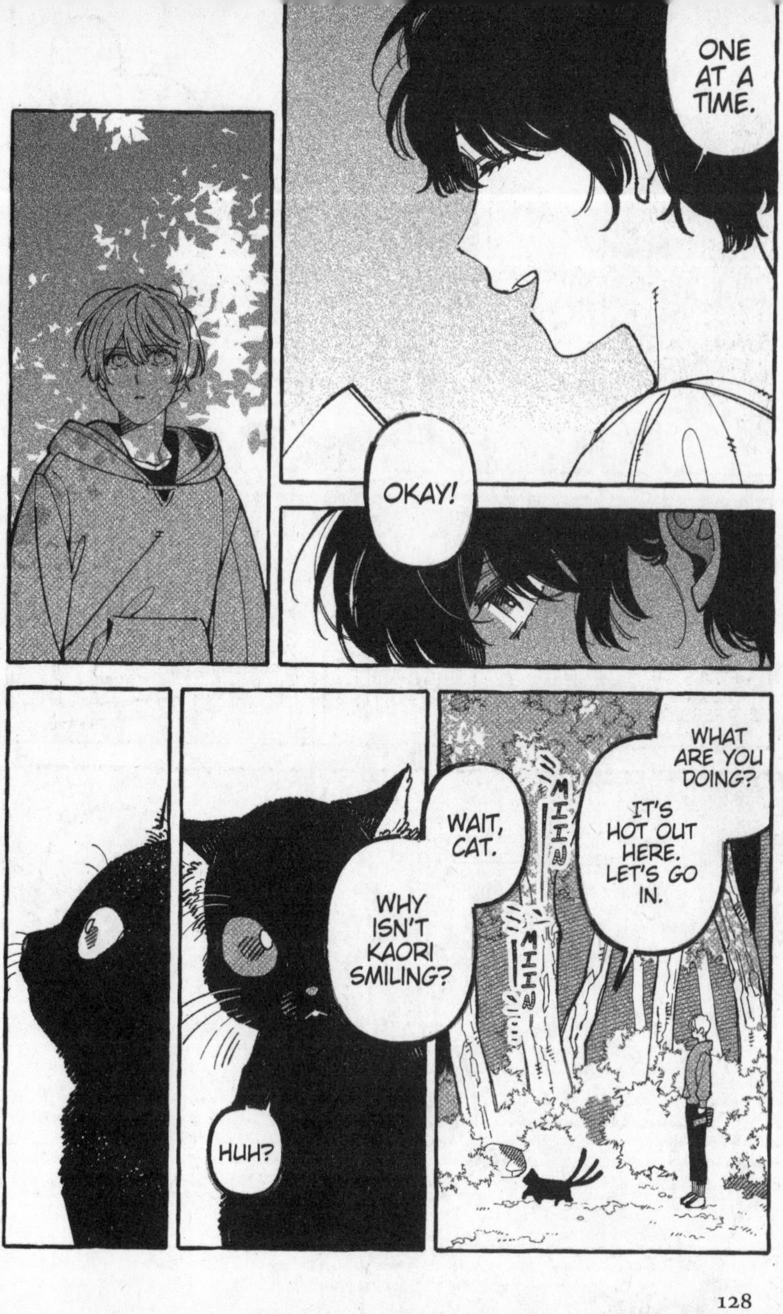
ONE AT A TIME.
OKAY!
WHAT ARE YOU DOING?
IT'S HOT OUT HERE. LET'S GO IN.
MIIIN
MIIIN
WAIT, CAT.
WHY ISN'T KAORI SMILING?
HUH?

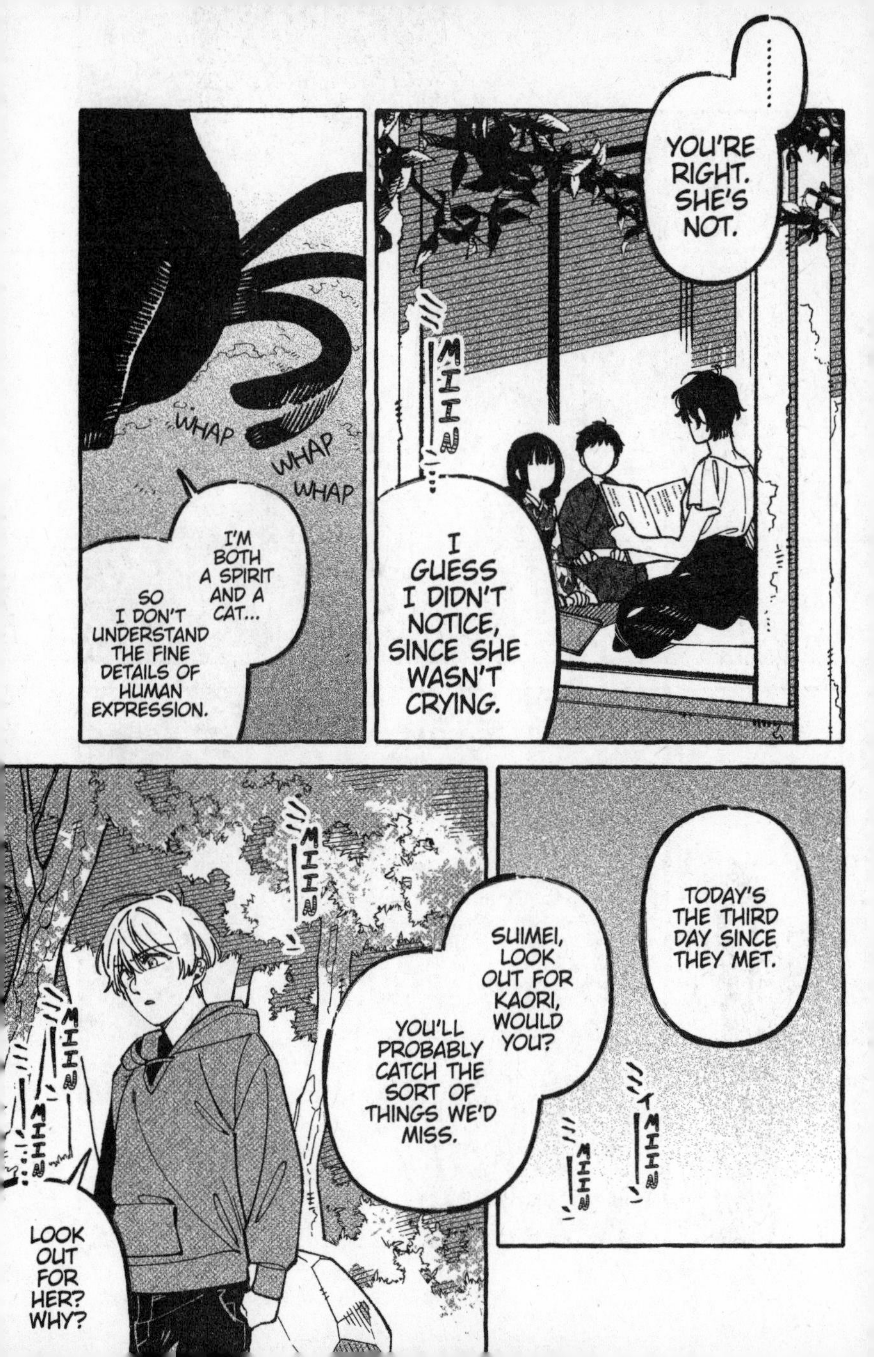
......
YOU'RE RIGHT. SHE'S NOT.
MIIIN
I GUESS I DIDN'T NOTICE, SINCE SHE WASN'T CRYING.
WHAP
WHAP
WHAP
I'M BOTH A SPIRIT AND A CAT...
SO I DON'T UNDERSTAND THE FINE DETAILS OF HUMAN EXPRESSION.
TODAY'S THE THIRD DAY SINCE THEY MET.
MIIIN
MIIIN
SUIMEI, LOOK OUT FOR KAORI, WOULD YOU?
YOU'LL PROBABLY CATCH THE SORT OF THINGS WE'D MISS.
MIIIN
MIIIN
MIIIN
LOOK OUT FOR HER? WHY?

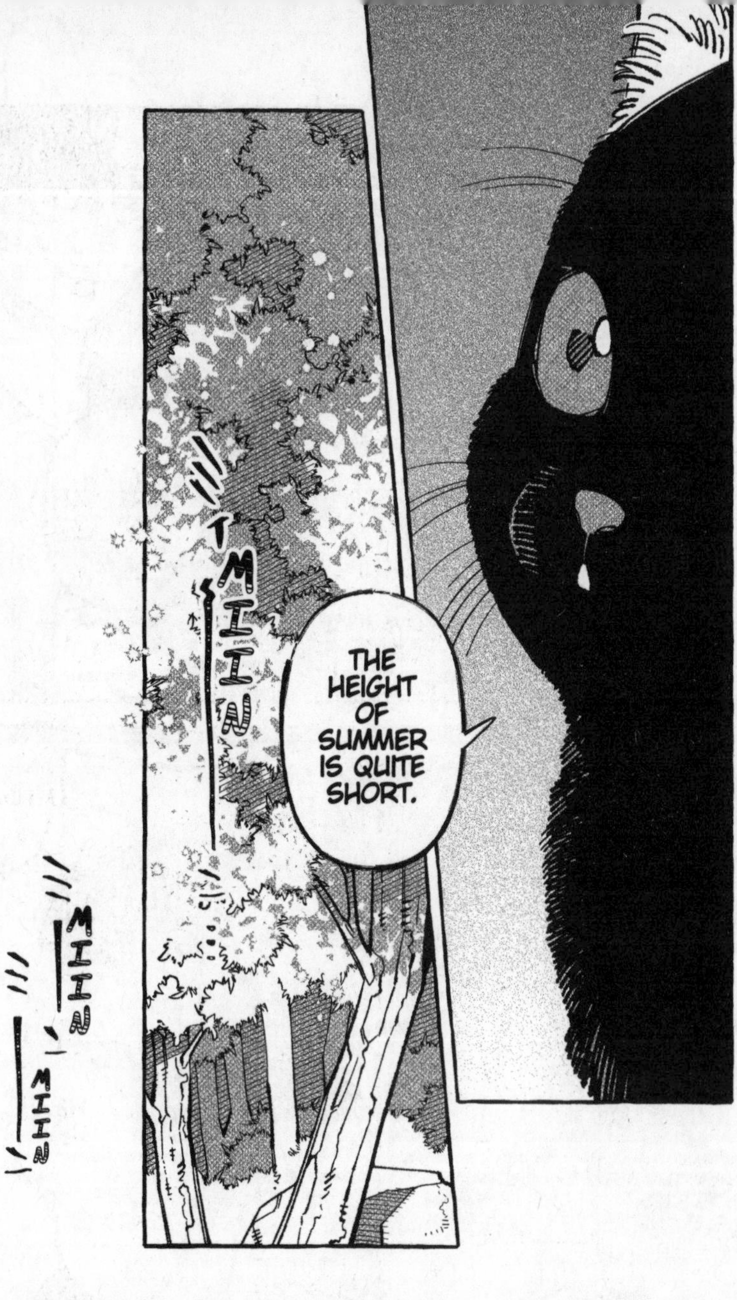
THE HEIGHT OF SUMMER IS QUITE SHORT.
MIIIN
MIIIN
MIIIN

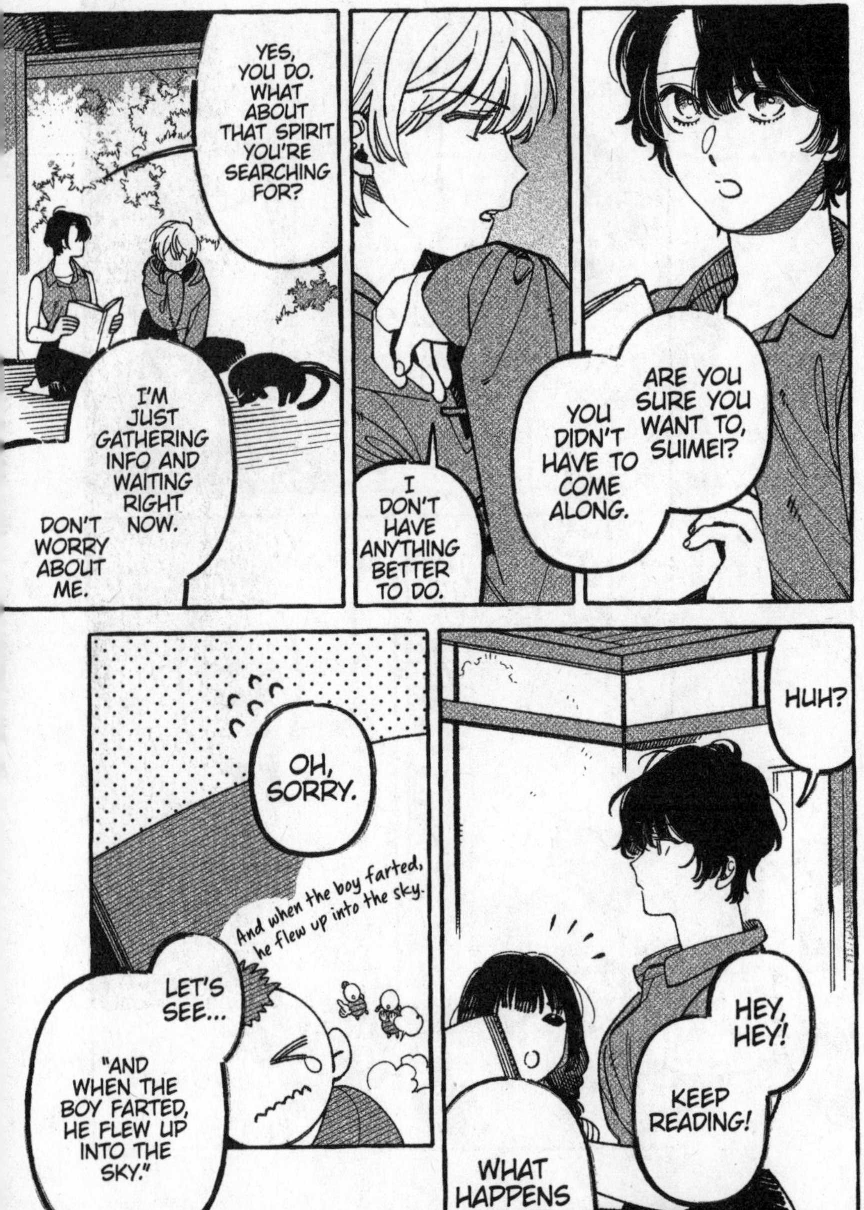
ARE YOU SURE YOU WANT TO, SUIMEI?
YOU DIDN'T HAVE TO COME ALONG.
I DON'T HAVE ANYTHING BETTER TO DO.
YES, YOU DO. WHAT ABOUT THAT SPIRIT YOU'RE SEARCHING FOR?
I'M JUST GATHERING INFO AND WAITING RIGHT NOW.
DON'T WORRY ABOUT ME.
HUH?
HEY, HEY!
KEEP READING!
WHAT HAPPENS NEXT?
OH, SORRY.
And when the boy farted, he flew up into the sky.
LET'S SEE...
"AND WHEN THE BOY FARTED, HE FLEW UP INTO THE SKY."

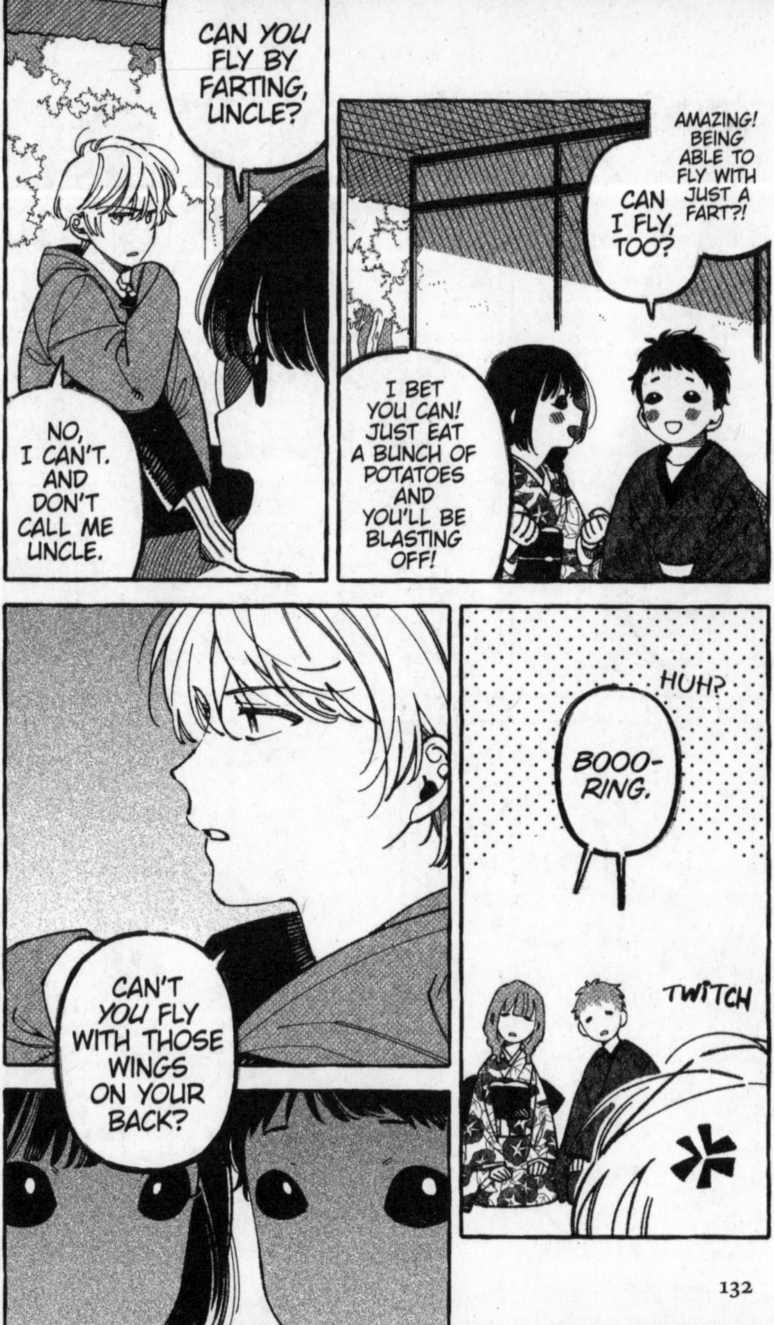
AMAZING! BEING ABLE TO FLY WITH JUST A FART?!
CAN I FLY, TOO?
I BET YOU CAN! JUST EAT A BUNCH OF POTATOES AND YOU'LL BE BLASTING OFF!
CAN YOU FLY BY FARTING, UNCLE?
NO, I CAN'T. AND DON'T CALL ME UNCLE.
HUH?
BOOO-RING.
TWITCH
CAN'T YOU FLY WITH THOSE WINGS ON YOUR BACK?

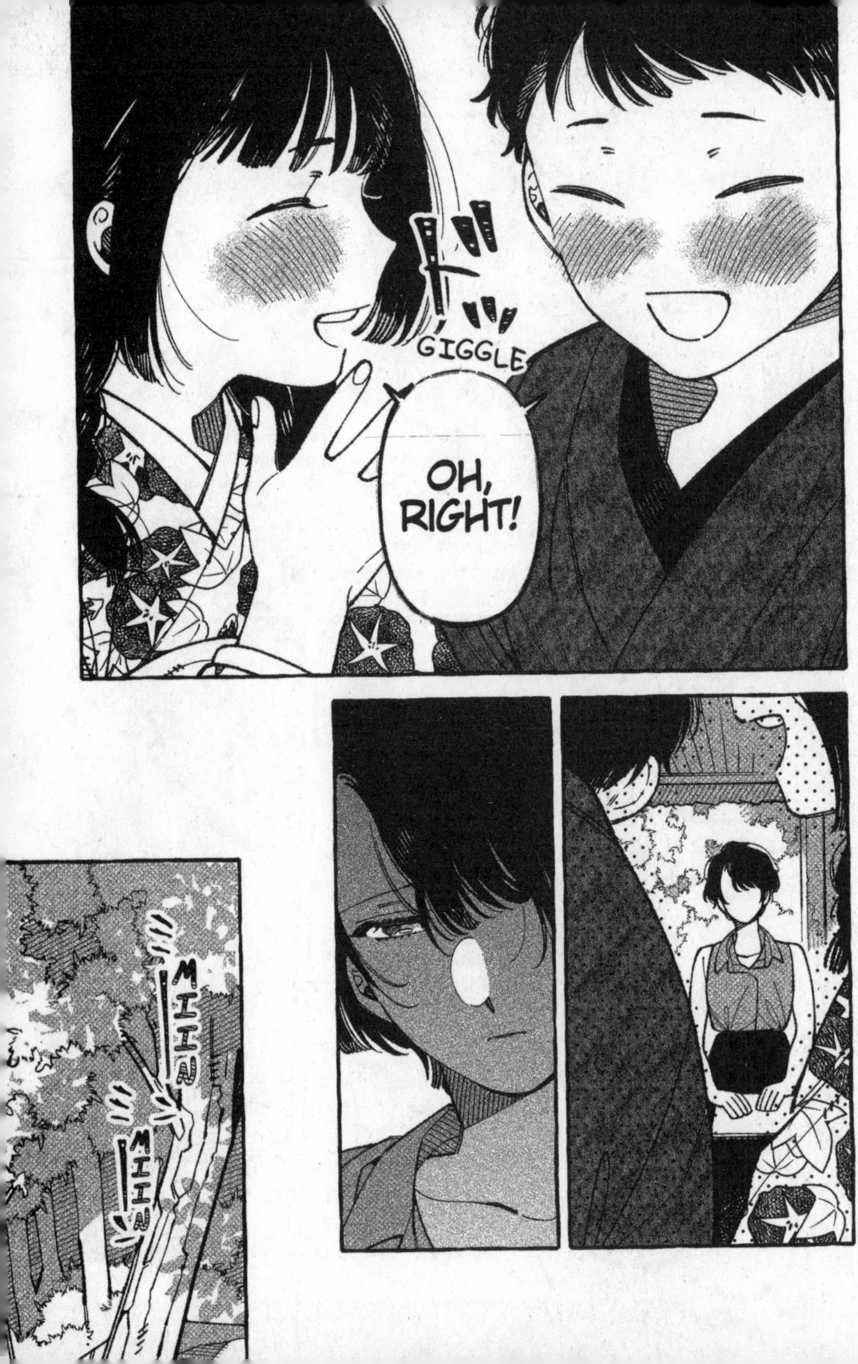
GIGGLE
OH, RIGHT!
MIIIN
MIIIN

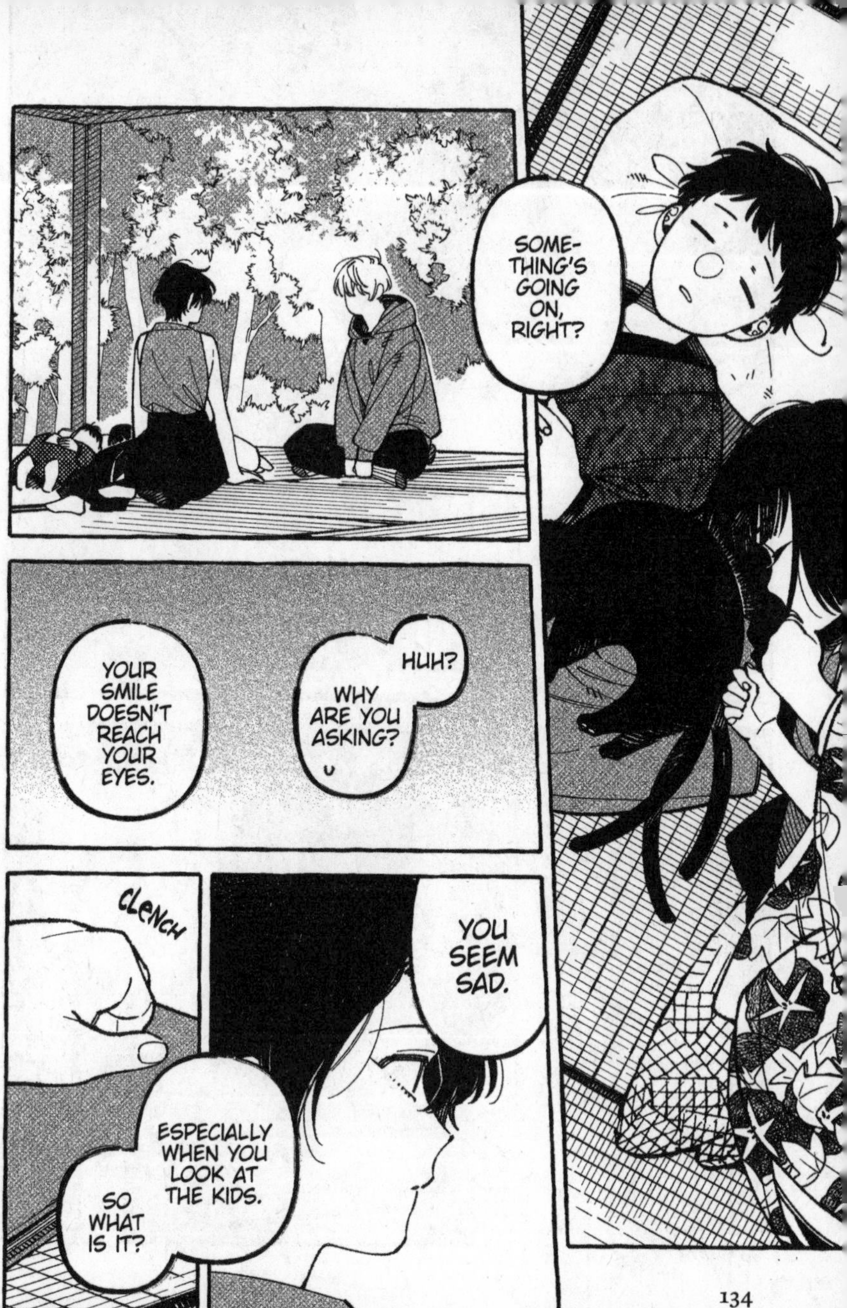
SOME-THING'S GOING ON, RIGHT?
YOUR SMILE DOESN'T REACH YOUR EYES.
HUH?
WHY ARE YOU ASKING?
YOU SEEM SAD.
ESPECIALLY WHEN YOU LOOK AT THE KIDS.
SO WHAT IS IT?
CLENCH

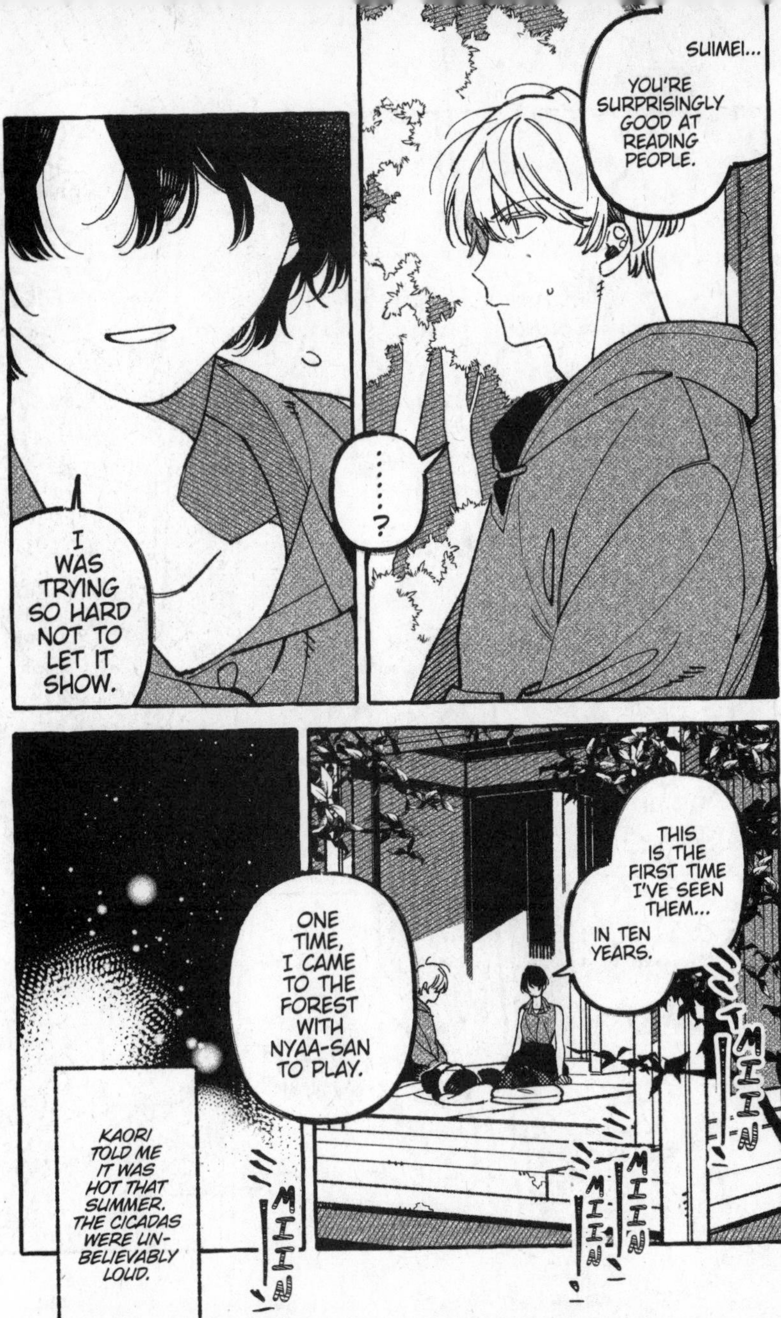
SUIMEI...
YOU'RE SURPRISINGLY GOOD AT READING PEOPLE.
.....?
I WAS TRYING SO HARD NOT TO LET IT SHOW.
THIS IS THE FIRST TIME I'VE SEEN THEM...
IN TEN YEARS.
ONE TIME, I CAME TO THE FOREST WITH NYAA-SAN TO PLAY.
MIIIN
MIIIN
MIIIN
KAORI TOLD ME IT WAS HOT THAT SUMMER. THE CICADAS WERE UN-BELIEVABLY LOUD.
MIIIN...

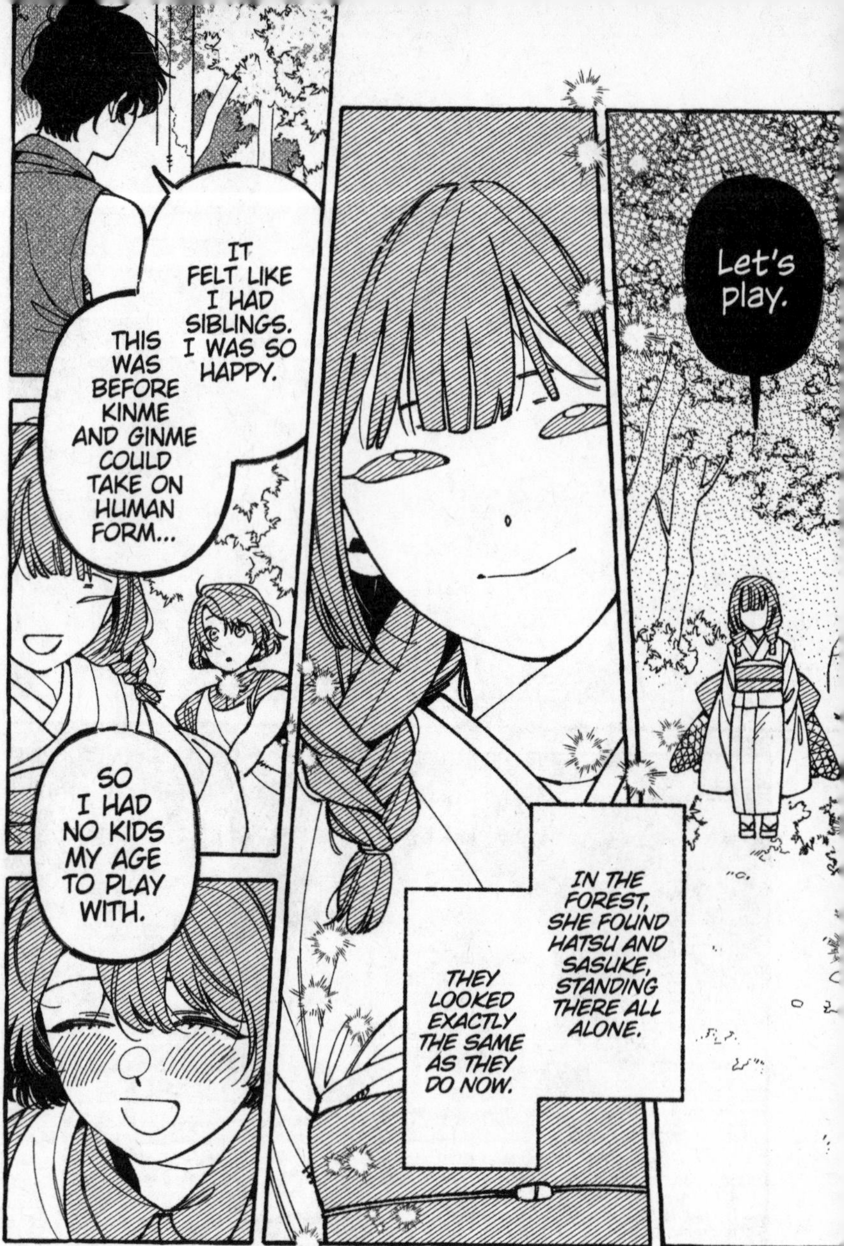
Let's play.
IN THE FOREST, SHE FOUND HATSU AND SASUKE, STANDING THERE ALL ALONE.
THEY LOOKED EXACTLY THE SAME AS THEY DO NOW.
IT FELT LIKE I HAD SIBLINGS. I WAS SO HAPPY.
THIS WAS BEFORE KINME AND GINME COULD TAKE ON HUMAN FORM...
SO I HAD NO KIDS MY AGE TO PLAY WITH.

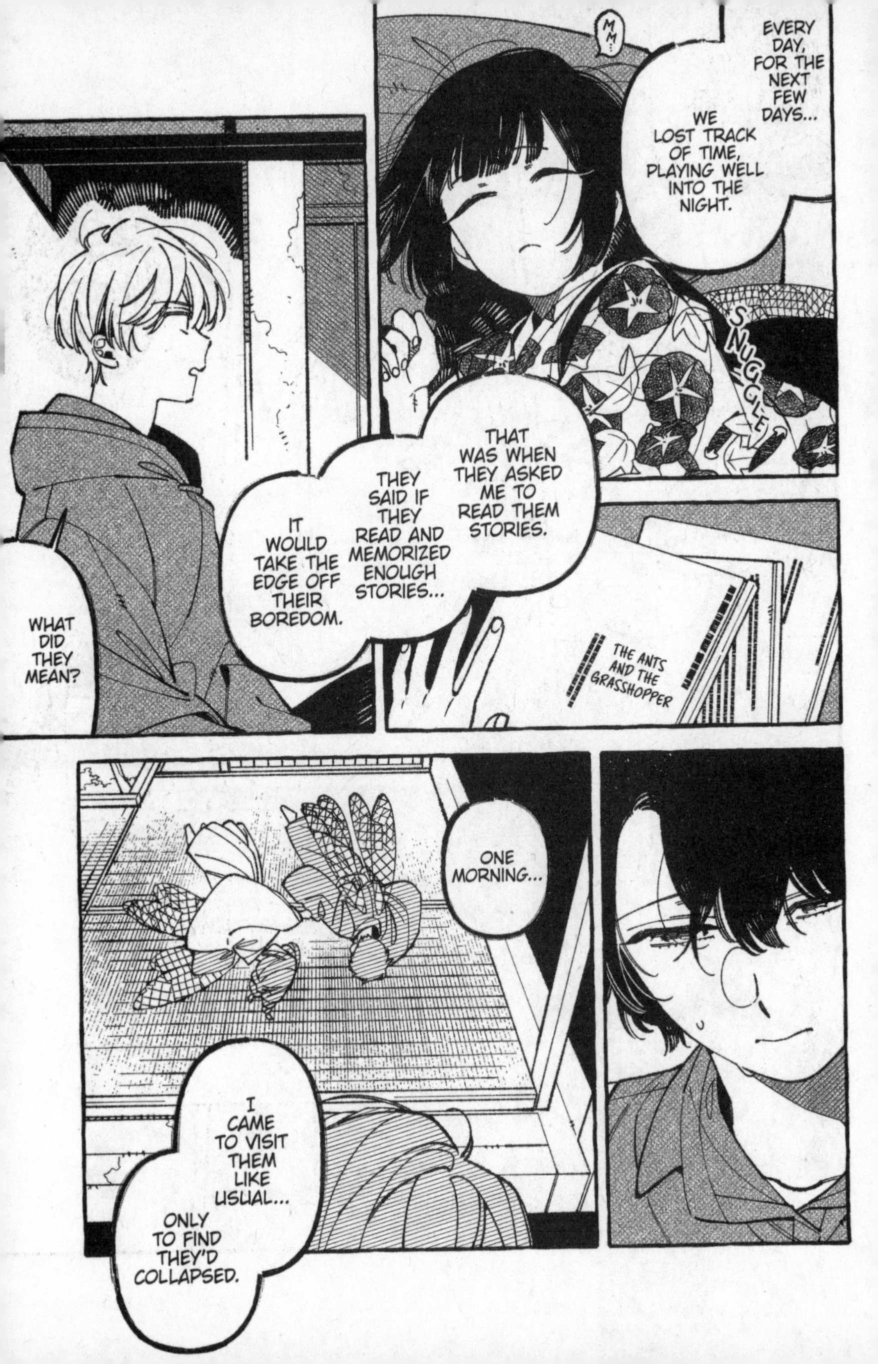
EVERY DAY, FOR THE NEXT FEW DAYS...
WE LOST TRACK OF TIME, PLAYING WELL INTO THE NIGHT.
MM...
SNUGGLE
THAT WAS WHEN THEY ASKED ME TO READ THEM STORIES.
THEY SAID IF THEY READ AND MEMORIZED ENOUGH STORIES...
IT WOULD TAKE THE EDGE OFF THEIR BOREDOM.
THE ANTS AND THE GRASSHOPPER
WHAT DID THEY MEAN?
ONE MORNING...
I CAME TO VISIT THEM LIKE USUAL...
ONLY TO FIND THEY'D COLLAPSED.

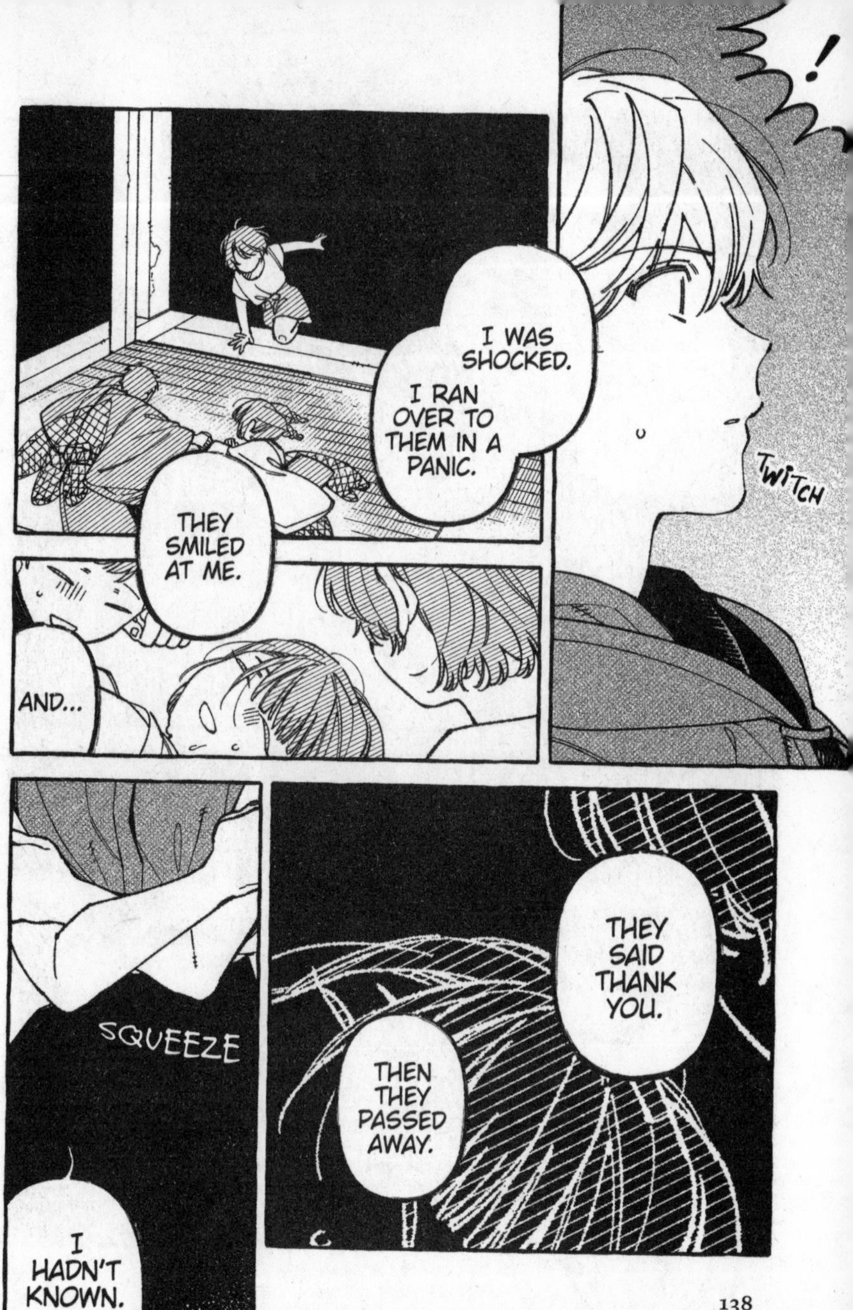
!
TWITCH
I WAS SHOCKED.
I RAN OVER TO THEM IN A PANIC.
THEY SMILED AT ME.
AND...
THEY SAID THANK YOU.
THEN THEY PASSED AWAY.
SQUEEZE
I HADN'T KNOWN.

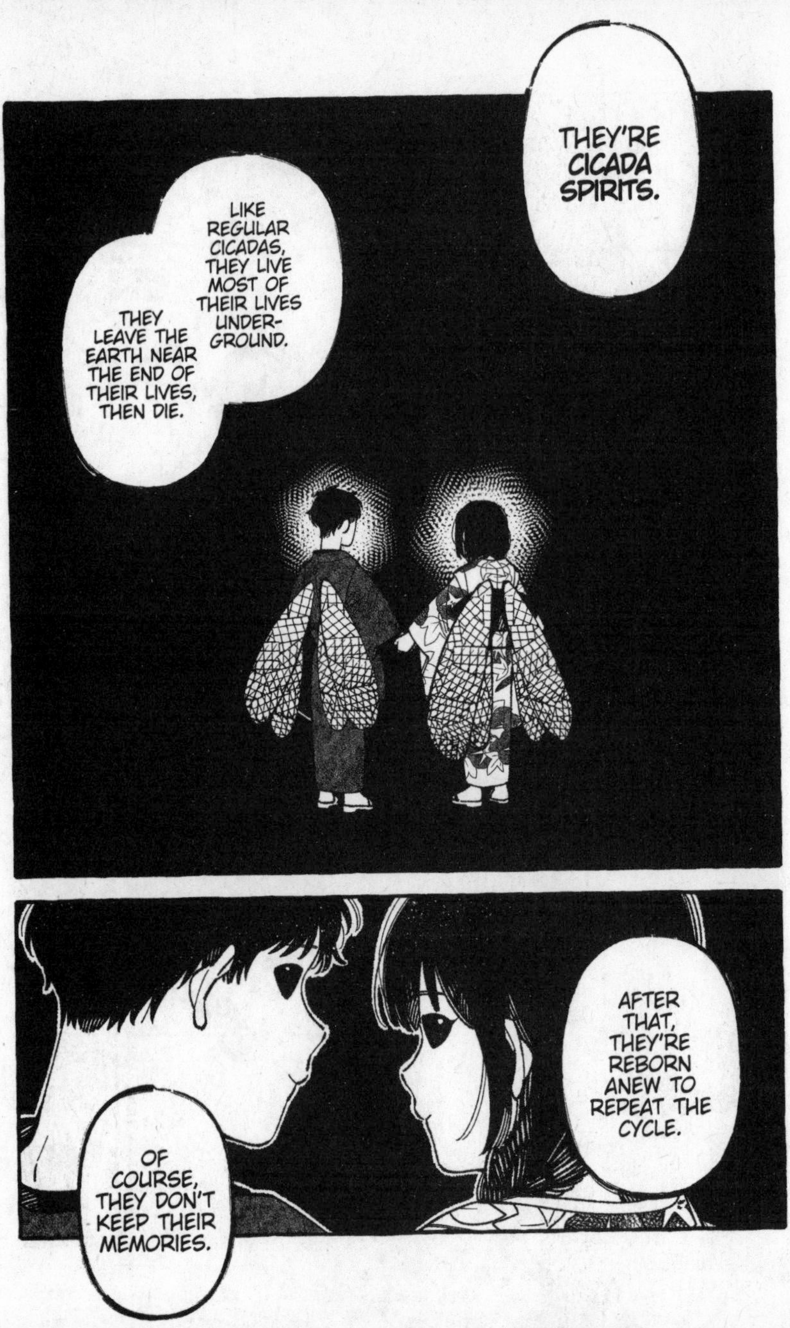
THEY'RE CICADA SPIRITS.
LIKE REGULAR CICADAS, THEY LIVE MOST OF THEIR LIVES UNDER-GROUND.
THEY LEAVE THE EARTH NEAR THE END OF THEIR LIVES, THEN DIE.
AFTER THAT, THEY'RE REBORN ANEW TO REPEAT THE CYCLE.
OF COURSE, THEY DON'T KEEP THEIR MEMORIES.

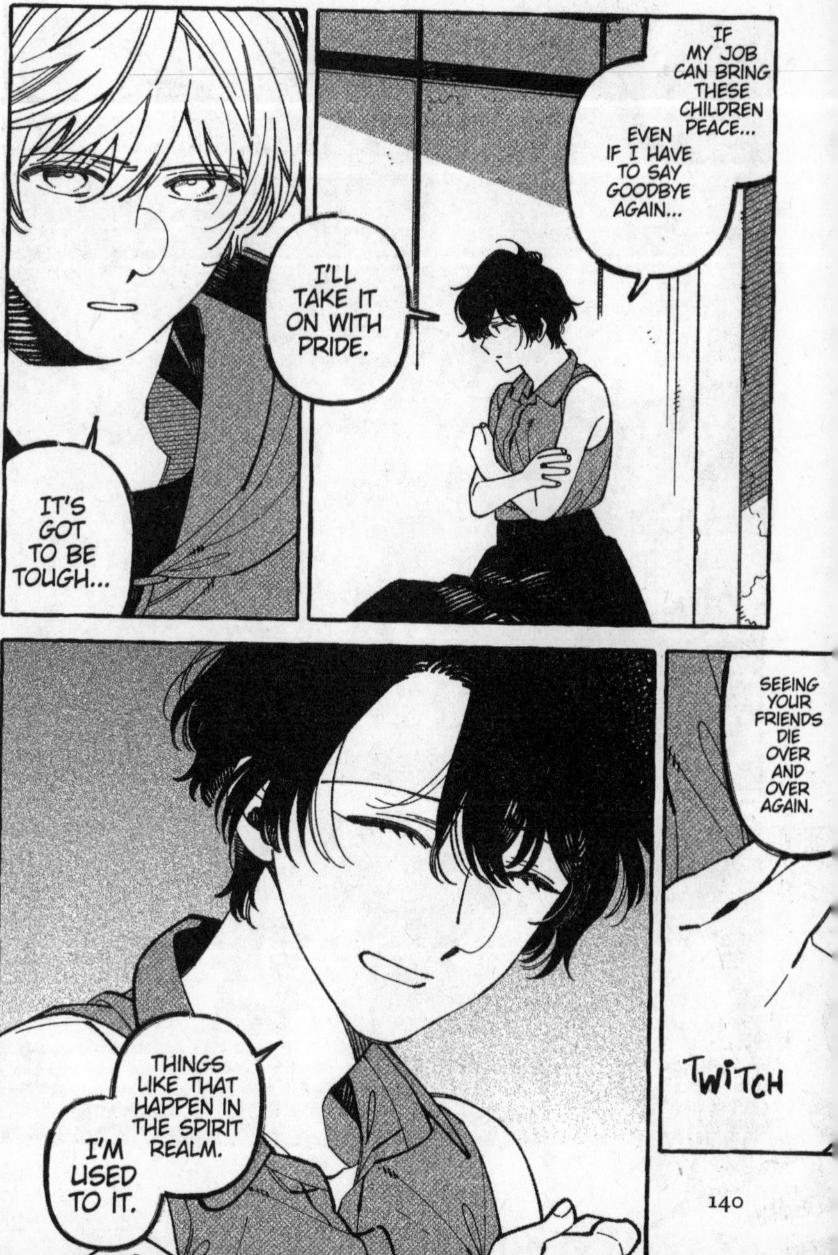
IF MY JOB CAN BRING THESE CHILDREN PEACE...
EVEN IF I HAVE TO SAY GOODBYE AGAIN...
I'LL TAKE IT ON WITH PRIDE.
IT'S GOT TO BE TOUGH...
SEEING YOUR FRIENDS DIE OVER AND OVER AGAIN.
TWITCH
THINGS LIKE THAT HAPPEN IN THE SPIRIT REALM.
I'M USED TO IT.

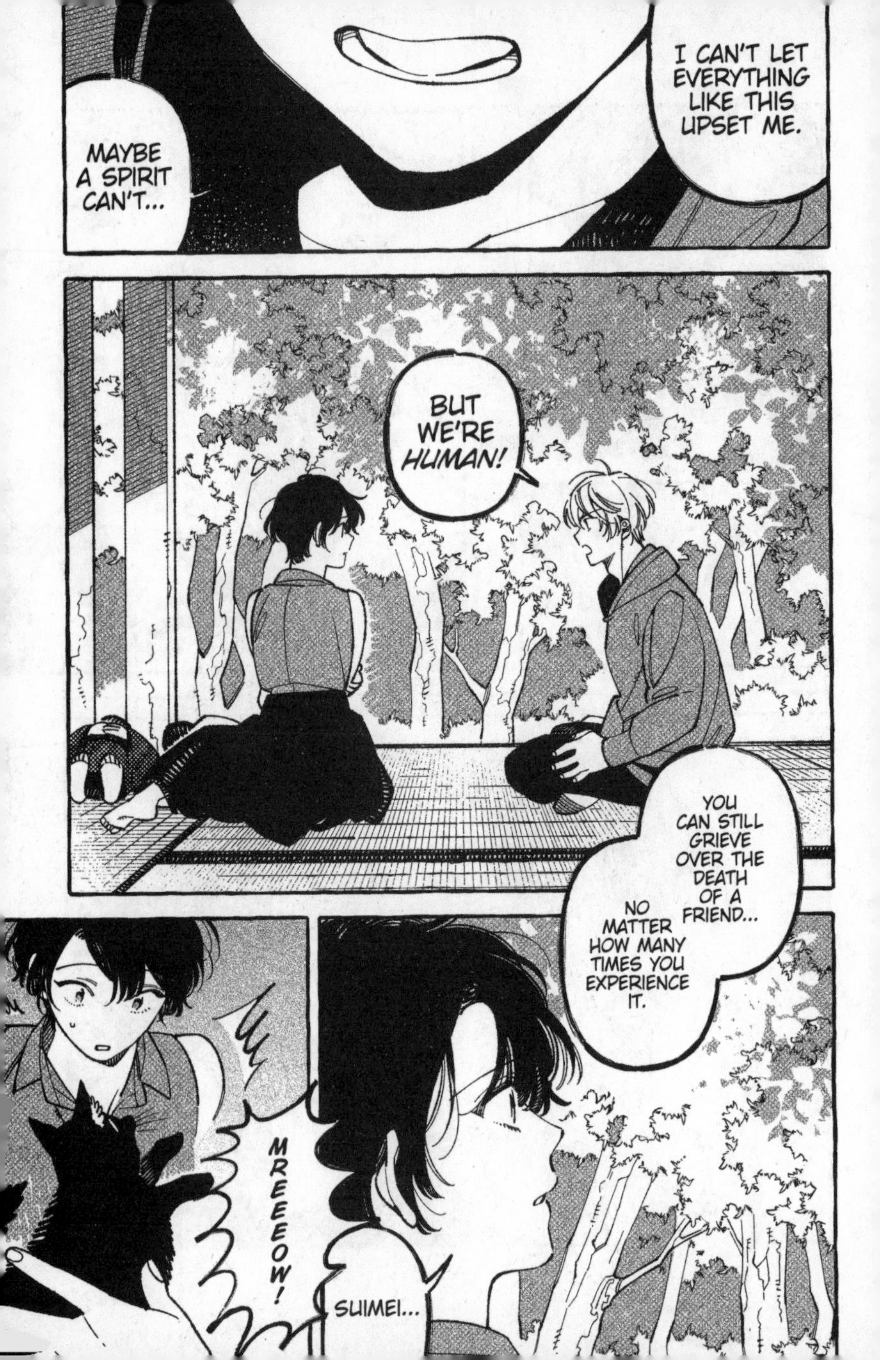
I CAN'T LET EVERYTHING LIKE THIS UPSET ME.
MAYBE A SPIRIT CAN'T...
BUT WE'RE HUMAN!
YOU CAN STILL GRIEVE OVER THE DEATH OF A FRIEND...
NO MATTER HOW MANY TIMES YOU EXPERIENCE IT.
SUIMEI...
MREEEEOW!

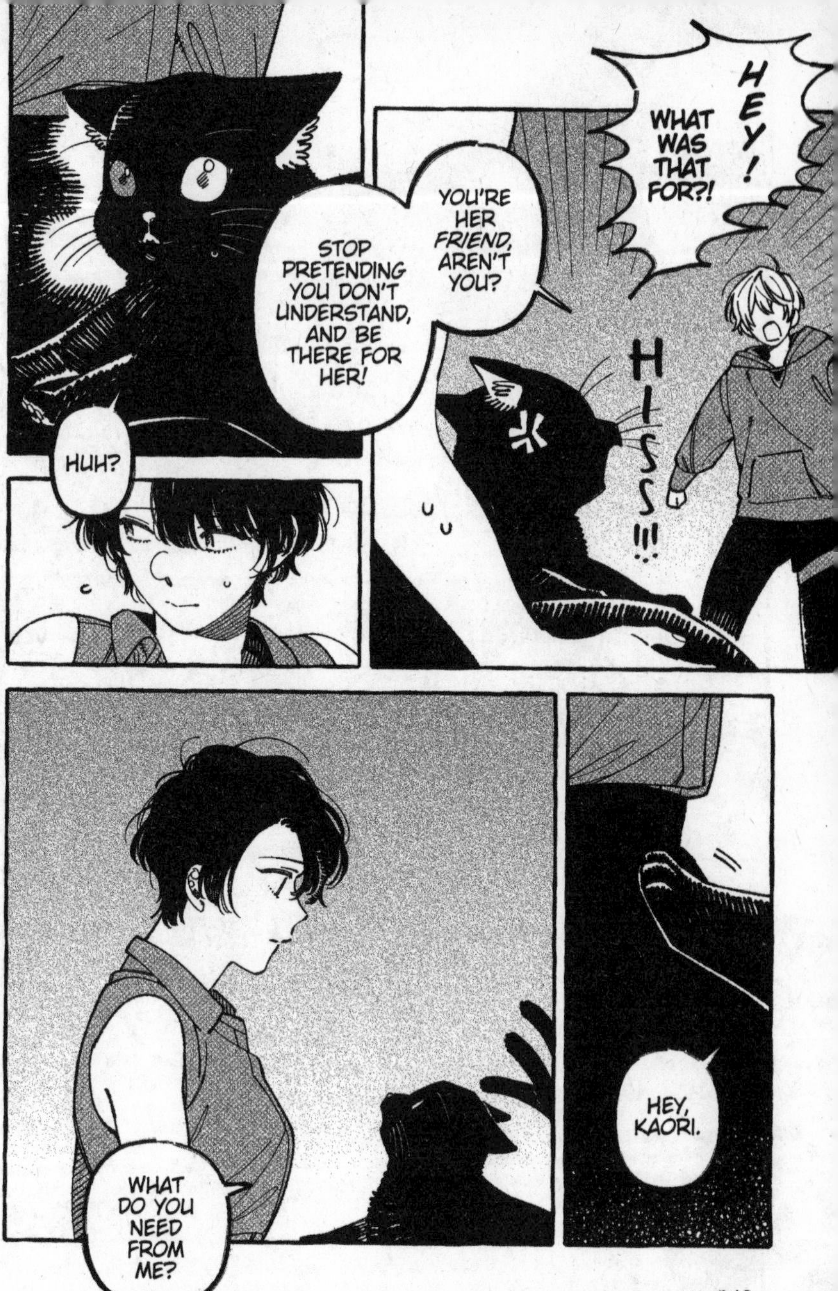
HEY!
WHAT WAS THAT FOR?!
HISS!!!
YOU'RE HER FRIEND, AREN'T YOU?
STOP PRETENDING YOU DON'T UNDERSTAND, AND BE THERE FOR HER!
HUH?
HEY, KAORI.
WHAT DO YOU NEED FROM ME?

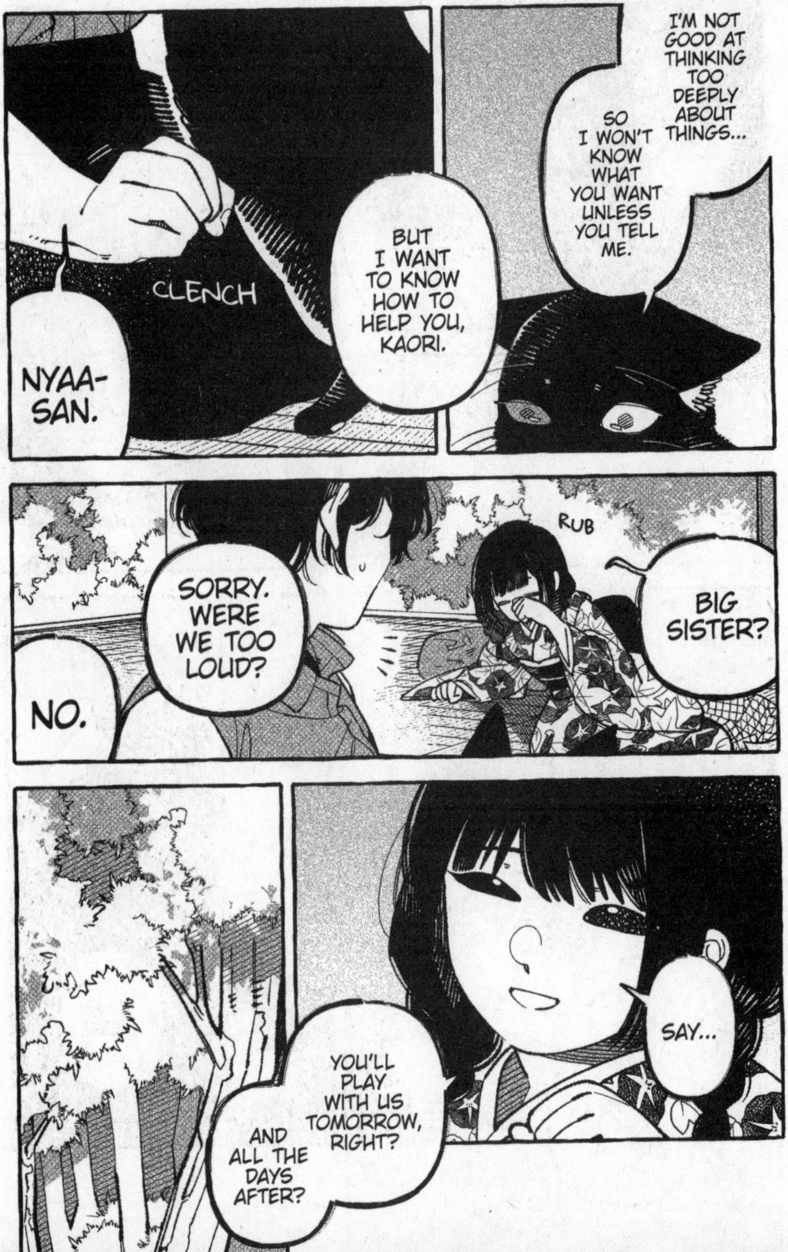
I'M NOT GOOD AT THINKING TOO DEEPLY ABOUT THINGS...
SO I WON'T KNOW WHAT YOU WANT UNLESS YOU TELL ME.
BUT I WANT TO KNOW HOW TO HELP YOU, KAORI.
CLENCH
NYAA-SAN.
BIG SISTER?
RUB
SORRY. WERE WE TOO LOUD?
NO.
SAY...
YOU'LL PLAY WITH US TOMORROW, RIGHT?
AND ALL THE DAYS AFTER?

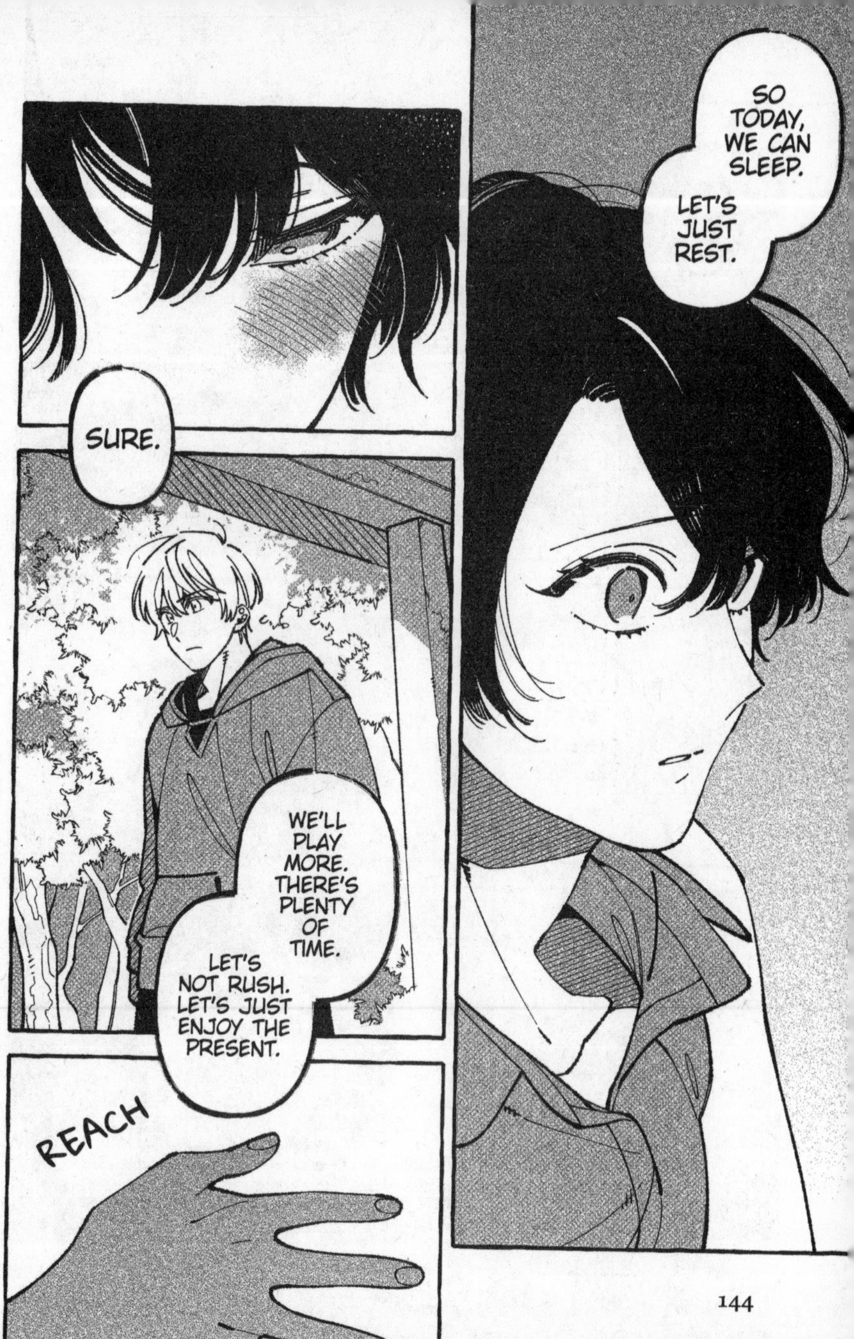
SO TODAY, WE CAN SLEEP.
LET'S JUST REST.
SURE.
WE'LL PLAY MORE. THERE'S PLENTY OF TIME.
LET'S NOT RUSH. LET'S JUST ENJOY THE PRESENT.
REACH

YOU, TOO...

SUIMEI.

ALL RIGHT.

A FEW DAYS LATER, HATSU AND SASUKE PASSED ON.

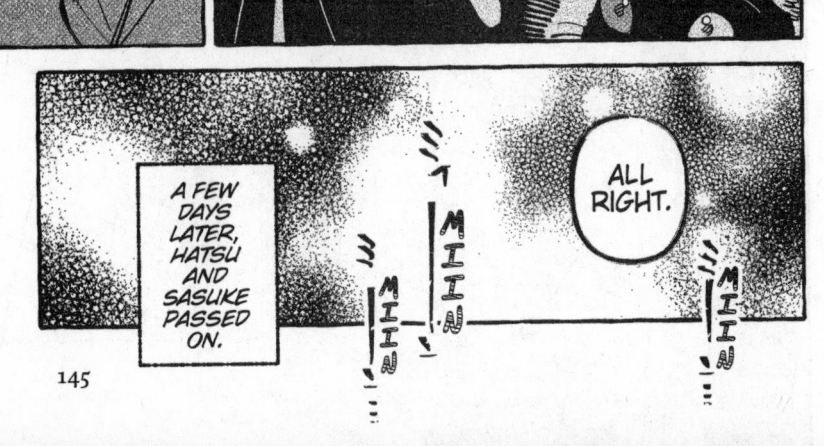

MIIIN

MIIIN

MIIIN

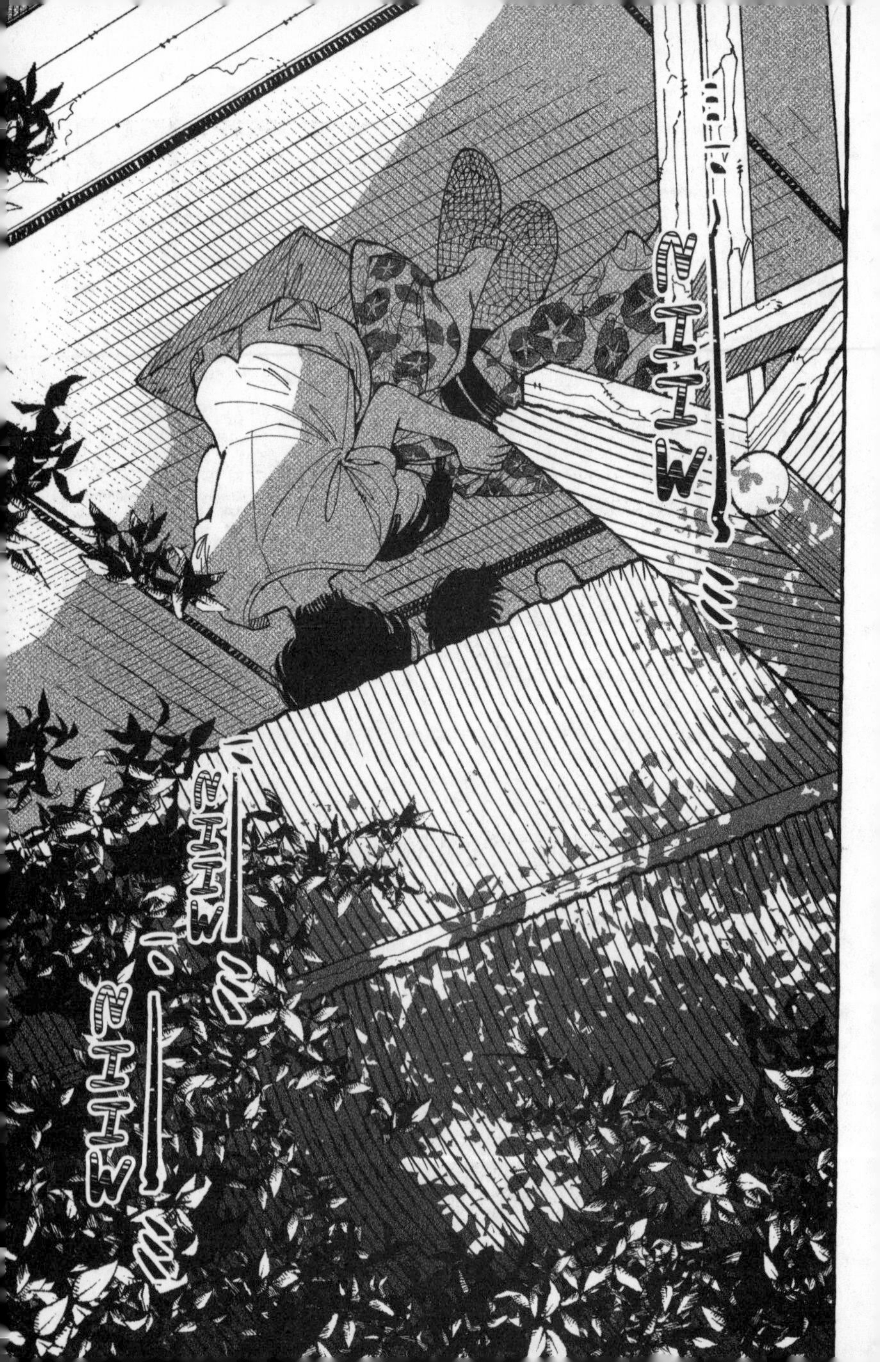
MIIIN
MIIIN
MIIIN

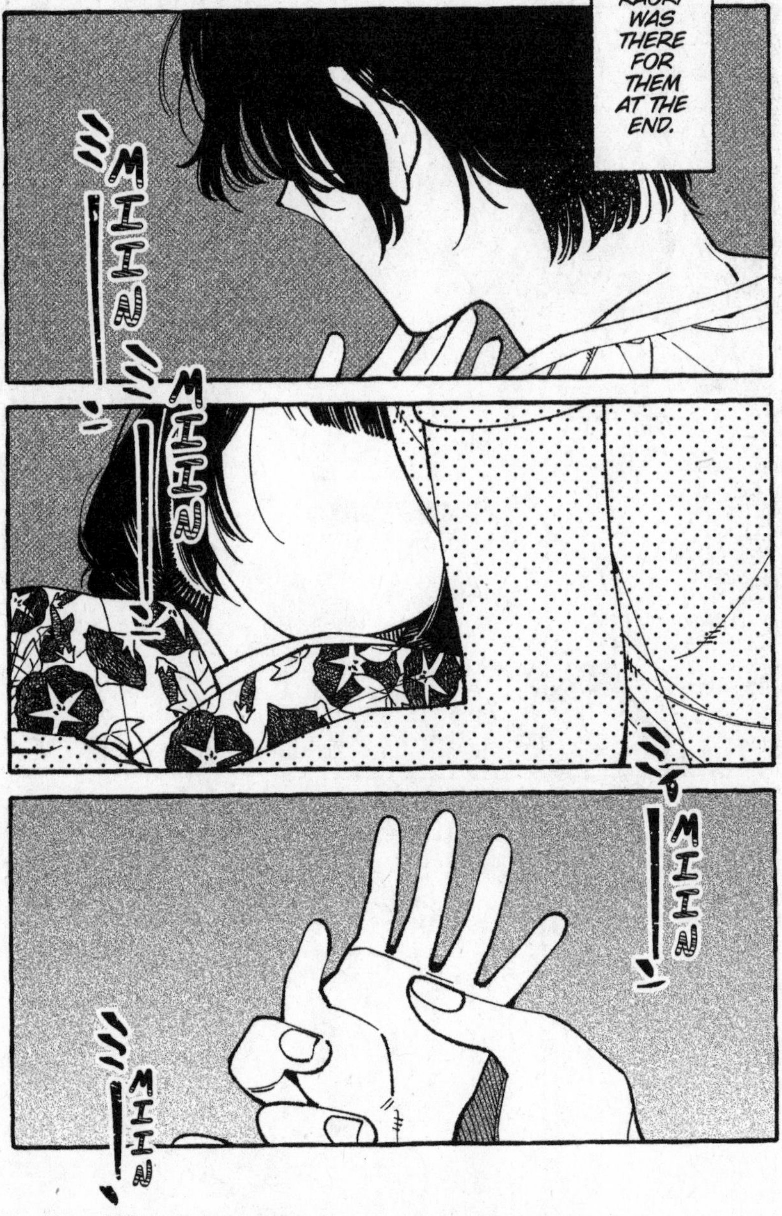
KAORI WAS THERE FOR THEM AT THE END.
MIIIN
MIIIN
MIIIN
MIIIN

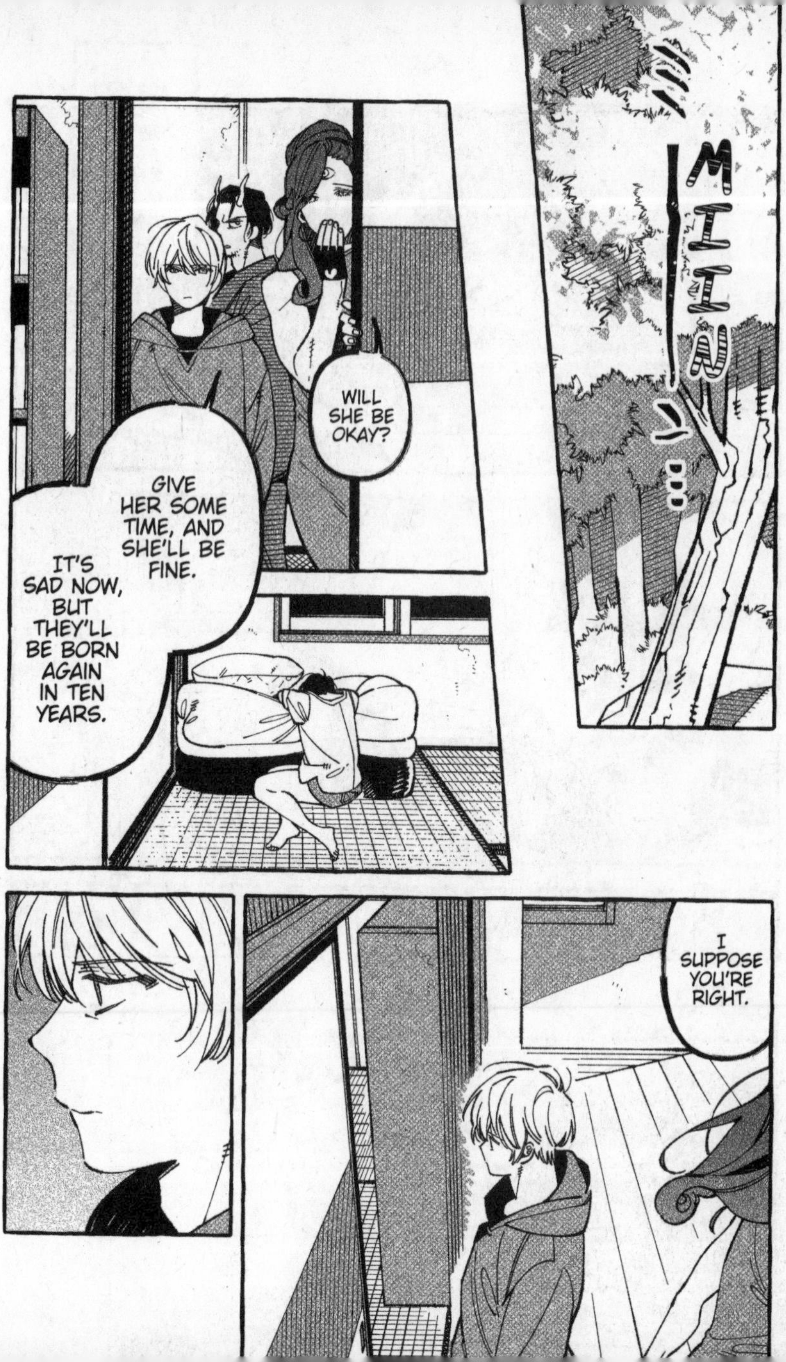
MIIN
WILL SHE BE OKAY?
GIVE HER SOME TIME, AND SHE'LL BE FINE.
IT'S SAD NOW, BUT THEY'LL BE BORN AGAIN IN TEN YEARS.
I SUPPOSE YOU'RE RIGHT.

SO, HATSU AND SASUKE...

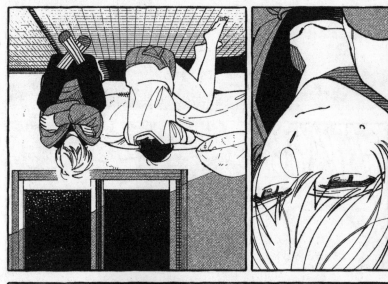

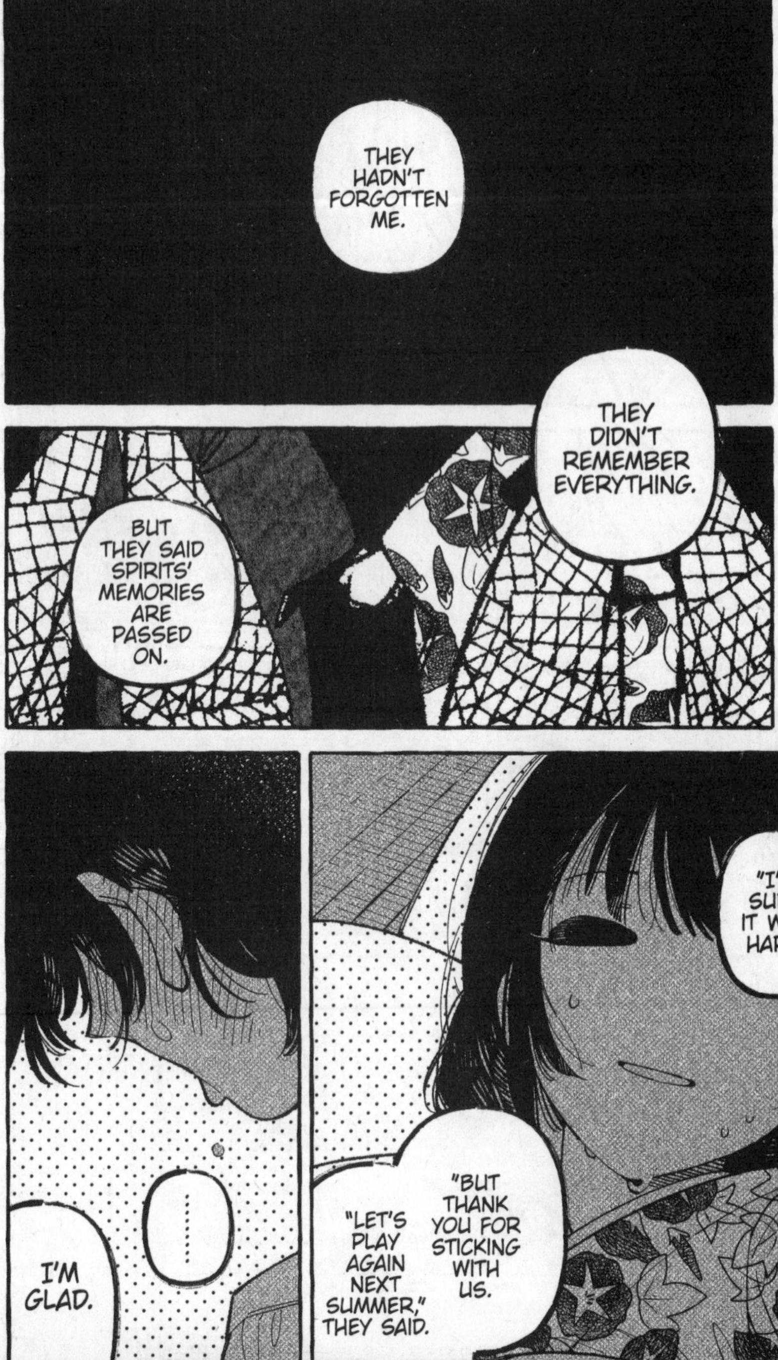
THEY HADN'T FORGOTTEN ME.
THEY DIDN'T REMEMBER EVERYTHING.
BUT THEY SAID SPIRITS' MEMORIES ARE PASSED ON.
"I'M SURE IT WAS HARD.
"BUT THANK YOU FOR STICKING WITH US.
"LET'S PLAY AGAIN NEXT SUMMER," THEY SAID.
......
I'M GLAD.

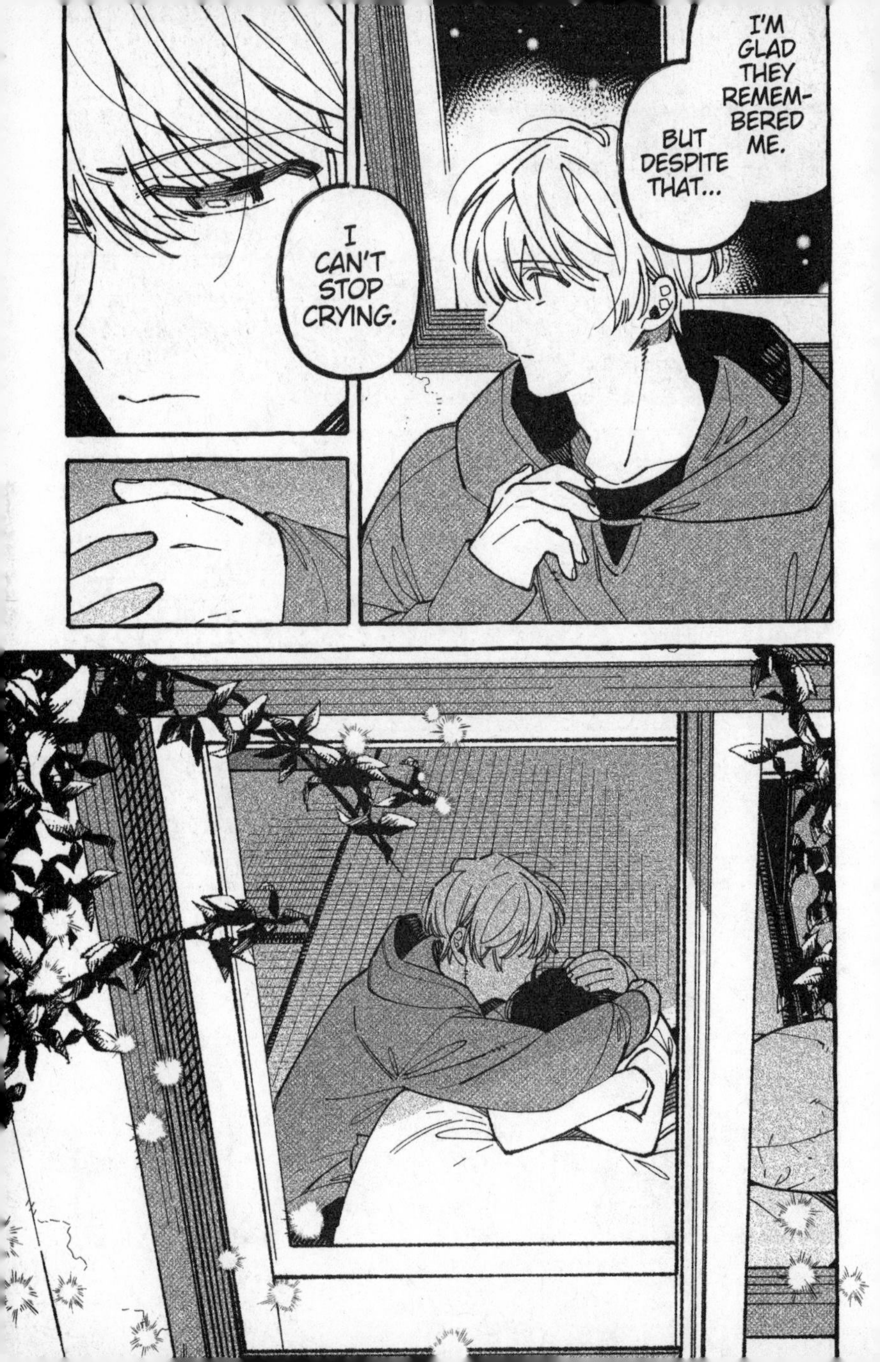
I'M GLAD THEY REMEMBERED ME.
BUT DESPITE THAT...
I CAN'T STOP CRYING.

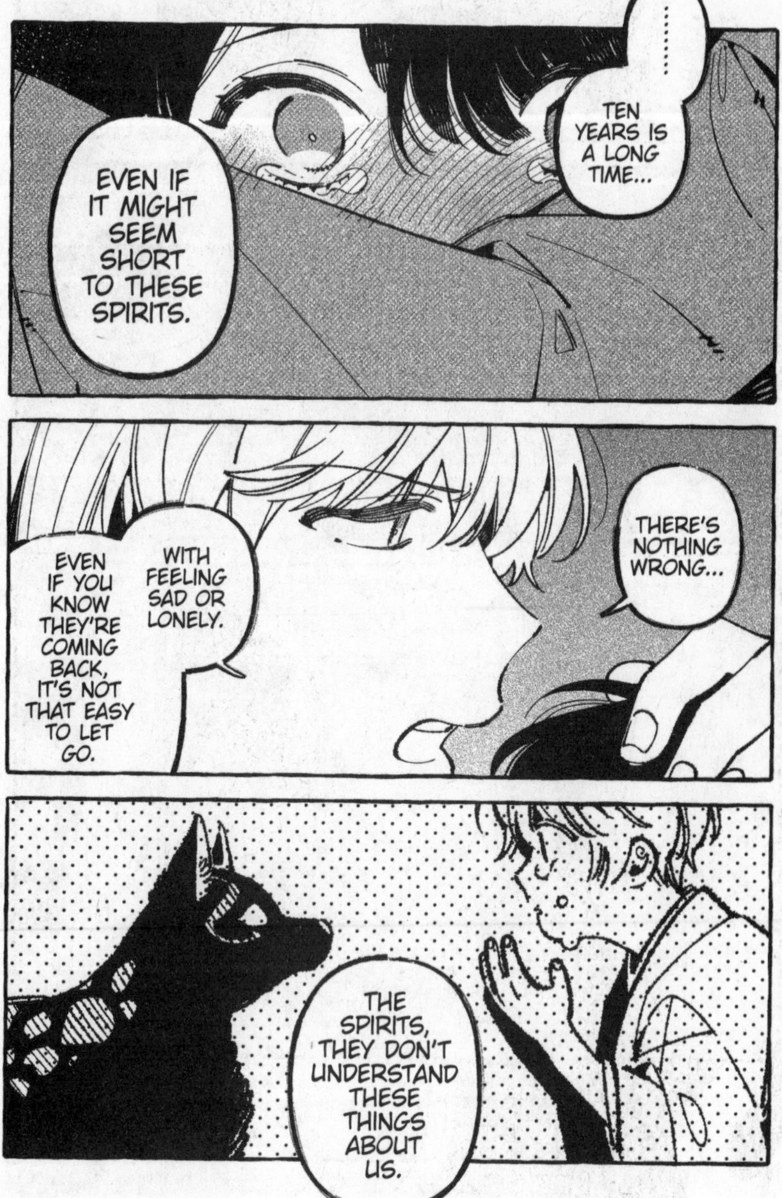
......
TEN YEARS IS A LONG TIME...
EVEN IF IT MIGHT SEEM SHORT TO THESE SPIRITS.
THERE'S NOTHING WRONG...
WITH FEELING SAD OR LONELY.
EVEN IF YOU KNOW THEY'RE COMING BACK, IT'S NOT THAT EASY TO LET GO.
THE SPIRITS, THEY DON'T UNDERSTAND THESE THINGS ABOUT US.

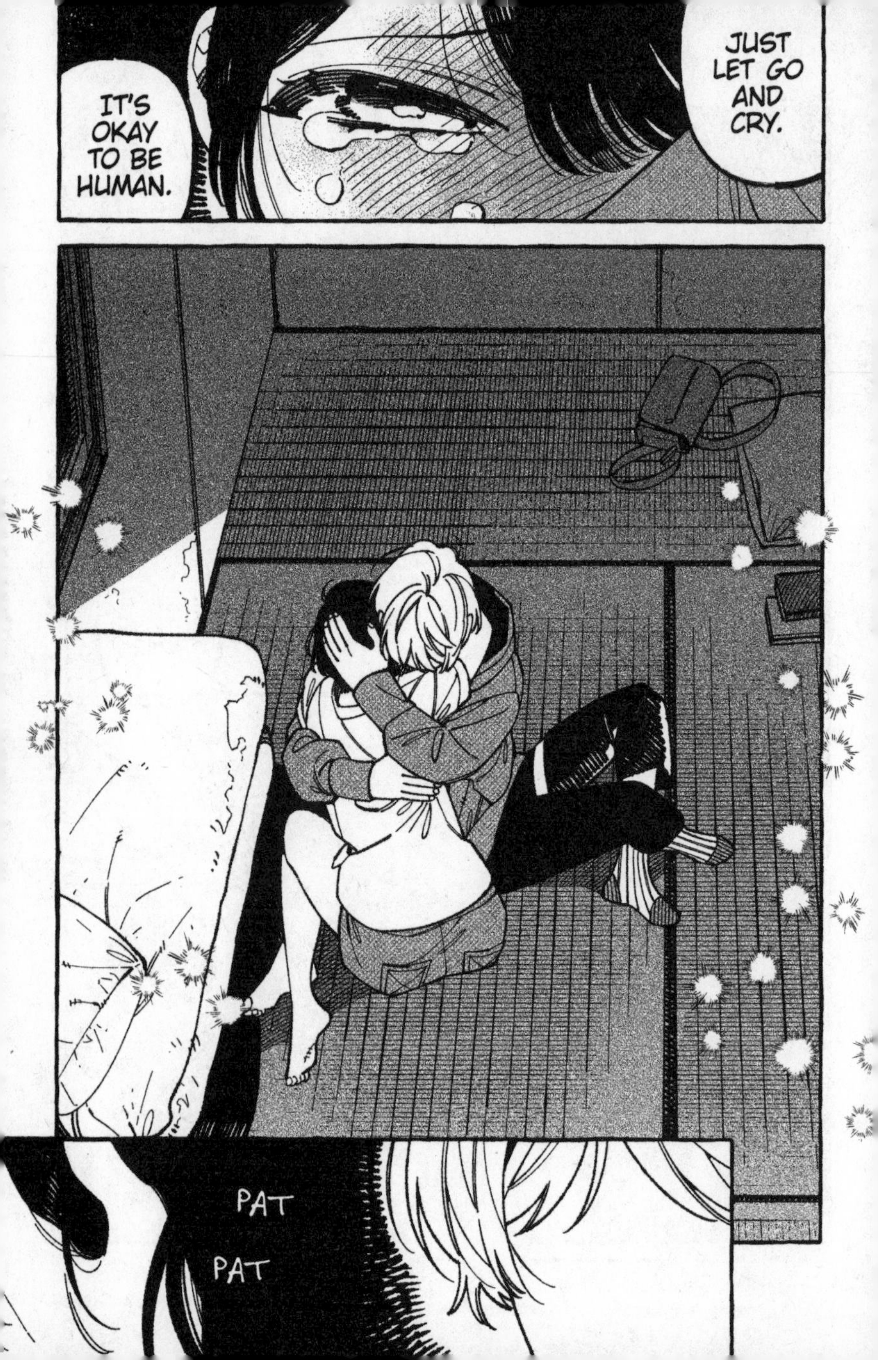
JUST LET GO AND CRY.
IT'S OKAY TO BE HUMAN.
PAT
PAT

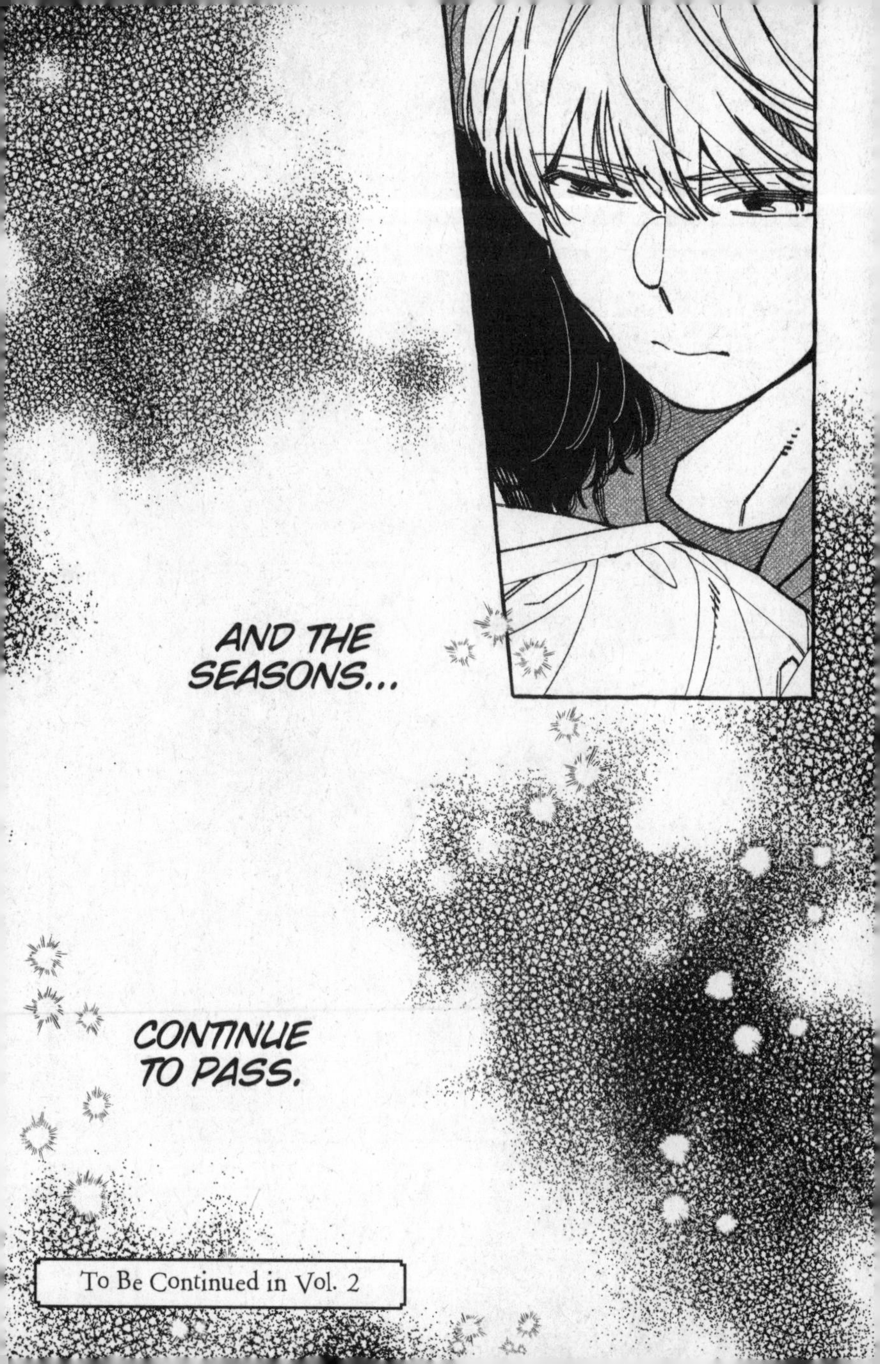
AND THE SEASONS...
CONTINUE TO PASS.
To Be Continued in Vol. 2

Kinme and Ginme's Friendly Guide to the Spirit Realm

BY SHINOBUMARU

"Hey, Suimei," a boisterous voice, paired with dark hair and cool eyes, said. "You're still a newcomer to the spirit realm, right? We'll give you a tour!"

"I don't need one. And I'm busy."

"Don't be like that. Come hang out with us!" A voice similar in tone—if a bit softer—joined in, coming from a face nearly identical to the first, except for the eyes.

The target of their attentions sighed. "In short, you're looking for a plaything, and I'm it."

"He found us out!" the twins shouted as one.

"You're just that transparent, birdbrains."

It was a sunny day. Suimei had been in the backyard of the bookstore, in the middle of his morning routine, when the raven twins called out to him—the elder, softer-spoken twin, Kinme, and the younger, louder twin, Ginme. As raven Tengu, they resembled birds in more ways than one. The biggest similarity, however, was their curiosity. And what they currently found most interesting was the young exorcist who'd wandered into the spirit realm, Suimei.

Suimei had silver hair and golden eyes, as well as a thin nose and equally thin lips. His face was almost like a porcelain doll's, except that he always wore an unpleasant expression. He'd come to the spirit realm searching for a specific spirit, but all the twins cared about was that a powerless exorcist was conveniently staying at the home of a close friend! What could possibly be more interesting?!

They latched on to anything that might drive some of the dullness from their lives. Carpe diem. Live in the moment, in the very second! This hedonistic view was exactly the philosophy Kinme and Ginme lived by. So the "tour" they were offering was merely a pretext to drag the boy out and have fun with him.

"You might find that spirit you're looking for!" Ginme said. "How about it?"

"We can even search with you!" Kinme joined his younger brother's attempts to persuade the young exorcist.

"Ghh..." Suimei's face twisted in displeasure, but only because he was seriously considering it. He'd had no luck finding the spirit, which made him relatively easy to goad. Of course, the twins were well aware of this fact. But this time, no amount of needling would convince him. He'd turn them down. "I shouldn't. Besides, today, Kaori and I are—"

He was interrupted by a cry of "Kinmeeee!" from the younger twin.

"I know, I know," the older twin said.

The two of them took hold of Suimei, each grabbing a hand. They were so quick, there was little Suimei could do to defend himself.

Smiling, the twins spread their massive black wings.

"Wh-what do you think you're doing?!"

They were quite tall, at least two heads taller than the young exorcist. Plus, Suimei had something of a small frame. He dangled between them, their grip unyielding, like he was a disobedient child they feared would wander off. And indeed, though he kicked his legs in protest, his resistance had little effect. The twins might appear to be somewhat slender, but moving those giant wings of theirs required an incredible amount of muscle.

Kinme turned toward the bookstore's main room and shouted, "Kaoriii! We're borrowing Suimei for a bit!"

"Huh? Kinme? Ginme? When did you get here?" Kaori poked her head out of the house.

Ginme's expression softened. Seeing the woman he had a (one-sided) crush on bright and early in the morning seemed to put him in a great mood.

He smiled with delight. "We figured we'd help Suimei with his search!"

Kaori smiled back. "Oh, really? That's nice of you."

"Yeah, well, you know me! I'm the kind of guy who can't abandon someone in trouble. Wa ha ha ha!" His bashful laughter came to an abrupt end once he felt Suimei's ice-cold glare.

"Stop using me to suck up to her."

Ginme twitched. If he let this sourness continue, his plan to have a good time with Suimei (at Suimei's expense) would fall apart. That wouldn't do.

"Ha ha ha ha ha!" Ginme laughed awkwardly. "*Use* you? Would I do a thing like that?" He flapped his wings. "A-anyway, we oughta get going! Come on, Kinme!"

The twins took to the air.

Suimei sighed as he watched the bookstore grow smaller. "Fine. Do whatever you want with me. It's not like it's going to kill me."

Having lost his powers as an exorcist, there was nothing he could realistically do to escape the talons of these meddlesome ravens. However, giving in to them was only the beginning of what was to be, quite literally, a hellish journey.

Not that Suimei knew that.

"All right, first up! Time to show you some things you'd never see in the human realm!" Ginme said excitedly.

His brother's eyes went wide. "Wow, there's a ton of dead folks in here today. Thanks for the hard work keeping them in line, devils!"

The twins had brought Suimei to a place just outside the spirit realm, the fifth of the burning hells: the Hell of Great Screams.

As it turned out, the human realm and hell were practically adjacent to each other. Open the right (or wrong) door, and you might discover a path overflowing with the dead. This particular path had been a favorite playground of the twins' since they were children.

"Suimei, did you see that?" Ginme nudged him, smiling wide. "Those guys are boiling well, aren't they?"

"Oof. That water looks so hot. Do you think they're being tormented?" Kinme perked up. "We should ask them!"

"C-cut it out, you idiots! We definitely should *not* ask!" Suimei, his face pale, shot down this idea.

The twins turned a pair of identical frowns on him.

"Really?" Kinme said. "This doesn't interest you? It's not every day you get to learn how hot the bathwater in hell is."

"Exactly!" Ginme chimed in. "And you might want to know before you end up in one of those cauldrons yourself."

"If I'm going to end up there anyway," Suimei shouted, "how's knowing the temperature going to help?!"

"Good point," they answered in unison.

"I can't tell if you two are actual idiots or not." Suimei let out an exasperated sigh. The twins laughed, their teasing expressions perfectly mirrored.

"Time to move on!" They grabbed him and took off again.

Their next stop was the city's shopping district. They landed in the middle of a road decorated with several rusted shop signs resembling those of the human realm in a bygone era.

Kinme approached one of the shops. "Old man, we'd like some meat skewers, please. Three of them, okay? Hot off the grill, if you can!"

"Gotcha covered!"

"The skewers here are the best!" Ginme turned toward Suimei. "Hey, you missed breakfast, right? Are you hungry?"

"Y-yeah..." Suimei found himself surrounded by the sound of meat sizzling on the grill and the mouthwatering aroma that came with it. While he was debating what to do, the twins finished making their purchase. They handed him one of the three skewers.

"This is what I live for!" Kinme sighed. "After I put some of my favorite seven-pepper spice on it, that is."

Suimei looked at his own steaming skewer, the juices dripping down off the large chunks of meat. That's when he noticed a sign casually hanging behind the vendor that read: *Human Meat in Stock*. Suddenly, he didn't feel quite as well as he had a moment ago.

"Hey...what kind of meat is this?"

"Hmm?" Ginme mumbled, his mouth full. He swallowed before giving Suimei a sunny smile. "Are you worried it's human meat? It's not. Human meat's too expensive for our tastes."

"Hold on. Hold on one darn second! Are you saying that with enough money, you *can* get human meat?!"

Ginme laughed. "I mean, that's what the sign says, so probably? Don't ask me, though, 'cause I've never bought it."

"Well, sir? Can you solve this for us? Do you carry human meat?"

The vendor narrowed his eyes in response to Kinme's question. He looked up and down the street before responding. "Can't say either way!"

Suimei shoved the skewer back at Ginme. "I can't eat this!"

"You're serious? After Kinme went out of his way to treat you?"

"But you don't even know what kind of meat it is!"

"You're making too big a deal out of it! I mean, it's beef... probably. It tastes sort of like beef, I guess?"

"Why are you throwing the question back at me?! Kinme! What kind of skewers did you get?!"

Kinme squinted at his skewer. Then, donning a smile similar to the vendor's, he said, "I'm not certain now."

Suimei could do nothing but turn his eyes heavenward and pray.

"And this is the last spot on the tour!" Having traveled through most of the spirit realm, Ginme and Kinme at last brought Suimei to the bookstore.

"If you need to borrow any books, this is the place!" Kinme smiled. "In fact, this is the *only* place for that, if it's human books you're looking for."

Ginme followed up with, "They have the cutest girl up front, a grumpy, shaggy old man running the place, and a black cat you do *not* want to make mad."

"I know all that already! Some tour this is. Sheesh!"

Suimei was exhausted, having been dragged here, there, and everywhere. And while it should have come as no surprise, he hadn't found the spirit he'd been looking for on this excursion, either. He'd spent the whole day serving as the twins' personal amusement.

"What was the point of all that?" he grumbled. "Am I nothing but a toy to you two?"

The twins looked at each other and smiled.

"Ha ha ha!" Ginme laughed. "We're sorry about that. We really did just want to give you an introduction to our realm."

Kinme picked up where his brother left off. "After all, Suimei, you came from what you might call the 'outside' world. Once we got it in our heads to give you the royal treatment, well..."

The twins' eyes, gold and silver like their namesakes, twinkled.

Together, they said, "We just wanted you to see what's so great about the spirit realm!" They spoke from a place of innocence and enthusiasm, and the love they bore for their precious home was plain to see.

"That you did," Suimei admitted with a sigh and a wry smile. "I learned a lot today. Thanks."

After a moment of shock, the twins, blushing with joy, flashed each other happy smiles.

Kaori spotted the three of them from inside the bookstore and called out. "Oh, hey! You're finally back! Dinner's almost ready!"

The twins, recovering from their surprise, relaxed once more.

"Say, Suimei!" Ginme grinned. "We've got some even better places in mind to take you next time."

Suimei rolled his eyes. "Tell me you're kidding. I don't want to go. And I'm busy."

"You'll like them," Kinme chimed in. "These other spots are sure to be a hit. Besides, we're friends, right?"

"I don't have the slightest intention of becoming friends with either of you."

"Whatever you say, best friend!" the twins spoke as one.

"Stop upping the ante!"

Their merry voices resounded throughout the spirit realm.

Kaori laughed to see them. "Boys make friends so fast."

In the span of only a few hours, they'd grown closer. Kaori found that to be a wonderful thing, even as she watched their antics with a somewhat exasperated smile.

THE HAUNTED BOOKSTORE

Gateway to a Parallel Universe

THE HAUNTED BOOKSTORE

Gateway to a Parallel Universe

The Ways of Love in the Spirit Realm

BY SHINOBUMARU

"Say, Kaori. Is there anyone you're interested in?" Noname's voice held a twinge of anxiousness that carried throughout the bookstore's main living space on that quiet afternoon.

I gulped down the last of my rice cracker. "Where did that come from? Did I miss something?"

Noname cupped her cheeks with both hands, looking like some blushing girl talking about her first crush. "Well, I mean, come on! You've reached the age where it wouldn't be weird for you to have someone special in your life! Furthermore..." Her eyes darted to the door leading to the interior of the shop. I was pretty sure Suimei was in there, running the counter. "You're sharing a roof with a boy just about your age. Oh my! I worry about you two!"

"You can't be serious." I smiled wryly at the spirit who'd been like a mother to me. Then I returned to sipping my tea. I'd made a stronger blend today.

"Honestly, there's no one I'm particularly interested in. Not even the guys at my part-time job. Anyway, Suimei is nothing more than a renter." I made my stance on the matter clear.

Noname's face drooped in disappointment. "Boo! That's no fun. I was hoping to see the fit you-know-who would throw if you brought home a lover. Then I could tease him about it!"

"Noname, sometimes I wonder if you and Shinonome-san actually get along."

"Why's that? We get along well, I think! We don't hold back around each other, nor are we particularly sweet. We're always the first to laugh at each other's failings."

"I wouldn't call that getting along well."

"From my perspective, I see us as good friends." Noname's bright red lips curved up in a smile, like a crescent moon.

I smiled faintly back. As long as the two of them were okay with that, I supposed it was all right.

Noname and Shinonome-san might hurl insults at each other, but I knew that deep down they respected one another.

"On the subject of love..." I paused, taking a moment to look back on my life. I'd been raised in the spirit realm, and it was where I spent the vast majority of my time, so the human concept of love was foreign to me.

I'd attended high school in the human realm, but I'd felt awkward the whole time I was there. I mean, for one thing, all my classmates had two eyes and two arms! No one changed their shape, no one could fly, and no one asked if they could have a finger or two of mine to sample the taste!

Humans are just the weirdest creatures.

That was my first impression of them. Of course, I'm human, too. But leaving that aside, I just couldn't see myself falling in love with one of them.

Not that I'd fallen in love with any spirits, either. They were just too different for me to imagine any kind of romantic relationship with them.

"Maybe there's something wrong with me." I frowned. I'd never felt my heart race around a human, nor did any of the spirits strike my fancy. Was I attracted to anyone at all?

Love. An emotion that could be considered intrinsic to human life. In many instances, it ends in procreation. It wouldn't be a stretch to say that falling in love leads to the prosperity of the entire species.

And that's where we hit a snag. If I have zero interest in such a fundamental emotion, does that mean...?!

"H-have I given up on being human?! N-no! I don't want that!"

"Kaori? What are you going on about?"

"Noname!" I sobbed. "I want to fall in love, too!"

Her amber eyes flashed with mirth, her cheeks flushing. "Goodness, me! I wasn't expecting to hear *that* from you!" She patted her chest in pride. "But I'll give you all the advice you need to have a fairy-tale romance! I might not look it, but I know plenty about love."

I clasped her hands. "Noname—no, *Teacher*—I'm counting on you!"

"Ho ho ho! I hope you're prepared for a workout! Just don't give up halfway!"

I shook my head. "I'll follow you anywhere!"

The two of us looked at each other half a second longer before we were overcome with girlish giggles.

"What is going on in here?" Nyaa-san entered the room, looking at us like we'd gone crazy.

That was how I came to apprentice under Noname in the study of love.

"Now, you can't just grab the first soul you get your hands on. You don't want to lower your standards. Make sure they're a good match. Someone you can open up to. Find your own prince on a white horse. That's how you'll end up with the love of a lifetime!"

"Yes, Teacher!" Notebook in hand, I asked Noname my first question. "What, generally, am I looking for in a good match?"

"That's a good question. Why don't I start off with a story to help you? This is about how *I* found the love of a lifetime." With the ease of a trained speaker, Noname began telling me her greatest love story.

"I remember it like it was yesterday," she said. "Yes, even though it was many years ago now. He was a man of unquestionable strength. He would even stoop to treachery and betrayal if it furthered his ambitions. And there were many who despised him for that. He was clumsy with his feelings, and conceited about his prowess in battle. He wasn't graceful in the ways of the world. But I knew him differently! I knew how kind he was, deep inside!"

I was awed. "Sounds like you fell in love with quite the guy, Noname!"

She laughed. "It was one-sided until the end. He had this woman of amazing beauty, always by his side. She was a lotus blooming in the marshy swamp that was that chaotic era. So you can imagine I wasn't even a passing thought in his mind. They really were suited for each other."

I saw the glimmer of tears in Noname's eyes. My own heart grew heavy, seeing her sadness.

It seemed to me like falling in love must be wonderful, if just the memory of it could bring you to tears! That thought got my heart racing. I wanted an experience of that caliber. Something to shake my emotions to their core.

"He sounds like quite a guy. So, should I be looking for someone strong, too, you think?" My mind was already at work, envisioning possibilities.

"That's my ideal type, without a doubt. I shiver just to recall his sculpted physique, all those bulging muscles."

Just then, Nyaa-san, who'd been listening quietly, cracked an eye. "Sounds made-up. Does this guy of yours have a name?"

Noname smiled. "Lu Fengxian."

Nyaa-san's entire demeanor changed. Her jaw seemed like it might hit the floor, it was hanging so low. "Lu Bu?! Are you an idiot?! I can't believe you'd use the famously chaotic warrior of the Three Kingdoms to talk about romance!"

"What's wrong with that? I *did* have a crush on him."

"You started out telling us it was 'many years ago,' but this was *centuries* ago! We can't have dangerous guys like Lu Bu wandering the streets, or everyone would be screaming in panic! Also, he's more than just strong! And you mentioned a prince on a white horse, but you said *nothing* about Red Hare! Ugh! This is why I hate spirits who've lived for a needlessly long time!" Nyaa-san had barely stopped to take a breath through all of that and was now panting.

Noname shook her head, as if to say, "How rude."

"I don't know if I want the strongest warrior of the Three Kingdoms as a boyfriend," I murmured.

Noname's lips twitched. "W-well, suit yourself. In any case, you need to narrow down what you're looking for in a partner. If you ask for too much, you're liable to find nothing at all. So let's start with a list!"

Nyaa-san and I looked at each other, tilting our heads.

"What do I want? Someone I can look in the eyes and talk to. If they've got hundreds of eyes all over their body like a Dodomeki, I wouldn't know which to look at."

"Kaori, how low are your standards?" Nyaa-san scoffed. "You've got to narrow it down to more than 'has a pulse.'"

"O-okay," I said. "How about someone with a good salary? I'm tired of living hand-to-mouth!"

Noname sighed. "Sounds like I have to go scold Shinonome again. That dolt!"

"What else..." I thought some more. "Someone close to me in age would be nice. A thousand-year-old mountain hermit would be too preachy, you know?"

"Agreed. A lot of people get really inflexible the older they live."

Now that I was thinking about it, I had more preferences than I realized. Maybe I really *did* want to fall in love, and it just hadn't happened yet because I hadn't met anyone who fit all my qualifications.

I felt a sudden sense of relief and began listing off even more traits. "As for their face...I like someone with sweetish looks. They don't have to be riding a white horse, but I think I'd like someone prince-like?"

"Okay, just what are you three talking about?" From out of nowhere came a sullen, exasperated voice.

Looking around, I spotted Suimei peering into the living room.

"You know it's almost lunch break, right? What are you doing lazing around? You said you'd help me in my search today."

I gasped. "You're right! I'm sorry!"

As I jumped to my feet, Noname said something curious. "By the way, Suimei, how old are you?"

Suimei knit his brows, wary. "Seventeen. What's that matter?"

"That makes you just three years younger than Kaori," Noname observed. "While we're talking about you, does being an exorcist pay well? I hear you're forking out quite the sum to stay here."

"I mean, I make enough to support a family."

"Interesting! That's impressive for someone so young! Oh, and do you have just the two eyes? No others tucked away elsewhere on your body?"

Suimei sighed. "What kind of cringey fantasy are we talking about here? Why are you wasting my time with all these questions?"

Noname grinned, pulling me close to whisper in my ear. "He's pretty close to your type, don't you think?"

"Huh?!" My face suddenly flared with heat.

Trembling, I looked over at Suimei. Two eyes...and a really good salary. He was younger than me, but not by that much.

But no! No, no, no! No one could meet my standards that easily! And there were other important qualifications, right?! Like personality and height and overall compatibility! And a bunch more, too!

From Suimei's perspective, I must have been freaking out over nothing. He looked at me curiously. "Pale with fright one minute and red as a tomato the next. You're so strange." But then his gaze softened, and I saw the light of one of the glimmerflies reflected in his eyes. They were a warm, honey-brown color, perfectly suited to his handsome face. In that moment, I found them particularly striking.

My heart leaped. Embarrassed by my own unexpected reaction, I looked away. Suimei returned to the front of the shop. Once he was gone, I placed my hand on my chest to feel my rapidly beating heart.

"Oh my. And to think, it was meant as a jest!"

Realizing Noname had caught on to what I was feeling, I blushed harder. "N-no! No, no, no! It's not happening! Suimei's selfish and rude!" I stomped into the kitchen.

But as I began cutting up vegetables for lunch, I noticed my eyes were particularly vulnerable to the tears the onions brought on.

Ugh! Why did love have to be so hard to understand?

Still, I couldn't help but wonder if the day would come when I had my own bittersweet love affair. I glimpsed the glimmerflies fluttering by the kitchen window, seeming to carry my dreams of an unknown future on their backs.

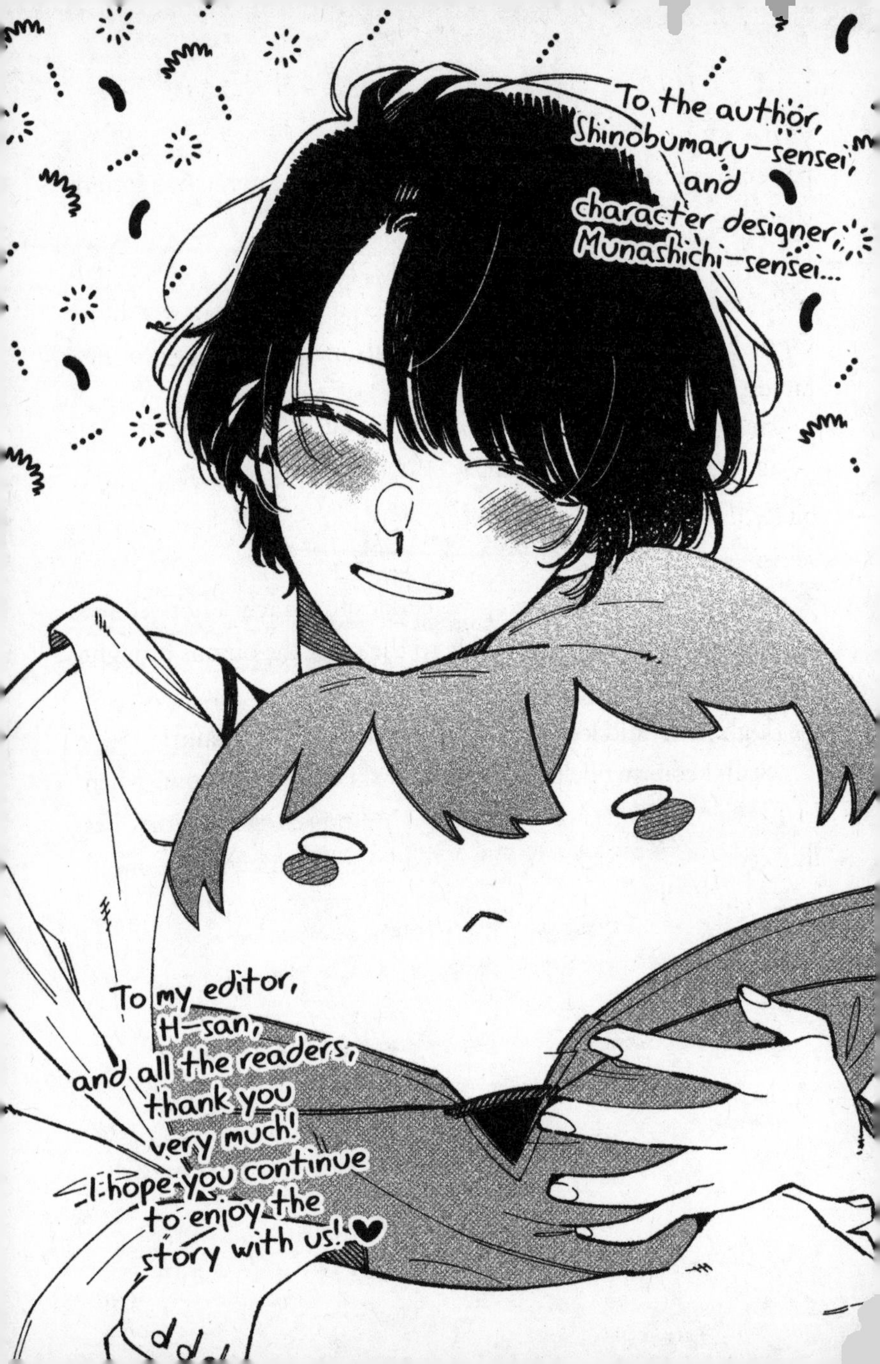
To the author, Shinobumaru-sensei, and character designer Munashichi-sensei...
To my editor, H-san, and all the readers, thank you very much! I hope you continue to enjoy the story with us! ♥

Author's Afterword

Firstly, thank you very much for picking up the manga adaptation of

The Haunted Bookstore: Gateway to a Parallel Universe!

I'm the original novel's author, Shinobumaru.

While I've been working on this title for Kotonoha Bunko, the idea of it receiving a manga adaptation never once crossed my mind, so I'm more than pleased to see it come to pass! And to have Medamayaki-sensei be in charge of drawing it... I remember the joy I felt at the news. (Especially since I teamed up with Medamayaki-sensei in our previous work.

Isekai Omotenashi Gohan.)

Unlike our previous isekai title, this one has a somewhat unique setting, which Medamayaki-sensei did an amazing job bringing to life. Kaori's many expressions, Suimei's coolness, Shinonome's shabbiness (with just a hint of that sexy older man charm!), Not to mention the playful raven twins and Nyaa-san, who's so cute! But my favorite may be Nurarihyon. That designs too much. I can't take it! Do I need to say it's the reason

Nurarihyon's appearing more in the original?

Things are getting exciting over on the novel side, so if you're interested, please consider picking up the original as well!

I'd be happy if everyone continues to enjoy

the story of Kaori and the others.

Shinobumaru